CHASING PARADISE

CHASING PARADISE

David Ewen

*Evening***Express**

BLACK & WHITE PUBLISHING

First published 2010
by Black & White Publishing Ltd
29 Ocean Drive, Edinburgh EH6 6JL

1 3 5 7 9 10 8 6 4 2   10 11 12 13

ISBN: 978 1 84502 311 9

A CIP catalogue record for this book is available from the British Library.

Typeset by Ellipsis Books Limited, Glasgow

Printed and bound by MPG Books Ltd, Bodmin

**796.
352**

CONTENTS

ACKNOWLEDGEMENTS

Thanks to *Evening Express* picture editor Alan Paterson for helping order the gallery of images; to Midas Media for allowing me to re-live press conferences; to Jake Molloy of the RMT Union; to the many experts in the fields of planning, law and ecology who kept me right; and to journalists around the world who helped inform my understanding of the bigger story.

FOREWORD

by

Donald J Trump

It is with great pleasure that I write this foreword for David Ewen. We have been through a prolonged battle in Aberdeenshire and the victory is therefore even sweeter. I'd spent years looking for a site and when I saw the Menie Estate, I knew it was the place. Therefore I was prepared to go for it with everything I've got – Scotland is worth fighting for.

Great battles should be remembered and David's account brings every battle we encountered to light in a colourful and riveting way. Along with business leaders, government supporters and others like Sir Sean Connery, we made our way through a labyrinth of obstacles.

My mother was from Scotland and this has truly been a labour of love for me. It is an honour for me to provide the citizens of Scotland with an opportunity for economic growth for many years to come and I am grateful for the support of so many people. Trump International Golf Links Scotland will be the greatest golf links course in the world. Scotland deserves no less.

PROLOGUE

It's the first day of the golf season at Bedminster, an hour west of New York. The Georgian clubhouse – rendered in red brick, grey flagstone and whitewashed wood – dazzles in the April sunshine. An American flag big enough to sail a boat rises into the blue sky. It's unseasonably hot, easily seventy degrees Fahrenheit.

On the eighth fairway, the club's owner – wearing a white polo shirt and red cap, both bearing his insignia, a sort of heraldic crest – is approaching his ball.

'Did you know Bedminster has just been voted the best new course in the last twenty years?' he says with fatherly pride.

Without rehearsal, he hits a wedge into the green, arms following the hips back to the target. The ball bounces once, twice, stunned by the soft ground, and rolls to within a few feet of the hole.

Donald Trump is smiling.

'The good news is we're winning,' he says, returning the club to his bag. 'The bad news is the tournament isn't over yet.'

Chapter 1

KISSING THE EARTH

Airport employees are still trying to flatten the red carpet as the Boeing 727 taxies to a halt. They are anxious that the April breeze does not disturb the welcome. A guard of honour is waiting, a phalanx of chief executives: Douglas Paterson from the city council, Jennifer Craw from Scottish Enterprise Grampian, and Geoff Runcie from Aberdeen and Grampian Chamber of Commerce. The Queen, who flies into Aberdeen for her annual holiday at Balmoral Castle, fifty miles west of the city, usually has to make do with a Lord Lieutenant and a few special branch detectives.

Long before he steps from the Boeing, you can tell Donald Trump is in town.

The four-foot lettering emblazoned on the black fuselage – TRUMP, in twenty-three-carat gold leaf – is something of a giveaway. A streaked red *T* on the tail is styled to convey motion: it looks as though the plane has taken off before the decal has dried. There is a further clue to the owner in the registration – VP-BDJ – the DJ standing for Donald John. A private number on a private jet. It's what you might expect.

Trump – black woollen coat, white shirt, striped blue tie – offers a Churchillian salute as he takes to the tarmac.

'I should almost kiss the ground,' he says. 'I mean, this is where my mother was born and raised. She was raised in Stornoway on the Isle of Lewis, and she loved Scotland. And, you know, my whole family loves Scotland, so it's great to come back to Scotland.'

Piper Andrew Macleod, from Stornaway, has piped the billionaire off his plane to the tune of Highland Laddie. Trump approaches the firefighter, drawn from his division's band, and poses beside him. He puts his hands playfully around the bagpipes, holding the instrument as though it were some kind of bewildering marsupial.

A room in the terminal has been set aside for a press conference.

'I'd like to introduce you to our new neighbour,' says airport boss Andy Flower, standing at a lectern.

'Thank you all for being here,' says Trump from behind a table. 'We appreciate the wonderful welcome.'

Trump, a big, broad-shouldered man with a rolling gait, is a dominating presence. He leans forward, as though imparting something intimate to a friend.

'I have to start off with my mother,' he says. 'She'd be very upset with me if I didn't. She passed away a few years ago but she to her last days loved Scotland. She was almost ninety years old. And she lost her husband, my father, a few years before that, and once she lost him she didn't feel like going forward too much anyway. They had an amazing relationship; they were married for sixty-four years. And I've always had a very warm spot for Scotland . . . I'm doing this to a certain extent . . . and maybe to a large extent . . . and maybe even larger than I know . . . in honour of my mother.'

Trump talks about his four US courses, about the associated challenges and successes.

'If I didn't get along with the environmentalists, I wouldn't have opened the course that's two-and-a-half miles along the Pacific Ocean,' he says. 'We have a thing called the Coastal Commission in the state of California, which is probably the toughest environmental group anywhere in the United States. Over a twenty-year period nobody has ever remembered getting something approved, so big, and so fast. And now that it's opened everybody loves it . . . If for any reason the community groups, the community, the local representatives, the politicians, if for any reason they feel we're not doing the right thing, if they let us know, we will go some place else.'

This curious blend of audacity and humility is stock Trump. It's what he does so well: prostrating himself before the people while leaving no one in any doubt about what he wants.

If for any reason they feel we're not doing the right thing, if they let us know, we will go some place else.

He sounds wounded and threatening at the same time.

'We're not looking to have any arguments,' he continues. 'We're looking to take a great piece of land and make it better. We're looking to take a great piece of land and on that piece of land build the best golf course in the world. Not the best in Europe, not the best in the United States. We're going to build the greatest golf course in the world.'

The greatest golf course in the world.

'There are a few other sites where we feel this could be achieved. But I really wanted to come to Scotland.'

Trump elongates the last sentence, adding four stresses.

'We hope the process can go quickly. The markets are right, the world is right. We hope the process can go quickly.'

Architects have spent four months giving form to Trump's vision. US firm Wimberly Allison Tong & Goo has brought along a 'rough rendering' of a 450-500-room hotel. 'A Victorian design, which I think is beautiful,' says Trump. 'Mark, why don't you show them?'

'This is very conceptual,' says Mark Yoshizaki, unfurling a drawing.

The hotel looks tiny.

'By the way, this is the clubhouse not the hotel,' says Trump. 'Otherwise the hotel just got a lot smaller.'

Everyone laughs.

Yoshizaki shows an interior from the hotel, a drawing room with a chandelier, armchairs before a fireplace, a decanter on a table. Trump notes the generous size of the room.

'The bad news is it's a very expensive space . . . for me.'

Trump suggests the hotel will persuade people to stay in the North-east, that the resort can lure golfers from St Andrews.

'It's going to be very good economically for Aberdeen and the whole area.'

He says he has 'all the land' he needs for the course: 'To build a great course you need 200 acres. We have 800 acres.'

Trump finishes with praise for Scotland's leader: 'Jack McConnell has been amazing as a representative of Scotland. He hasn't discussed the specifics of the site. All he wanted to do was make sure we came to Scotland; he's made absolutely no commitments to us. He's done nothing except work very hard to get us to come and spend hundreds of millions of dollars or pounds or whatever you want to say in Scotland.'

It had taken Donald Trump six years to reach the point where he was thinking about getting intimate with Scottish soil. During that time, he scoured the planet for the right piece of land. His team had looked at 211 sites but perhaps inevitably, Trump had settled on a strip of Scottish coast: the finest courses in existence are on the edge of Scotland's cold grey seas, formed among the tumult of sand dunes and grassy hillocks known as links.

This is where the game originated, where the oldest clubs are based, and where golf's pre-eminent tournament is staged. The Open Championship, one of the sport's 'majors' along with the US Open, the Masters, and the Professional Golfers' Association Championship, is played every year on one of nine seaside courses in the British Isles. Five are in Scotland. Carnoustie Golf Links is within an hour's drive of Aberdeen and the St Andrews Old Course, the most hallowed crucible of all, is another forty minutes along the east coast.

Rumours about Trump's interest in the North-east coast emerged in January 2006.

Ashley Cooper, a former Wall Street broker and managing partner of Trump Golf Properties, confirmed the company was looking to expand overseas, and that a site in Scotland was under considera-tion. Cooper added they were hoping to make an announcement in four to five weeks but said releasing details before then might be 'damaging' to on-going negotiations with landowners. The announcement, when it came, was suitably grand. They were planning not one course but two, as well as housing and a hotel.

The site turned out to be the Menie Estate, lying between the settlements of Balmedie and Newburgh, ten miles north of Aberdeen.

Trump bought 800 acres from Tom Griffin, an American lawyer who in the 1970s made a fortune selling his legal expertise to the flourishing North Sea oil industry. Griffin had stocked the property with pheasant and partridge and turned it into a shooting gallery. On a hunting trip in England, Griffin met Patrick O'Connor, who co-owned The Old Head of Kinsale, a spectacular golfing promontory on the south-west coast of Ireland. Griffin mentioned his interest in having his links valued and O'Connor invited him across to talk about making the most of his land.

Griffin ended up being shown round Kinsale by a Scottish photographer. Brian Morgan had visited 1,000 courses in fifty countries. He also knew how to play the game of building courses, having pointed Lyle Anderson to the Loch Lomond site, home of the Scottish Open.

Morgan explained: 'As things turned out Patrick was busy, so I took Tom around the course and told him all about golf development. From that first meeting I was invited by Tom to visit Menie and to view the land. I thought it was the perfect links site, where, like Turnberry, the non-links land or farmland rises to overlook the spread of the dunes. But I knew the only way this might get planning was with a big name architect like Nicklaus, Norman, Palmer or Player, and with a lot of money behind them.'

To help find a partner or buyer, Morgan photographed the site from the ground and the air and personally delivered folios to Jack Nicklaus, Greg Norman, Tom Doak, Tom Fazio, and other leading designers and developers.

Herb Kohler, whose family owned a US plumbing empire, made

the trip to Menie. Kohler had bought the Old Course Hotel in St Andrews for £40 million and built Whistling Straits on the edge of Lake Michigan, one of the top courses in the US, contrived from a Wisconsin plain. Kohler wasn't tempted by the lumpy canvas that was Menie. A year later, Trump was speaking to M.G. Orender, president of the Professional Golfers' Association of America, about his desire to own a links golf course. Orender contacted O'Connor, who contacted Morgan.

'Patrick called me to tell me to get a set of prints to Donald Trump,' said Morgan. 'I did that and Mr Trump sent his representative to Aberdeen where we met and right away he knew it was what Mr Trump was looking for.'

Trump then added parcels of land totalling 600 acres, acquired on his behalf by project director Neil Hobday.

Menie, Hobday believed, represented an almost mythical find, the treasure at the end of a quest. Hobday himself had spent more than a decade searching thousands of miles of Scottish coastline for a mix of grass and dune from which something sublime might be fashioned, a links to be cut and polished like diamond. He had been planning his own golf complex near Nairn, ninety miles north-west of Aberdeen, next to the Spey Bay Hotel, where a classically-styled but threadbare course runs between shingly beach and pine forest. However, the cost of connecting the resort to a sewage plant (a belated request from planners) proved prohibitive and the venture collapsed.

Hobday, the first to shake Trump's hand when he landed in Aberdeen, understood success too. As a former director of golf at Loch Lomond, he had helped set up the World Invitational tournament at the venue. He was a member at Prestwick, where the first Open was held in 1860, and at IMG had managed Colin Montgomerie, Sam Torrance and other sporting talent. Hobday was quick to reassure locals that Trump was ready to invest emotion as well as money in the North-east.

'Make no bones about it, everything Mr Trump does is five-star and everything he does here will be five-star plus,' he said. 'This development is very special to Mr Trump. It involves his two passions in life – property development and golf.'

For £6 million, Trump ended up with the castellated Menie House, three miles of sugar sand beach, and a jumble of dunes. The purchase was all about potential. Between Aberdeen's River Don and Menie repose two fine courses, Royal Aberdeen, the sixth oldest golf club in the world, formed in 1780, and the century-old Murcar Links. Beyond Forvie National Nature Reserve, to the north of Menie, is another revered course, Cruden Bay.

Trump had come to Aberdeen not just to share his dream but to see where it would be realised.

He had bought Menie Estate without setting foot on it.

Three days after arriving in Scotland Trump was ready to offer a judgment during a tour of the land with designer Tom Fazio II, nephew of the legendary American golf course architect of the same name. Fazio had already described the job of producing a layout as a 'once in ten lifetimes' opportunity. When he first saw the Menie links he said he 'couldn't believe anything like it existed on earth'. Trump, now seeing it for himself, suggested Fazio would be 'doing as little as possible' to the land. He wanted Fazio to go easy on the bulldozing because, as he put it, 'you can't really make perfection any better'.

In the majestic juxtaposition of sea and land and sky, he divined the influence of someone with a reputation for creative excellence that surpassed even that of the Fazio family's.

'That was cut by God,' said Trump from atop a hillock. 'He was the best golf architect of all. Better than Tom Fazio.'

Fazio laughed and said: 'And he'll get all the credit.'

He meant God, not Trump.

Given that Trump had come to Scotland looking to make heaven on earth, it maybe wasn't surprising he figured The Almighty was on his team.

*

When Donald Trump acquired the Menie Estate, he already owned courses in Canouan in the Grenadines, New York, New Jersey, Florida and California. The latter was the most expensive on earth. Trump spent $265 million remaking the three-year-old Ocean Trails Golf Course on a peninsula near Los Angeles. He bought it for $27 million in 2002 after the owners went bankrupt. The eighteenth hole had crumbled into the Pacific Ocean, the landslide wrecking three other holes. Undaunted, Trump reclaimed the eighteenth from the sea, raising it up on a matrix of steel platforms. The resurrection cost $61 million.

In Scotland, a top-end course rarely costs more than £5 million ($8 million).

A Trump course is like a supermodel: long, narrow and freakishly pretty. The fairways are sinuous, the rough perfectly variegated, the putting surfaces preternaturally green. In California he filled the bunkers with milled granite. His clubs have tennis courts, equestrian centres, swimming pools, ballrooms, restaurants. The buildings are airy, the furniture opulent. Trump's clubs have a slightly colonial feel. You expect to be greeted by someone waving a cooling palm frond.

But despite the millions lavished on land for golf, which now included Menie, Trump's business was still very much about high-rise.

Donald Trump builds buildings. That's what he does, year in, year out. His wealth made him a celebrity, and graft made him a billionaire. He knots a tie each day and takes his place behind a desk, where he eats his lunch. In *Think Like a Billionaire*, Trump said: 'I have a talent for making money; some people don't. But part of my "talent" is my drive and my work ethic.'

Trump is always on message, ever optimistic. He acts like a politician who actually believes what he says.

When Trump started building in Manhattan in the early 1970s, New York was a cheerless, crime-ridden metropolis, the original Gotham City. Central Park evoked muggings and murders. As with

Menie, Trump was interested in what Manhattan might become. And when he moved there in 1971 from Brooklyn, he was ready to lead the transformation.

Trump had already proved himself while studying economics at Pennsylvania University after spotting a 1,200-unit apartment block in a listing of repossessed federal housing projects. His father's real estate company, the Trump Organization, spent $800,000 refurbishing Swifton Village block in Cincinatti, Ohio. Trump oversaw the work, installing white doors and window shutters to soften the red brick walls, and landscaping the grounds. He was fastidious and within a year the block was brimming with tenants.

The Trump Organization sold Swifton Village for $12m, more than double what it paid for the complex.

Manhattan was, however, very much Trump's own show. While his father Fred stuck to developing cheaper land, Trump moved in on the Commodore Hotel, next to Grand Central Station. He partnered the Hyatt Hotel Corporation, won a forty-year tax abatement from the cash-strapped city government, gave the building a landmark glass façade as part of its makeover, and made a resounding success of the new Grand Hyatt.

When the renovation of a municipal ice rink in Central Park foundered, Trump stepped in to complete the job, cheered on by the local media after his offer of help was initially rejected by the mayor. He finished the Woolman Ice Rink in time for Christmas, doing in six months what civic leaders had failed to do in six years. Trump didn't take a fee. He was New York's very own Santa Claus.

In 1983 he treated himself to a new base in the heart of Manhattan, the fifty-two-storey Trump Tower on Fifth Avenue.

Trump spent money on hotels, casinos, even an airline. He built big and borrowed big, so when the real estate market collapsed in 1990 he found himself somewhat exposed. He came close to bankruptcy before renegotiating more than $2 billion in loans and making one of the great commercial comebacks in US history. The turnaround made it into the *Guinness Book of Records*.

Trump's story now had a compelling dramatic arc – rich boy, poor man, even richer man. It had become a very human story, a tale of hubris, downfall and redemption, given extra resonance by his divorce from the sassy Ivana. Trump emerged in the mid-1990s as a global celebrity but kept the day job. He built. He licensed. He became The Donald. Fallible, yes, but irrepressible.

By the time his attention turned to the North-east of Scotland, Trump had a share in several million square feet of Manhattan. His television show *The Apprentice* was raking in millions for Trump, who was both its star and executive producer. *Forbes Magazine* estimated that Trump Tower, Trump World Tower, 1290 Avenue of the Americas, and 40 Wall Street (four of Trump's best-known buildings) were together worth more than $1 billion, and put the owner's net worth at $3 billion. Trump, never one to put himself down, insisted it was nearer double that.

So why bother with Menie? Golf, after all, accounted for less than two per cent of his turnover.

Yes, he wanted to make money on his courses – that's what helped pay for the next one – but his interest in a Scottish links derived from something altogether more profound. The clues were there in his meticulous reinvention of Swifton Village. They were evident in his immaculate personal grooming, in the scrubbed nails and carefully coiffed hair.

Menie would be all about the pursuit of perfection.

Belhelvie is an unremarkable village. In 1983 two horses and a Shetland pony were found grazing in the church cemetery. The police were called after a man discovered the animals trampling and eating wreaths on his wife's grave. 'It was a terrible thing,' he reported. The parish minister called the desecration a 'most distressing experience' and expressed sympathy for families who had lost flowers to the beasts.

For the next twenty-three years nothing much happened.

And then in November 2006 Donald Trump hired the church hall to unveil his plans for the world's greatest golf course.

Trump could have chosen St Andrews, home of the sport's governing body, the Royal and Ancient (R&A). He could have picked the country's capital, Edinburgh, the seat of the Scottish Parliament. But Belhelvie had a more pertinent association: it was just two miles from Menie.

A black banner hanging outside the Forsyth Hall read 'Trump International Golf Links Scotland'. Inside, aerial photographs were pinned to boards, draped with sashes of yellow and black tartan: Trump's ancestral colours. A large flat-screen television played a loop of business leaders expounding the benefits of embracing Trump. Stewart Milne, a local man who had become Scotland's biggest housebuilder, applauded the Trump Organization for its detailed research on the North-east.

Letters, embossed with the company's name in gold letters, had gone out to residents, inviting them to share in the 'vision' for Menie. Aberdeenshire councillors were asked along too but the council's legal chief Neil McDowall had cautioned them against accepting, warning that their attendance could be 'easily misconstrued'.

The event coincided with the submission of an outline planning application to Aberdeenshire Council on 27 November 2006. Trump International Golf Links Scotland proposed two eighteen-hole courses; a 25,000 sq ft clubhouse; 950 holiday villas; a 450-room, five-star, eight-storey hotel with an accommodation block for 400 staff; thirty-six four and eight-bedroom golf lodges; a spa; tennis courts; a golf academy; a turf research centre; and land reserved for future residential development.

More than 200 people turned up at the hall. Ashley Cooper, wearing a lapel badge with intertwined US and Scottish flags, sat at a table covered with yet more tartan. Six people flanked him, ready to take questions. They included an economist, a transport planner, and professor Bill Ritchie, director of the Institute for Coastal Science and Management at the University of Aberdeen. Neil Hobday was there too.

Cooper started his pitch by explaining that Trump had phoned him from New York at 9am that day.

'That's 4am East Coast time – in Trump Tower,' said Cooper. 'He gave me a couple of last-minute tweaks . . . This is very much on his radar screen and something the entire company is extremely, extremely excited about. Simply put, our goal is to build the greatest golf resort development in the world and we've always set the bar very high. And we've found a site that's worthy of those lofty words.'

Cooper predicted surrounding houses would put on twenty per cent in value and assured locals they would be able to play the course. Cooper added: 'I wouldn't be surprised if Tiger Woods and Colin Montgomerie were out batting a ball around the links.'

The meeting ended with a round of applause.

Afterwards, one Balmedie woman said: 'Opportunities like this only come along once in a lifetime and this would be fantastic for Aberdeen.'

Cooper was buoyant and declared the project, valued at £300 million, as 'a win-win, a home run for the residents'. 'We go into every one of the developments we do globally with realistic antici- pations,' he said. 'If we didn't think something close to this would be permitted, we wouldn't be wasting our time. We want to go where we are welcome.'

It is a natural wonder to compare with the formation of a pearl in an oyster, a miracle spun around a speck of grit. A single blade of grass traps a single grain of sand, borne by the wind. A second grain lodges, then a third. More sand is amassed. After several decades the dune stands maybe fifty feet high: it cannot get any bigger now. As the wind continues to heap sand, the dune collapses under its own weight, its slopes dissolving, the grains dispersing; and waiting nearby to seed the next dune is new marram.

The Menie dunes sit back from the beach, swept into shape by the wind. The landscape looks primeval but the dunes are like a mound of leaves on an autumn day: a fleeting manifestation, an apparition almost.

For 4,000 years they have risen and fallen between Aberdeen and Cruden Bay. The sediment, rippling northward, makes up one of the biggest expanses of sand in Britain. Trump stressed that building a golf course on the Menie Links would be a personal dream, one involving his own dollars, but in chasing that dream he was obliged to take on a silent partner, the toughest and most redoubtable of all: Mother Nature. Any course would be as much hers as Trump's.

Seaside golf has always been subject to the caprices of weather and topography, a game where the ball's trajectory depends on the will of the wind and the run of the ground, where good fortune lies next to bad. A links course can appear open and benign, featureless even. That is an illusion. It is styled that way so the breeze can have a say in how it plays, land and sky often working in concert to sucker the complacent or impatient golfer into being too bold. The canny player, the one who understands the subtle interaction between the elements and his ball, can exploit this blank canvas. He can mix his shots – high or low, fade or draw, punch or bump-and-run – to startling artistic effect.

Donald Trump has no shortage of strategies for getting what he wants. As he teed up his plan for the 'greatest golf course in world', the question was which to deploy in dealing with the chary folk of north-east Scotland.

Chapter 2

AN UNFORESEEN PROPOSITION

If you fly in to Aberdeen from the south, you pass over one of Europe's biggest puddles. Rubislaw Quarry is nearly 500ft deep. This is Aberdeen's womb, the place from which the Granite City was brought forth, naked and unformed. In 1775 it was a sixty-foot hill. By the time it shut in 1971 it had yielded six million tonnes of stone. The closure foreshadowed the demise of other traditional industries – paper mills, textile factories, fishing. This exhausted, barren quarry might well have become a symbol of the city's decline, a black hole at the centre of its galaxy, ready to suck everything back down.

But the city's economy didn't collapse upon itself.

On the fringes of the old quarry, new office blocks have appeared. They serve an industry that has made stone and paper and textile production look like a corner shop operation; that harvested a natural resource that had been under north-east noses for aeons.

For years fishermen had been bringing up tar balls in their nets. In the early 1960s a Texan prospector sailed from Aberdeen Harbour with a pile of dynamite, which was detonated at sea. Bill Mackie, then a young reporter with the *Evening Express*, recounted the story of boarding the boat in his book, *The Oilmen: The North Sea Tigers*. 'The geologist told me the companies "ain't spent spending millions for nothing",' said Bill. Equipment used to measure earthquakes revealed what was in the rock below – organic matter crushed and cooked for 150 million years.

Oil.

In 1964, Britain ratified the Geneva Convention, a move that divvied up the North Sea and opened the way for exploration.

Nobody had tapped oil and gas in such deep, dangerous water but equipment advanced quickly, much of the technology homegrown. Innovative and enterprising new companies supplied everything from drill bits to pipelines. People became millionaires providing catering to offshore platforms.

The BP's Forties Field – which would yield up to 500,000 barrels a day – put the energy province on the map in 1970. The North Sea oil and gas was the making of companies like Shell and BP and has generated more than £100 billion for the UK Treasury. Aberdeen – a settlement for Bronze Age fishers, home to one of the world's oldest universities, a frigid northern city with cobbled streets and cautious attitudes – became the steel-and-glass Oil Capital of Europe. And the whole of the North-east, stretching from the coast to the Grampian Mountains, encompassing the fishing ports and rolling farmland of Aberdeenshire and Moray, benefited.

It took the Piper Alpha disaster to expose the brutal nature of the relationship with the North Sea.

The Piper Alpha platform had once been the biggest producer of oil. When output slowed, a gas production module was tacked on to the platform, right next to the control room.

Just before 10pm on 6 July 1988, a pump used to compress the gas for transport onshore stopped working. A second pump was activated but the on-coming nightshift didn't see paperwork warning that a pressure safety valve, removed for maintenance, had been replaced with a flange. Gas built up, forced the steel plate, and escaped, shrieking in the night. The condensate exploded (a welding spark was the possible ignition source), disabling the control room and triggering oil fires. The searing heat ruptured a gas pipeline, and a fireball engulfed the platform. A nearby platform continued to pump oil to Piper: commercial imperatives denied the crew authority to shut off production. Flames rose 400ft. Steel melted. Men jumped 175ft into the sea.

One hundred and sixty-seven people died, including two rescuers aboard a vessel searching for survivors.

The legendary Red Adair spent three weeks bringing the fire under control, filling the wells with cement and capping them. The accommodation module, where many had sought shelter, was later raised from the seabed with eighty-seven men entombed. Thirty bodies were never recovered. Just sixty-two people survived. A bronze memorial statue stands in Aberdeen's Hazlehead Park. An inscription reads: 'Dedicated to the memory of the one hundred and sixty-seven men who lost their lives in the Piper Alpha oil platform disaster.'

In Piper's aftermath, safety, particularly evacuation procedures, was dramatically improved. The industry continues to provide 40,000 direct jobs in the North-east and supports other businesses: bed and breakfasts, helicopter operators, taxis, pubs. The North-east, home to half-a-million people, has the lowest regional unemployment in the country and the highest average wage in the UK outside London. But, like granite, oil is a finite resource. There is plenty of fossil fuel left in the North Sea – at least as much as has been taken out – but extracting the dregs is becoming harder and more expensive.

When Donald Trump arrived in Aberdeen, production was already slowing as energy producers explored cheaper provinces abroad. The North-east has responded by trying to restyle itself as a centre for renewable energy instead of just a hydrocarbon power base. A concentration of pioneering technology companies, and high quality housing, is envisaged for a thirty-mile coastal corridor between Aberdeen to Peterhead.

Sitting in the middle is the Menie Estate.

Trump described himself a 'big fan of all forms of alternative electricity' but said he wasn't 'thrilled' about a plan for thirty-three wind turbines running up the coast, close to the shore, from Aberdeen towards his estate.

'I don't think, Scotland, for the sake of some electricity, you want to ruin the beauty or the majesty of your country,' he said after unveiling his golf course plans. 'If you can find a location where they're not too obtrusive, we wouldn't object. From the eighteenth hole, to be honest, what I want to see is ocean. I don't want to see windmills.' Trump said he believed the company behind the wind-farm plan was 'willing to make certain concessions' and added: 'I do warn Scotland on this. You just can't do this to yourselves.'

When the windfarm proposal was scaled down and moved away from Menie, Aberdeen Offshore Wind Farm Ltd felt compelled to explain changes were made to accommodate migratory birds on the Ythan estuary and the flight paths of offshore helicopters. David Hodkinson, managing director of AMEC's wind energy business, a partner in the project, said: 'While confirming that we have had constructive discussions with Mr Trump's representatives, I can state that they have not resulted in any further modifications to the layout beyond those incorporated previously to address concerns by other project stakeholders.'

Trump suggested another way to help replace oil and gas: back him.

He wasn't the only one who thought a golf resort could act as a catalyst for investment and might help fill the void left by heavy industry.

Jennifer Craw, chief executive of development agency Scottish Enterprise Grampian, said: 'We have benefited in the North-east for thirty years from the oil and gas industry and will continue to do so for decades to come. But this development has the potential to help us diversify the local economy for future generations and show-case Aberdeen City and Shire on a global stage.' Ian Dunlop, area director for VisitScotland, the country's tourism agency, said it would 'immeasurably enhance' the North-east's profile. Aberdeen's Lord Provost John Reynolds called it the 'biggest thing in Scotland for many, many years' and Stewart Spence, owner of the city's only five-star hotel, declared it 'the biggest thing since the oil'.

Trump's plan, if approved, promised to partly satisfy at least one economic hankering.

Strategic planners estimated the North-east would need at least 50,000 new homes in the next twenty-five years to maintain a critical population mass – big enough to keep companies in skilled employees, to make the airport viable, to attract and retain big-name retailers. Aberdeen's population was shrinking as families headed for satellite towns and villages where housing was cheaper. The mood, however, was testy: people wanted what space they found all to themselves. Menie was not, as things stood, zoned for residential development on that scale.

Local councillors, those faced with finding room on the ground for thousands of new and replacement houses, often balked at the challenge. They talked about the need to preserve the 'green belt' when in reality land zoned as such was often just empty fields. The concept was introduced post-war to stop London burghs coalescing but became an ideological ligature: planning policy across the UK requires housing to be concentrated around existing settlements, away from open countryside.

But Menie wasn't just any piece of countryside.

There were Sites of Interest to Natural Science and Sites of Environmentally Sensitive Areas. Aberdeenshire Council had labelled it an area of Undeveloped Coast and an Area of Landscape Significance. The estate's highest dunes formed the southern third of Foveran's Site of Special Scientific Interest (SSSI), a UK designation affording an extra degree of protection from development. The Menie Dome – formed after a breach in the coastal dune ridge funnelled sand further inland – was the most dramatic manifestation of the system's dynamism. And it was here Trump wanted to put his championship course.

As well as the unusual geomorphology, Menie's SSSI designation recognised the community of animals supported within the grassy folds and swampy hollows of the old and new dunes. Menie was home to otters, bats, water voles, badgers, bank vole, brown hare, grey squirrel, hedgehog, mole, pygmy shrew, rabbit, stoat, red fox, weasel, wood mouse, great crested newt, smooth newt, palmate newt, frogs and toads. Lichens, fungi, mosses and liverworts thrived too.

There are thirteen SSSIs in Scotland located wholly or partly on golf courses. Eleven of the courses pre-dated the notification. A nine-hole course in the far north of Scotland at Durness needed retrospective permission. The other, at Machrihanish on the west coast, had static dunes but these contained rare orchids. Major sections were declared off-limits, necessitating long walks between some holes. Earth-moving was restricted to tees and greens, leaving players to hit over blind brows from sunken fairways. Rough couldn't be cut.

Brian Morgan, who had discerned the golfing promise of the site, and secured American and Australian money for the course, noted that cows and sheep were free to stomp and chomp their way across the dunes during winter. Machrihanish, he said, was previously a dumping ground for farm machinery and a playground for the military. Abuse and neglect appeared more acceptable than golf. 'Only a person with lawyers and money could force their way through the planning problems which confront golf developers today,' he lamented.

Menie's conservation designations were largely unknown to Donald Trump when he bought the estate. His resort plan, while promising jobs and wealth, could not have been more contentious had he proposed squeezing eighteen holes into Princes Street Gardens and turning Edinburgh Castle into a hotel.

Aberdeenshire Council is the sixth biggest of Scotland's thirty-two local authorities. It has six settlements of more than 10,000 people and a hinterland that runs to the edge of the Cairngorms, Britain's highest mountain range.

Planning officers are there to ensure Aberdeenshire renews itself and grows in an orderly fashion – that there are enough schools and roads to cope, that natural and human heritage is respected. They assess a development proposal against policy, collecting and collating views, weighing the positives and negatives, before producing a detailed report with a recommendation to grant or refuse. A typical planning application might involve turning a steading into a house or erecting a wind turbine next to a farm. A big deal would be a new supermarket. Nothing the size of Trump's dream had ever crossed the desks of Aberdeenshire Council's planners.

On 30 March 2007 an Environmental Impact Assessment (EIA) was submitted by Aberdeen-based agents S.M.C. Jenkins & Marr, accompanied by economic and transport studies. The intention had been to submit the EIA before Christmas but it could not be completed until thousands of pink-footed geese (winter migrants from Iceland) showed up on the estate where they fed on the farmer's barley. The birds would not be rushed, even by Donald Trump.

Details about housing were also included.

More than two months before Trump first visited Aberdeen, his representatives had discussed with planners the inclusion of housing at Menie. Two senior architects from Jenkins & Marr met with Aberdeenshire Council planning director Christine Gore and the Scottish Government's Chief Planner Jim Mackinnon at the council headquarters. Also present was Keith Newton, who managed the Formartine area, which covered Menie. A minute from the meeting, obtained under the Freedom of Information Act, stated: 'Without wishing to sound negative about the project overall, it was agreed one area where the development does not sit easily with local policy background, is the inclusion of 250 houses for private sale.' Selling holiday homes was seen as easier: 'The closer his connection between the housing and the resort, the better the fit with local policy.'

Trump's plan now included 500 residential houses.

That summer, Donald Trump wasn't the only person planning a golf course with housing in the North-east.

During the week of the Open, Jack Nicklaus flew into Aberdeen to join the party. The eighteen-time major winner had agreed to design a course on the Ury Estate, fifteen miles south of the city, next to the coastal town of Stonehaven. On a sodden July afternoon, the Golden Bear arrived by helicopter. He was chauffeured around the 160-acre estate before setting out his vision for the Nicklaus Signature Golf Course.

In a marquee, Nicklaus – hair still boyishly blond, hands like baseball mitts – enthused about the project.

'It's a beautiful piece of property,' he said. 'We can do something very special and hopefully something that's going to complement Stonehaven and the community, something that people are going to enjoy. The goal is a golf course for the community, not a golf course for the guys who are playing the Open at Carnoustie this week. We're not coming here to do a course for the sake of it but to make this a successful development and enhance the value of what happens in Stonehaven and the community . . . Hopefully it will create jobs, bring tourism here, and hopefully an awareness of the area. It will make golf more important to Aberdeenshire than it has been in the past. I haven't known a golf course yet that hasn't benefited the local economy.'

Local company FM Developments wanted to invest £40 million in the estate. There were to be four hamlets with a total of 230 houses, leisure facilities and holiday accommodation. The housing would help pay for the restoration of ruined Ury House, a listed building, which would become the clubhouse and hotel.

When asked if the course would be better than Trump's, Nicklaus replied: 'I would certainly hope so. I've got to believe that.' But he added: 'I don't want to put down his property or project because I don't know anything about it.' After the press conference, Jack was happy to sit and chat. People wanted to know if he thought Tiger Woods, then on twelve majors, would overtake his tally. Nicklaus wasn't sure. He gave one of those wincing smiles. Nor was he convinced Trump's course would be acclaimed as the world's greatest. 'He's a businessman, not a designer,' Nicklaus observed.

Aberdonian Paul Lawrie, who won the Open at Carnoustie in 1999, was designing a course as part of a £115 million development four miles west of the city. The Muir Group wanted to convert Blairs College, a former Roman Catholic seminary, into a 150-bed luxury hotel, with health club, restaurant and conference centre. The pitch sounded familiar. 'We're going to provide a fantastic golf course for everyone,' said Lawrie. 'This has the potential to provide a wonderful asset for the North-east as well as attracting visitors to the area.'

The Muir proposal included 260 houses. Like Ury, this would be an 'enabling' development. That is, profit would pay for the renovation of the historic college, a cross-subsidy acceptable under planning policy.

If that wasn't enough, there was a proposal to reinstate Aberdeen's premier municipal eighteen-hole to its original design. The gently undulating Hazlehead course, framed by pine trees and heather, had been laid out by Alister MacKenzie, architect of the revered Augusta National, in the late 1920s. A consortium wanted to lease the course for ninety-nine years and invest £10 million while maintaining public access. Eight-time major winner Tom Watson was spotted measuring yardages one Monday morning, accompanied by PGA chief executive Sandy Jones. Now, that would have been a sight to put you off your putt.

No detailed designs were required at this stage for Trump's resort but preliminary sketches for the clubhouse, hotel and resort facilities showed ornate structures with turrets and flags. Wimberly Allison Tong and Goo (the architecture firm represented at the airport) specialised in what it called 'Victorian vernacular', and had been hired because of its reputation as one of the world's leading holiday resort developers. Previous projects in the US included Disney's Grand Floridian Resort and Spa, the Walt Disney World Resort in Florida, and the Venetian Resort-Hotel-Casino complex in Las Vegas.

Scotland's architectural watchdog was unimpressed with the drawings.

The body, set up to review nationally important projects and provide guidance, wrote to Aberdeenshire Council urging it to reject the plans. Angela Williams, Architecture and Design Scotland's head of design review, said:

Should a world-class golf facility be located in such a sensitive land-scape, it needs to be realised through an exemplary design process to secure a built development and reformed landscape of exception-ally high quality. We do not see such an aspiration in the designs as currently submitted. They would not only have a negative impact on an area of high landscape value but would also devalue the Scottish architectural tradition that they attempt to emulate . . . We do not believe that the designs submitted are of sufficiently high quality for this unique location, for a project with such an international profile, or for Scotland as a whole.

The design of buildings could always be changed. What really rattled some people was the prospect of the dunes being stabilised for the championship course.

Conservation charity the Scottish Wildlife Trust (SWT) lodged a formal objection with the council. Its planning co-ordinator Paul Gallagher said: 'The application maintains an unacceptable level of impact on habitats and uncertainty remains in relation to the effect on species. The process of stopping sand from getting on the golf course would destroy the natural process which keeps the sand moving.'

Government agency Scottish Natural Heritage reckoned Trump's plans would neither conserve nor enhance the dunes, and instead cause irrevocable damage. SNH's Grampian manager Robin Payne said: 'This stunning site at Menie with its huge sand dunes is part of the largest dune system in Scotland, stretching from Newburgh to Bridge of Don . . . As the development of a golf course at this location would cause such significant damage to the SSSI, and the dunes to the south of it, we have submitted an objection to this part of the proposal.'

Scotways, the former Scottish Rights of Way Society, was con-cerned about references on the drawings to security gates.

The Royal Society for the Protection of Birds (RSPB), which had taken to calling itself an environment charity, objected too. Area manager Dr Ian Francis said: 'Within the application site, the breeding bird community includes a range of species typical of sand dunes and slacks, with significant numbers of skylarks plus some breeding waders, particularly lapwings and redshank.' He worried about Birds of Conservation Concern – a 'red list' of birds that had suffered a sudden or historical decline, or whose habitat had been lost. Species in the Foveran Links that had seen a big fall in populations included the corn bunting, linnet, reed bunting, and thrush. The 'red-list' also featured the house sparrow and starling, both common garden birds in the North-east.

The entrance to Menie Estate is easily missed driving north from Aberdeen. There is no giant red T to mark the spot, no heavily reinforced steel gate, no gold or marble or waterfall. Just a low wall and a huddle of trees.

A narrow driveway, bordered by fir and willow, runs flat and straight for quarter-of-a-mile before kinking right. The land opens out: you have a sense of it falling away towards the sea. You turn again, sharp left, and enter what feels like a country park. There are several ponds and lawns girdled by ancient beech and sycamore trees. Below the road is the resplendent Menie House, built in 1835 on the foundations a fourteenth century castle. It has a pleasingly compact symmetry, neatly offset by a fairytale tower. From a distance the tall thin chimneys, sash windows and stepped gables make it look like it was made from Lego.

A sign reading 'Trump International Golf Links' directs you to a steading, which has been converted into an estate office, but I'm heading for the big house.

Up close, Menie House is the quintessential country mansion: gravel forecourt, imposing black door, riotous ivy. Local building magnate Donald Stewart put it up for sale in 1959 and hundreds of people queued up to buy the fittings and furniture. Auctioneer Charles Crighton of Aberdeen and Northern Marts described the turn-out as 'the largest audience I've seen at a sale'. Shifting the house, which came with a ghost, the ubiquitous green lady, took that bit longer and it came close to being demolished.

George Sorial, Trump's director of international development, greets me. He is dressed like a golfer. Chinos, open-necked shirt, heavy watch loosely worn, short navy blouson embroidered with 'Trump International Golf Links', the same curly font as the sign.

Sorial joined the Trump Organization after first becoming a customer. Home is the seventy-two-storey Trump World Tower, next to the United Nations' base in New York. Sorial got to know Trump as president of the board of residents. There was a closer connection, though. His mother, like Trump's, emigrated to New York from the Isle of Lewis in the Outer Hebrides, off Scotland's west coast. Both New Yorkers are just one generation away from being Gaelic speakers.

Sorial, then, understands the pull of the past.

'Mr Trump takes great pride in what he does and has wanted to do a project in Scotland for a long time,' he says. 'He loves golf, he loves building courses. This is something he has contemplated for years, something he may view as a legacy. There is a very significant emotional attachment. If you're in a room with him and start to discuss this project, he can't conceal his excitement, his passion. He has said he wants to build the best links course on earth – and he'll do it.'

We're sitting at a table in the front room. Sorial has replaced Ashley Cooper on the project. Five feet of separation lends the interview a formal air. I suspect Sorial wants to establish boundaries. He is very particular about what he says and the context, checking that I've understood what he considers to be the salient points, where the emphasis has been laid, how the message should be distilled. The precision of his conversation reveals his training as a lawyer: he is Assistant General Counsel for the Trump Organization.

'My experience of working with the council has been very posi-tive,' he says. 'I've found them to be very business-minded, fair, reasonable people. Based on all our discussions, all our meetings, I'm fairly confident they're going to do the right thing for the people of Aberdeenshire. I recognise what we're asking them to approve is a challenge for them on many levels. But they've handled everything with professionalism and dignity, and there's been a mutual respect. In my experience in business and life in general, when you have those things together the outcome is always positive and works for everyone.'

Do the right thing for the people.

No presumption, a hint of deference, but there's a clenched civility too. Sorial, a detail man, is hard-ball.

'In any project there comes a point when you have to make an unemotional, detached business decision. You ask, is it worth it if there's going to be a fight or a dispute? You look at costs and you look at options – are there other places you can do what you want to in a quicker, more cost-effective time frame? But we're not any-where near that.'

If for any reason they feel we're not doing the right thing, if they let us know, we will go some place else.

Sorial knows the case is going to hinge on the environment. He mentions that the Trump National Golf Club in New Jersey has just become the recipient of the first annual Metropolitan Golf Association Foundation Environmental Award for its construction and opera-tion. And he ventures that the Trump Organization's own environ-mental study at Menie, commissioned from UK scientists, will comfortably comply with council standards.

'Not only did we hire the best, but we put them out there and said, go take a look, we are not going to restrain you, we're not going to influence you. We want you to paint an open and honest assess-ment of what we're dealing with. The council has an obligation to be rigorous in examination of what we're doing. Any good developer doesn't mind that and will do everything they can to give them comfort and assurance that the end product is a high quality one.'

Sorial's manner has lightened when we finish. He is less defensive, perhaps because the questions have related to planning procedure rather than Trump's celebrity, to prosaic fact. He tells me later Trump has a motto, a bit of advice to keep handy for those long trans-Atlantic trips. Get it done, have fun.

IT is just a whim of one rich individual.

The area does not need any more golf courses.

The enjoyment of the area would be detracted from by the visibility of such a monolith of a development.

The development is solely to line the pocket of Donald Trump and money raised would not remain in the North-east.

Residents were 'sold' a much smaller scheme when the Trump Organization made approaches to local residents to buy their homes.

These were some of the objections recorded in the planning department's report on the Trump resort, published on 12 September 2007. They numbered 985.

Trump has a proven record of long-term employment.

The benefits to tourism and leisure far outweigh any concerns.

We must not squander the opportunity of a lifetime.

If objectors had been around hundreds of years ago as golf evolved along the coast, they would have objected then and if they had been successful then Scotland may have never given golf to the world.

The whole of Europe and the rest of the world are watching us with envy that this corner of Scotland has been chosen before other destinations.

27

These were arguments in support of the scheme. They numbered 1,850.

Planning officer Lesley Aitken reported that the resort would cost £953 million to build. The inclusion of housing, which raised land value from £21 million to £112 million, was non-negotiable. Aitken said: 'The applicant has made it clear that the housing is proposed in order to make the development as a whole financially viable, and that effectively the proposals stand or fall on the inclusion or exclusion, respectively, of the housing development.' Price tags would range from £400,000 to £1 million. Golf club membership was put at a steepish £3 million, a figure disregarded as a 'mistake' by the Trump Organization on its publication: the course would be pay-and-play. The resort was forecast to generate £47 million a year for the local economy while supporting more than 1,000 permanent jobs.

On the negative side, the Trump Organization's own environment study predicted 'significant adverse' impacts to the land. Some sand would no longer shift. Habitat would be lost.

Despite its linkages with a new bypass for Aberdeen and a runway extension at the city's airport, Aitken indicated sustainability was 'very much at the heart of this proposal'. She did concede the location – far from any railway, poorly served by buses, and a twirl of the globe from the homes of potential US and Far Eastern tourists – was 'not on the face of it very sustainable'. She took some comfort from the Trump Organization's 'commitment' to reducing the use of fossil fuels. Aitken said: 'Any locational disadvantages can be offset by enhanced transport linkages and the provision of "smart cars".'

That was Smart, the manufacturer, which had an electric vehicle. Yes, Trump was proposing to provide residents with free cars.

Here's how Aitken summarised the £1 billion question being asked of the council:

Given the steady growth of new golf facilities in Scotland in the last twenty to thirty years perhaps it was only a matter of time until Aberdeenshire saw the level of interest currently at its door. However, this period of growth has also seen an increasing emphasis on environmental concern and various pieces of legislation have led to more scrutiny of such proposals . . . Striking a balance between the applicant's ambition of building the best golf course in the world with the environmental sensitivities of the site and the significant economic benefits to be derived from the construction, operation and worldwide prestige of the golf and leisure resort proposal are exactly the competing issues, which must be addressed . . . The development will undoubtedly have a substantial beneficial impact on the regional and local economy but conversely it is also clear that there are significant adverse effects on natural heritage.

Aitken was not there to vacillate. The biggest professional judgment of her career read:

There is no doubt that the proposal does conflict with many heritage designations but taking all of these landscape, natural, built and cultural heritage considerations together along with other relevant matters, it is considered that these are not compromised to such an unacceptable degree as to justify refusing the application. The view of Development Management, in line with Government guidance, is that this is an occasion where the social and economic benefits are of national importance and that these do override the adverse environmental impacts. Even the severe impact on the SSSI and some of the wider environmental and biodiversity issues must be set aside in this instance to allow this level of economic and tourism invest-ment to take place. This is a proposal which no planner or Development Plan could have foreseen and such an opportunity to diversify the economic base must be grasped. The housing element of the proposal does not currently sit very comfortably with policy either but if this is the level of investment which is going to be needed to allow the wider economic and tourism investment to take place on such a grand scale, then it cannot be seen as a precedent and only applies in extremely rare circumstances.

Aitken recommended approving the scheme in principal. Before undertaking any work on the ground, the Trump Organization would have to come forward with detailed plans for landscaping, building work, access and transportation. Aitken suggested attaching fifty-five conditions, including the establishment of the Menie Environmental Management Advisory Group (MEMAG) from representatives of Aberdeenshire Council, SNH, the Scottish Environment Protection Agency, the Scottish Coastal Forum, and the local community, as well as Trump's own team.

George Sorial received the news around noon in New York. 'I went into Mr Trump's office with it and explained it in detail to him. He said, "That's great." He was very happy with the tone of the report.'

The Scottish Wildlife Trust was distinctly unhappy. Chief Executive Simon Milne said: 'The recommendation totally disregards the impact that this development will have on a very special place for wildlife.'

Opponents of the scheme, including those drawn from Aberdeen Campaign Against Climate Change, responded by forming a single-issue campaign group. Sustainable Aberdeenshire described itself as 'a pressure group of concerned environmentalists, local residents and the broader community who are united in opposition to the Trump steamroller'. Its slogan was *Menie Not Money*.

One of its most articulate members was Mickey Foote, who had lived on a houseboat in London prior to moving to Scotland. Foote produced The Clash's first album in 1977. He was a bona fide dude, someone who made blue-tinted Ray-Bans look like the most natural accoutrement in the world. His cottage, where his mother once stayed and which he visited as a child, overlooked the Menie Estate. Foote, who didn't believe Trump's financial case stacked up, was passionate but pithy too. Even George Sorial, who found himself chatting to Foote during cigarette breaks at public meetings, admitted to a sneaking admiration.

The newly-formed Sustainable Aberdeenshire decided to march

on Menie – or rather along its beach. On a blustery October day around 200 people gathered at a car park near Newburgh Golf Club for the five-mile walk south to Balmedie Country Park. Organiser Rob Ashlin, a post-graduate ecology student, said: 'There were mothers and children and local residents taking part along with university students and campaigners. It was a very representative cross-section of people.' Not everybody finished. Some were repelled by the wind slicing northwards across the beach, the same prevailing wind that shaped the dunes.

Trump – in a black tammy and quilted jacket – is back among the dunes. He claims it is in his 'genes' to withstand the cold. What about the coastal haar, the thick fog that rolls in from the North Sea? 'I love the fog because I can't see my bad shots,' he jokes. As he swings a club for the cameras, Trump says to no one in particular that he wants Scottish golfer Colin Montgomerie to know Menie will be the best course in the world. 'But it's going to be tough,' he adds. 'Tell Nick Faldo too.' Trump is relaxed about the planning process. 'If Scotland wants to have the finest golf course in the world, everything will go smoothly.'

Today, Trump is 'walking every blade of grass' with the studious Dr Martin Hawtree, who has taken over from Tom Fazio II.

Hawtree has been hired on the recommendation of Peter Dawson, Chief Executive of the R&A, golf's governing body, following a meeting a year earlier in an office overlooking the St Andrews Old Course. Dawson proffered the name at the end of a forty-minute conversation about what it might take to land The Open.

Hawtree, a doctor of philosophy, is in the habit of setting up courses for the event, recommending subtle tweaks to the layout. He is a past president of the British Institute of Golf Course Architects, now the European Institute. Hawtree Limited, of Woodstock, England, is the oldest golf course architectural practice in the world, having been involved in building or improving more than 750 courses since 1912.

The recruitment does much to stress the Trump Organization's affinity with the links landscape.

Hawtree wants to make sure the course is 'in harmony' with its surroundings: 'I am intrigued by balance in the composition of a golf hole, trying to ensure that the wider landscape surrounding a hole, in the case of this project, towering dunes, is fully balanced.'

'We had the club house in the dunes, but we are moving it back,' says Trump. 'The dunes will hardly be touched.'

The group re-convenes in a marquee on the grounds on Menie Estate. Trump, now in a suit, sits at a table bedecked with tartan. George Sorial is to his left. Hawtree is at the table end. Small and bespectacled, there is something of the cleric about him. When speaking, he clasps his hands as though in prayer. Quietly spoken and self-effacing, he is the antithesis of Trump. The designer is introduced to the media.

'I've really gotten to know him over the last couple of months, and he feels as strongly about the environment as I do and he wants to do as little as possible,' says Trump. 'He lives by that motto and that's why the Royal and Ancient has him every Open that they have for the last . . . how many years? Ten or so, Martin?'

'Not as many,' says Hawtree bashfully.

'Not as many as ten,' says Trump, shrugging. 'But they *have* used him. I just think he's a spectacular person and a great architect, so it was very important for me to get Martin.'

Trump is asked about the housing.

'I need to do the homes in order to get – and I wouldn't even say return on my investment – some of my money back. It's possible I could lose a great deal of money. It's a very, very expensive job to do it properly. It would be a lot less money if I didn't care about the environment.'

Trump expects to win over doubters.

'Often I have resistance and the people that resisted in the end fall in love with the project.'

He is asked about Michael Forbes, a local quarry worker who

lives within a wedge of the planned championship course. Forbes has vowed not to sell his home to him.

'Go down and take a look at how badly managed that piece of property is,' says Trump. 'It's disgusting to look at – rusted tractors, rusting oil cans. I actually asked him, "Are you doing this on purpose to try to make it look bad, so I pay you more money?" And then he gets publicity, you know, sitting there like, "Oh, he's an angel."'

Trump is imitating an angel, praying meekly to the sky. He lowers his hands.

'He's not an angel, he's a tough guy. He's a tough, smart guy. And it's too bad, that's one case.'

His voice trails off with faux sadness.

'Look, the right thing to do is approve it in the sense that we're stabilizing the land. The environment will be far superior when we've finished and the economic development aspects of the job are beyond anything probably proposed here for many, many years . . . I hope it gets approved. I can't say that it will. I can say this. That everybody in this room will come back in ten years and everybody will say, "That was a great job."'

And with that Trump is finished, ready to return to New York to sit and wait.

The time for talk was at an end. For the people who would decide what became of the golf resort plan, it had never really started.

Planning law in Scotland requires councillors and politicians to keep their mouths shut until an application is determined, lest they influence the outcome. Opposition MSPs (members of the Scottish Parliament) were accusing First Minister Jack McConnell of breaking the ministerial code of conduct by talking up Trump when the tycoon first turned his attention to Scotland. Though both the First Minister and Trump stressed no specific sites were discussed, Balmedie resident Debra Storr's nose twitched at the claim. She said: 'I haven't seen anything that's a clear breach but it has a bad smell about it.'

Planners could only offer *advice* about development. A £1 billion project was now in the hands of Aberdeenshire councillors, part-time politicians elected with a few hundred votes. And the vice-chairwoman of the committee that would rule on Trump's resort was a certain Debra Storr.

Chapter 3

A REGRETTABLE DILEMMA

They look like they have gathered for the Last Supper. Eleven councillors arranged at a long table, the leader flanked by her disciples, some loyal, others bent on betrayal.

Rather than facing each other, the Formartine Area Committee (FAC) finds itself fanned out towards an audience. On a dreich November night, 200 people have packed Balmedie Primary School gym hall. In the public gallery, on a hard plastic seat, sits George Sorial. Like everyone else he has come to hear the committee debate Trump's proposed golf resort and vote on its worth. The austere hall, with its pale green paint scheme, wooden wall bars and harsh fluorescent lights, has the feel of an interrogation centre.

'Okay, then, we open with the main item on the agenda . . .' says chairman John Loveday, seated beneath a basketball hoop. The main item is the only item on the agenda.

Lesley Aitken outlines the Trump proposal and asserts that the economic benefits will outweigh any detrimental impact on the environment.

And then – nothing. A £1 billion golf resort plan is on the table and nobody has anything to say.

Protocol requires a councillor other than the chairman to initiate debate. Loveday leans forward and looks along the table, to his right, then left. Rather than facilitating discussion, the committee's curious orientation has put the emphasis on public performance. Sighing, Loveday surmises 'nobody is prepared to do it' and grudgingly opens.

He mentions Trump's demand that any offshore windfarm be

sited away from the course. 'The arrogance that was put forward has not made things very easy,' he says. 'This is the North-east. I wish the applicant had taken more notice of that.'

Sorial *is* taking notice and makes a note. You can't believe it's anything nice.

Loveday describes plenty of positives – meeting the shortage of hotel accommodation, the economic benefits – but also negatives, especially the requirement to stabilize some of the dunes. 'I don't like interfering with nature,' he says. 'Nature is a very powerful beastie.' He also has a 'big, big problem' with the housing. 'Suddenly we've got 500 homes being plonked in the middle of the country-side.'

It's a slam-dunk.

Council leader Anne Robertson immediately puts forward a motion to grant. She urges colleagues to be objective about 'a once-in-a-lifetime opportunity' and draws comparisons with the offshore energy industry: 'Can you imagine where we would be now if our predecessors said no to the oil and gas industry thirty-seven years ago?' Robertson continues: 'This is an exceptional application and it needs to be considered as such. The eyes and ears of the world are literally upon us. The people of Aberdeenshire and beyond are looking for us to take a positive decision.'

A deflated Paul Johnston says he was hoping for more of a natter. He is left to offer an alternative motion, known as an amendment, calling for the applicant to produce a plan that avoids the SSSI altogether. 'Once it's gone, it's gone,' he says ruefully.

Debra Storr goes further and calls for a flat refusal. 'There's no policy that supports building houses to support a business venture.' She suggests housing in a 'closed' community is 'against everything we have spent ages trying to establish', that there is no case for development on the SSSI, and compares the scale of job generation to building three Asda supermarkets.

Her speech brings the first round of applause of the evening.

Rob Merson, who seconds Robertson's motion, thinks Storr is

missing the point. 'How many tourists would we take in to visit three Asdas?' he says, prompting laughter.

The atmosphere hardens again as the committee moves towards the vote.

First, councillors must decide which of the two amendments to accept – refusal or deferment.

Johnston's gets the nod 7-4.

Sorial cannot relax. Johnston's amendment calls for one golf course, just 300 holiday apartments, restrictions on the height of the hotel, and nothing in the way of housing. Trump has stressed there is no room for compromise. Deferment will be as bad a refusal.

Davidson – grant
Duncan – grant
Gifford – grant
Hendry – grant

Trump just needs two votes.

Loveday – defer
Johnston – defer
Merson – grant

Now Sorial can relax. Robertson surely won't vote against her own motion.

Norrie – defer
Owen – grant
Storr – defer
Robertson – grant

The result brings a brief whoop from the impeccably behaved crowd. It's hard to tell if that's because they're on Trump's side or just glad to be out of those hard plastic chairs after three hours.

George Sorial isn't, however, smiling. He looks livid. He makes for John Loveday and upbraids him for the personal attack on Trump. 'If he can't keep his emotions under control, he shouldn't be a councillor,' he says afterwards.

In the car park, he tries to find a quiet spot to call the boss back in New York where it's late afternoon. 'It's a go – we won,' he says, standing in the drizzle.

After explaining events to Trump, Sorial passes me the phone.

'I'm very happy the way it happened,' says Trump. 'I'm honoured by the support, I'm honoured to be a part of this. It's going to mean jobs for the North-east of Scotland, economic benefits, tourism. And all of this is going to be around long after the oil has gone.'

If anyone was well placed to enjoy the splendour of Trump's proposed championship golf course, it was Michael Forbes. But when it came to relaxation Forbes wasn't interested in golf. He preferred mending cars in his barn or fishing for salmon off the coast in a small boat. Forbes, who had worked at a quarry in Belhelvie for nearly twenty years, was fixing nets when Trump had dropped by. Forbes judged the meeting a 'waste of time': 'He said, "You're beautiful people, and I hope if we can't work things out, we can be good neighbours," and I just thought, what a load of rubbish.'

Forbes claimed he was offered £350,000 for his twenty-three acres – more of a demand is how he describes it – which prompted him to return the offer to Menie House in its original envelope with 'shove it' penned on the outside. What had riled Forbes was Trump's description of his home as 'disgusting'. 'It's none of his business,' said Forbes when I visited him. He rubbished reports that he'd asked for £1 million for land he had paid £24,000 for in the early 1980s. He said: 'I've never asked for money. I just want to be left in peace and quiet.' And what, I asked, if Trump offered him £10 million? 'He can shove it,' he said. Forbes sounded scunnered of the whole business. He said if you mentioned Trump to his wife Sheila, you would have to 'scrape her off the ceiling'.

Forbes was being styled by the world's media as David to Trump's Goliath, as the principled Scot standing firm against American imperialism. He was hailed as a Local Hero, after the 1983 film shot partly in the North-east about a recalcitrant local who thwarts an American oil baron's attempt to buy an entire village for a refinery. The Trump Organization thought Forbes was being manipulated – when, for example, he lifted his kilt and bared his backside for Trump in a documentary. Either way, Forbes was ready to resist any attempt by Trump to manicure Menie. He was the ultimate immovable object.

The *New York Daily News*, which had a journalist at the FAC meeting, reported: 'Donald Trump's $2 billion dream golf course in Scotland got a key vote of approval Tuesday – but not from the feisty fisherman whose refusal to sell his farm has knocked the billionaire's plans off-kilter.' News agency Reuters described the same 'fly in the ointment'. It reported: 'The salmon farmer's ramshackle old smallholding nestles behind the sand dunes, just below what may soon become a five-star hotel on Trump Boulevard, an elite golf academy and a turf research centre.'

In nearby Balmedie, the talk was mostly positive. Tracy Leiper, a garden designer and mum of three, said: 'Golf is a good way forward. The whole world can be involved.' Irene Williamson, a housekeeper at Balmedie's White Horse Inn, said: 'It's a brilliant thing. If he's willing to put his millions here I think we should take it.' Alana McLaren wondered if she would still be able to walk her spaniel along the beach but didn't think the dunes would be trashed. 'Trump's putting his reputation on the line and I don't think he's going to risk it,' she said.

In securing the backing of the FAC, all Trump had done was clear a bunker off the tee.

Because the application was contrary to existing planning policy, which presumed against building on unsullied coast, it was always going to have to go before the more powerful Infrastructure Services Committee (ISC). Victory at the FAC had set up an easier approach shot for Trump but he still wasn't in a position to hole out: the ISC could only indicate a 'willingness' to approve a plan at odds with council policy, and would be required to pass it to the Scottish Government for determination.

The ISC could, however, reject Trump's plan – declare it out of bounds – and end his game there.

The policy committee was chaired by Martin Ford.

Ford grew up in Exeter and moved to Scotland in the late 1980s to work with the Scottish Agricultural College. He had a doctorate in plant ecology and saw the planet as something to be cherished and protected. He didn't drive, choosing instead to cycle while on ward business. Twice vice-chairman of the Scottish Liberal Democrats, he joined Aberdeenshire Council in 1999 as the member for Newmachar and Fintray, the village where he lived. His election promise was to 'ensure the council continues to give high priority to its environmental responsibilities'.

The meeting in the committee room at the council headquarters begins jovially enough with chairman Ford reminding members the applicant's Scottish background should not be a material consideration. The planning report on this occasion is presented by the department's director Dr Christine Gore, who informs the committee the proposal is an 'exceptional one' and, as such, one where policy exceptions can be made.

Debra Storr, who sits on the ISC, has a list of objections ready to circulate but Ford says there won't be enough for the public.

'I've got fifty copies,' she pleads, but it's still no-go. Picking up from where she left off at the FAC meeting, she insists the scheme and the projected 1,000-plus jobs are not of 'national importance' and therefore unexceptional. Marcus Humphrey dismisses Trump as a self-styled 'white knight', riding into town to save the post-oil economy. 'The applicant's attitude has bordered on patronising,' he says. 'Visitors come to this part of the world for its beauty and solitude, not for Disneyland.'

Councillor Alastair Ross takes issue with the housing. 'He doesn't need the houses, he *wants* the houses,' he says of Trump. 'It's property speculation. We've got to do business but not business at any price. We need more affordable houses. I'm not anti-rich but I'm pro-the-people and I think that's where we should all be.'

Ross puts forward a motion to refuse.

'I think we have to play hard ball,' he says. 'I fully expect and hope the applicant will come back and negotiate.'

This is shaping up as a game of bluff. A handful of Aberdeenshire councillors ranged against the might of Manhattan.

'The rest of the country would think us mad if we turned it down,' says retired farmer Albert Howie.

SNP member John Cox puts forward an amendment to grant.

'Are we going to scrutinise every major development and say who's going to make money out of this?' he asks. 'Think about what we can do here for the North-east.'

Jill Webster explains how she had holidayed near the dunes and studied them at university. She says they are 'close to her heart' and that she doesn't want to see the landscape destroyed – but suggests neither does Trump.

Paul Johnston, also on the ISC, again puts forward an alternative amendment to defer.

The committee must choose between two amendments – grant or defer.

Ford – defer
G J Clark – defer
Cox – grant
Gifford – defer
Howie – grant
Humphrey – defer
Johnson – defer
Mollison – defer

If one more councillor votes to defer, the best Trump will get is a tie.

McRae – grant
Pratt – grant

Sorial knows what's coming.

Ross – defer
Storr – defer
Tait – defer
Webster – grant

It's 9-5 in favour of deferral. The option to approve is off the table. This isn't what George Sorial has travelled 3,500 miles to hear.

The vote now is between defer and refuse – either way, Trump is being left to think again.

Ford, casually dressed in a jumper and open-necked shirt, doesn't have the floor until nearly three hours into the meeting.

'This is the first time we've been asked to put our money where our mouth is,' he says. 'The dilemma is regrettable.' Ford suggests it would be 'hypocritical' to approve an application out of kilter with planning policy. 'We're not saying, "Go away, we don't want you." We're saying no to the destruction of our natural heritage. We're not saying no to golf courses and investment.' Is he advocating refusal or deferral? 'This is a kind of moral balance. We're told we can only have it if we sell our soul. Well, we don't have to sell our soul.'

Ford – refuse
G J Clark – refuse
Cox – defer
Gifford – defer
Howie – defer

Humphrey – refuse
Johnson – refuse

Johnson has just voted against his own amendment.

Mollison – defer
McRae – defer
Pratt – defer

It's 6-4 to defer.

Ross – refuse
Storr – refuse
Tait – refuse

Jill Webster, who loved the dunes as a kid, is last to vote.

Webster – defer

Seven-all. The chairman has the casting vote.

Ford votes to maintain the status quo – that is, to refuse.

It isn't quite 'you're fired' but as good as. Billionaire Boeing 727-owner Donald Trump gets his marching orders from a man who travels by bicycle.

As a beaming Storr hugs her supporters, a thunderous George Sorial exits the committee room.

'It sends out a message that if you want to do big business, don't do it in the North-east of Scotland,' he says. 'The councillors who felt by this decision they would attempt to strong-arm us and use that as a negotiating point were greatly mistaken. Ultimately, we can go and develop the project somewhere else. We'll be fine, it's the people of Aberdeen and the Shire that they really let down.'

*

It wasn't what you usually found in the foyer of a five-star hotel. The framed front page of a local newspaper.

The Marcliffe at the Pitfodels, four miles west of Aberdeen, displayed a montage of the seven councillors who had dumped Donald Trump's golf plans. Headshots had been arranged against a black background with Ford in the centre. The *Evening Express* story carried the headline 'TRAITORS'. The tone of the headline was inspired by the Marcliffe's owner, Stewart Spence, who branded the councillors as traitors and was quoted as saying: 'The councillors who voted against it should be tried for treason. They are numpties. They've let 500,000 people in the North-east down and the whole of Scotland because there is such a tiny minority against it.'

That day, the *Evening Express*'s editorial thundered:

These are the seven bright sparks we today accuse of betraying the North-east, its people and its future.

Once in a lifetime a man like Donald Trump – a man with vision and business acumen – comes calling, offering to pump £1 billion into the region.

He wanted to put us on the world map, pulling in thousands of visitors from across the world . . . and what happens? These misfits send him packing.

On a day when we needed brave councillors with enough vision to steer us to a bright future beyond oil, we got small-minded numpties, unable to see beyond shifting sand dunes and migrating birds.

We are now a laughing stock to the world, a backwater where our most important economic decisions are driven by buffoons in woolly jumpers, and women who are so out of touch with reality that they ask how people will get to the golf course when the oil runs out.

These traitors to the North-east were intent on making a name for themselves, not putting this area and its people first.

We truly hope Mr Trump appeals this decision. He knows the vast majority of North-east people back him.

As for these no-hopers, they should do the honourable thing and step down as councillors. The North-east will not forget or forgive their treachery.

While Spence couldn't wait to hang the *Evening Express*'s front page on his hotel wall, the coverage troubled others. Some thought the vilification of councillors 'disgusting'. Others, even those agreeing with the sentiment of the editorial, wondered if in joining the clamour for Trump to stay, commentary and reportage had been allowed to blur, and the newspaper's impartiality compromised.

People, of course, are no longer passive consumers of news. The internet has created a publishing platform where anyone can tell a story, however vainglorious or egocentric; where they can broadcast the most outlandish conspiracy theory or provide vacuous commentary on the minutiae of their lives. Email has been equally empowering, giving people an immediate and penetrative voice, the means to contribute to breaking news stories or critique its coverage. Here are some of the hundreds of emails the *Evening Express* received in the hours after the ISC meeting:

An absolutely ludicrous decision by those people who pass themselves off as councillors. They are denying the North-east and its population, who they are elected to represent, long-term prosperity and an opportunity to put this part of Scotland on the world map as a tourist resort. Shame on them.

Have you heard the disgusting response of Trump's UK representative to the democratic decision of the Aberdeenshire infrastructure committee? He said the North-east could never do big business. Trump just wants to make a quick buck out of our amazing country and disappear. We do mega-business. Fishing, oil, gas, agriculture, universities, research, IT. Bog off, Trump and go and bully someone else.

Congratulations to those who rejected the Trump proposal, and shame on your treatment of these people. Please give us the e-mails of those other councillors who are yet to be convinced that Aberdeen does not need the arrogant Trump, and are prepared to sacrifice the environment they have a duty to protect.

Hollywood gave us the Magnificent Seven, Aberdeenshire gives us the Myopic Seven. Seven elected officials who clearly have difficulty even seeing the nose on the end of their face. The Myopic Seven should consider this debacle their last gunfight and ride off into the sunset, hang up their six-shooters and hang their heads in shame. Resign now!

Councillor Marcus Humphrey stated that 'visitors come to this part of the world for its solitude and beauty – not for Disneyland'. Get real Cllr Humphrey, we don't need Donald Trump or Disneyland. If we want Disneyland we don't need to look any further than the Mickey Mouse outfit calling itself the Infrastructure Services Committee.

Just as readers are no longer passive consumers of the news, newspapers are no longer passive providers.

It isn't enough to wait for news to happen – the bank robbery, the football signing, the record-breaking rainfall – not when an increasing number of competitors are also waiting. Newspapers strive always to be first with the news, but there is another way a newspaper can distinguish itself from its rivals: by acting as a strong collective voice for the community it serves. The *Evening Express* prides itself on being a campaigning newspaper, on canvassing the views of readers and championing what matters to them. An independent poll commissioned by the *Evening Express* found 80.3% of people thought the Trump scheme should get the go-ahead. The vast majority of readers thought the ISC decision sucked and the newspaper said so.

Kate Dean, leader of neighbouring Aberdeen City Council, said it was 'beyond belief that such a short-sighted decision could have been made'.

None of this undermines a newspaper's role in preserving democracy, in scrutinizing the workings of government and keeping politicians accountable for their actions. Reportage can be ardent and provocative, but there must always be a balance.

The councillors who voted Trump down were all invited to explain their stance. Ford said: 'We voted for a unique piece of natural environment. You can build a golf course somewhere else but there is no alternative site for a number of rare species.' Paul Johnston, a retailer, said: 'You cannot say the North-east is a laughing stock because we took a rational, reasonable decision, democratically debated. If Trump picks up his ball and walks away he is devaluing his brand.' Alastair Ross, who runs a business consultancy, said: 'I think this is a much longer game. We would have looked very silly if we had rolled over at the first tickle of our tummies.' Debra Storr, an IT worker, said: 'If Donald Trump loves Scotland as much as much as he says he does, he will not go off in a huff.'

The council's policy, Ford laboured, was not one of development per se, but *sustainable* development. When people castigated Ford for 'not seeing the bigger picture' he must have allowed himself an ironic smile. What, to his way of thinking, could have been more important than cutting fossil fuel usage and safeguarding species? But Ford had voted to reject the plan in the expectation it would be resubmitted in a form more to his liking. It was, essentially, a gamble, a £1 billion roll of the dice, using assumptions based on the behaviour of Scottish developers.

Stewart Spence was still fulminating over the ruling when I called at the Marcliffe the following morning to meet George Sorial, who was staying there. The Lord Provost, there for another meeting, spoke of flying to New York to persuade Trump to appeal to the Scottish Government rather than withdraw from Scotland altogether. Amid the hysteria, Trump's official release was ominously restrained: 'We are surprised by the decision – it would have been a great development. We are considering an appeal and also considering doing something very spectacular in another location. Sadly it will not be in Scotland.'

Over bacon and eggs, Sorial told me they were looking at land for a course in Northern Ireland. As for any appeal in Scotland, he was still thinking about that.

Within hours of the ISC decision, council bosses announced plans for an emergency meeting that might overturn the vote blocking Donald Trump's proposal. Leader Anne Robertson needed the signatures of sixteen other councillors, or the signature of Aberdeenshire's provost, to be able to convene the meeting. 'The email system at the council has been struggling to cope with the number of people getting in touch and my phone has been going non-stop since this morning,' she said. Councillor Stuart Pratt, who voted for the resort at ISC, said: 'This is not democracy. Seven out of sixty-eight possible councillors turned this down.'

Some years earlier the council decided to let the ISC determine planning applications. The aim was to stop the full council being overwhelmed with referrals from the council's six area committees. Officers were now feverishly looking for loopholes in their own rulebook.

Trump called me from New York the day after he got dumped by the ISC. 'The decision is very sad for Scotland and certainly sad for Donald Trump,' he said. (I figured billionaires were allowed to talk about themselves in the third person.) 'I feel a little bit guilty because I feel like I let my mother down in a certain way.'

He announced he would attend an emergency meeting if it might help win approval.

'If they feel it is appropriate for me to be there, I would fly in immediately. If they wanted me there, I would be there. It might have been a mistake not to be there at the committee this week. But honestly, I thought this was going to be routine. You would think the whole council would have power over a committee. I don't know

Mr Ford. I feel badly that he voted against us. If I sat down with him I really think I could convince him that what we're doing is going to be great environmentally. We're going to be great to the bird and animal population and great to the dunes. Those dunes are totally unstable. They could blow away very quickly with one or two bad storms.'

Ford, of course, would have that countered that what made the dunes special was the fact they *did* blow about.

Trump was overwhelmed by messages of support, more than 1,000, he reported, to his office. 'I've never had so may people sending me letters saying please don't leave. It's from people in Aberdeen and Aberdeenshire, and Scotland. The support is so universal and so big. It's absolutely amazing.' Trump, however, wasn't to be cajoled. 'I was called by two major governments immediately,' he said solemnly. 'I haven't decided about appealing. The problem with the appeal is that it's a long process.'

On 3 December, hopes of any appeal were dashed by George Sorial, who said the process carried 'too much uncertainty at the end of it'. Short of a guarantee they would succeed, it was a no-go.

Sorial also revealed that the Trump Organization had signed a thirty-day option on the land in Northern Ireland. Sorial didn't say it precluded building at Menie but there were advantages in leaving people, not least Aberdeenshire councillors, to infer it must be one or the other. Sorial said: 'It is up to them now, they are the elected officials. They got themselves into this mess, and now they have to find a lawful way out of it. The planning processes are a disaster and have to be changed, but knowing that it will be different in the future is not going to help us. We are not asking for special treatment, we just want to be treated fairly, which we don't think has happened.'

The following day it fell to Anne Robertson to break the dread news. Nothing in the council's rulebook allowed the ISC's decision to be overturned. The emergency meeting would still take place the following Wednesday but without the possibility of reviving the Menie plan.

MSPs went into mourning. 'The situation is about as grim as it could get,' said Aberdeen Central MSP Lewis Macdonald, Labour's tourism spokesman. Tory North-east MSP Alex Johnstone said: 'I am afraid that it looks hopeless. This is what happens when people with no business sense come up against big business. Big business does not hang around. It goes elsewhere. It's a disaster for the North-east and Scotland.'

The years spent searching for a site, the millions invested in land, the hundreds of hours devoted to drafting plans: they had come to nothing. The dream, spun and shared by Trump, woven into a tantalizing tapestry of jobs and riches and an economy beyond oil, was dead.

Chapter 4

A SMELL OF SLEAZE

It was a star's entrance – preceded by a hum of excitement, guided by police, garlanded by flashbulbs. This was his moment, his destiny, his accession. Alex Salmond swept into the Aberdeen Exhibition and Conference Centre just before 3am. Suddenly the evening was alive. Here was a professional politician, the main act. As soon as he arrived, his opponents – the vanquished – were called to the stage. Not for Salmond hanging around, waiting, wondering, hoping. In the May election of 2007 he took the Gordon seat with 14,650 votes to Nora Radcliffe's 12,588, sweeping away the Lib Dems' 2,072 majority.

'The people of the North-east are the most independent-minded and generous people in the world,' he said, bristling. 'It has been a privilege all my political life to serve them. I intend to continue to do so.' Even in victory, Salmond sounded combative. He heralded the SNP's performance as the start of a 'new political dawn'. Salmond continued: 'It will be up to every party to see how a platform can be built to take Scotland forward, on public services, on the economy, on continuing to build the confidence of the Scottish people, to take the determination of this country's future into their own hands.'

The SNP came to power largely on the independence ticket. Many supporters hadn't really looked at the small print, at policy. What the country had inherited was a government with leftist leanings but also a love of the spotlight. The party's socialist agenda could not disguise Salmond's defining characteristic: ambition. He wanted Scotland to be a global player, certainly to hold its own in Europe, and as MSP for the Gordon constituency he had what might have seemed like the perfect light sabre: Donald Trump's golf resort proposal. He passed the Menie Dome on the drive to Holyrood from his home in the North-east village of Strichen.

But Trump's dream was dead, killed off by seven councillors before the year had ended.

Or rather it was, until the Scottish Government intervened on 4 December.

The day Aberdeenshire Council had declared there was nothing more they could do for Trump, Ministers asserted their authority and 'called in' the application to rule on it (though without saying how they would do it or when). A statement from the Scottish Government said: 'Ministers recognise that the application raises issues of importance that require consideration at a national level. Calling the application in allows Ministers the opportunity to give full scrutiny to all aspects of this proposal before reaching a final decision.'

The move was unprecedented. The year before, only eighteen out of 40,000 planning applications dealt with by councils had been called in for determination by the Scottish Government, and they all had been *approved* (they required a ministerial opinion because they were contrary to planning policy).

Trump presumed the intervention was a response to public outcry. 'I've never seen anything quite like it,' he said. 'The support has come not just from the people in Aberdeen and Aberdeenshire, but all over Scotland. People in the office are asking me, "Is something going on in Scotland?" because of all the calls we're getting. We are honoured by the fact that the Government has taken it as a matter of such great importance – and it *is* a matter of great importance. From day one, it has been so popular with the people. We want to do something very, very special.'

He finished the call with his customary refrain: 'Hopefully it will be positive because we are ready to start work on what will be the greatest golf course in the world.'

There was only one little hitch. It emerged that Salmond had spent almost an hour meeting George Sorial and Neil Hobday at the Marcliffe hotel on the day before the call-in. During the get-together, the First Minister raised the country's Chief Planner Jim Mackinnon on the phone. He passed the phone to Sorial, who arranged to meet Mackinnon the next day at his office on Victoria Quay in Edinburgh – a meeting which took place just hours before the application was called in. What's more, it emerged that the Cabinet Secretary for Finance and Sustainable Growth, John Swinney, who would rule on the plan, had attended a tourism function at Trump's Westchester Golf Village in New York on 2 December.

Two weeks into December, Martin Ford was sacked from his job as ISC chairman. His Lib Dem colleagues left SNP councillors to deliver the fatal vote on the back of a motion from John Cox that went largely unresisted.

Mickey Foote compared the ousting at the council's emergency meeting to the 'machinations of a banana republic'. While celebrated by many, the calling in of the Trump planning application raised questions about devolution and democratic rule. The SNP had advanced the vision of a united Scotland, awaiting liberation, but the country's history was one of internecine strife. Scotland was a changing aggregation of people, born of bloodshed and economic necessity. Highlander and Lowlander arguably had never felt a special kinship. They just happened to dislike everybody else – the Romans, the Vikings, the English – more than each other.

Independence – in Scotland, in Europe, across the world – was as much about power grabbing as power sharing.

Dr Michael Dyer, a senior lecturer in politics at Aberdeen University, saw the Scottish Government's intervention in the Trump case as being consistent with demands that local authorities freeze council tax and talk of a national police force replacing Scotland's eight regional ones. It was about political consolidation. 'Holyrood has become a super regional council, imposing national standards,' said Dr Dyer. 'Power has been devolved from London to Edinburgh, but within Scotland power is being centralised in Edinburgh. It's in line with a move towards centralisation.'

The leader of the UK Commons agreed. Harriet Harman pledged to raise concerns about the handling of the application with Des Browne, the Scotland Secretary. She said: 'The point of ensuring there was a Scottish Parliament was to devolve power from Westminster to people in Scotland, not to suck up power from local authorities and place them in Edinburgh.'

Ford stood accused of being partisan, but could local decision-making be anything but?

In fairness to the Scottish Government, the problem was not so much the binning of the Trump plan but that its fate had been entrusted to so few. No one disputed it was of at least regional significance yet it had been determined by a committee of fourteen. The emergency meeting didn't just curtail Ford's power but the ISC's, re-writing the rulebook so that the full council would take major planning decisions in the future.

So how would the full council have voted if presented with the Menie proposal?

The chamber was asked for a show of support as an 'enhanced consultee'. Of the sixty-five councillors present (Wendy Agnew, Alan Buchan and Mitchell Burnett were absent), only two registered their dissent, Martin Ford and Debra Storr. The other five ISC members who had voted against Trump just two weeks earlier sat in craven silence.

Trump hailed the uncontested motion as 'a tremendous victory'. 'The public should feel vindicated because they want it so badly,' he said. 'This sends a terrifically positive message to Ministers.'

Salmond's explanation for meeting Trump's representatives was simple: he had been asked to as Gordon MSP. Salmond accepted that as First Minister he was excluded from the 'planning decision process' but suggested that under Parliament's code of conduct he had to make himself accessible in a constituency capacity. 'I have met many people on all sides of the debate as I am duty bound to do so,' he said. 'I had no idea that the application was going to be called in the next day. I had absolutely no idea about that – that was never discussed.'

The Opposition wasn't letting the matter go, especially when it turned out Salmond had travelled to the Marcliffe in his ministerial Mercedes. West Aberdeenshire and Kincardine Lib Dem MSP Mike Rumbles said: 'The car alone makes it look like he was attending as a Minister and not as a constituency MSP as he claimed.' A Government spokesman responded: 'The First Minister was at an official engagement in Inverurie on 3 December, using a government car. It made practical sense for him to travel with his special advisor to complete government business and prepare for government business in Aberdeen the next day.'

There was something faintly trite about the exchanges – it felt like they related to an employee who had popped into the shops for a pint of milk on the way back to the office – but this was inescapably a matter of trust.

Trump wrote to all sixty-eight Aberdeenshire councillors, ostensibly to thank them for their 'time and effort' spent reviewing the application and to promise that the North-east would profit:

I believe that many tourists will come to play Trump International Golf Links and they will need a place to stay. They will shop in your shops, eat in your restaurants, and be very good for the local economy. Additionally, many jobs will be created, and, importantly, some day in the future when the area can no longer rely on oil, this wonderful complex will not only be a great source of pride, but a source of revenue and employment.

He signed off with:

I want to express my gratitude to local MSP Alex Salmond and the Scottish Government's Chief Planner James Mackinnon for agreeing to meet with my representatives last week. Although they would not discuss any particular details of our planning application and did not in any way indicate their support or opposition to our application, the meetings were important in that they demonstrate a great commitment for the people of Aberdeenshire and Scotland.

Aberdeen South MSP Nicol Stephen grabbed the chance to skewer Salmond and his government. The Liberal Democrat had been a golden boy of local politics after being elected to the former Grampian Regional Council in his early twenties. He was a former party leader and the country's deputy leader during Scotland's Lib Dem-Labour administration. During First Minister's Question Time, Stephen wanted to know why the developers were 'present with the Chief Planner on the very day that their application was called in'. He wondered about the 'pressure' put on Mackinnon by Ministers, and whether the project had been jeopardized as a result.

His voice was heavy but his heart must have been skipping a beat.

Stephen told the Parliament: 'This is a serious situation for the First Minister and his government. Every step of the way there is contradiction, concealment and cleverness from his government on this issue. It smells of sleaze.'

Sleaze.

That was the word that did it – the insinuation of immoral behaviour, not just impropriety.

George Sorial was incandescent and demanded an immediate apology for what he called a 'reckless and unsubstantiated attack' on his company's character. He said the Trump Organization had never been so insulted, which was quite something as it wasn't exactly short of detractors in the North-east.

Salmond was incensed too. He took a call from the *Evening Express* early next morning, interrupting a speaking engagement to accuse Stephen of 'wildly irresponsible gutter politics'. 'He launched a cowardly attack on Jim Mackinnon, a public official of outstanding probity, who does not have the right to defend himself,' he said.

It was too late, though. The Opposition succeeded in pushing for a parliamentary inquiry. Salmond would face a cross-party grilling in the New Year, and it was inconceivable Trump's planning application would be dealt with until the Local Government and Communities Committee hearing was completed.

At first the Trump Organization refused to field a representative. When the committee threatened to use legal powers to petition Neil Hobday, a Scottish resident, Sorial acceded to their request. On his appearance in Edinburgh he was still smarting over Nicol Stephen's allegations, and further irritated by the MSP's absence. He said: 'I am surprised the politician who made that comment isn't at the hearing today. I would have liked to ask him to justify what he said. As important as any project is for us, our global reputation is more important. We have never had the word sleaze associated with us before.'

Of course, the New York lawyer was there to answer questions, not to ask them. Glasgow Pollok MSP Johann Lamont wanted to know why Trump hadn't just appealed.

Johann Lamont: I am interested in the balance in the planning system. The right of appeal is often seen as a balancing mechanism. You described the situation in Aberdeenshire as 'chaotic', but others might argue that the council was following its processes, which had been agreed. However, there is a balance, because you have the right to appeal. Why did your organisation choose not to exercise that right of appeal, which is well founded in planning law?

George Sorial: I am very willing to answer that question, but I have to say that I am a little surprised that the issue is of such interest. Much of the advice that we receive from counsel is privileged and confidential. It amazes me that I have to sit here and have these

discussions in a public forum. However, I am willing to do so . . .
Our answer to your question is simple: we have tremendous opportunities everywhere else in the world to do our projects. I could name
dozens of countries that will more than welcome the development
of a Trump project. Why did we not appeal? We were not willing to
wait. We do not have the time. We had other options available to us
– which we still have.

The Trump Organization, Sorial explained, had requested the
meeting with Salmond because the council was unable to say if the
emergency meeting might be able to reverse the ISC decision. 'You
never have enough information,' he said. 'It is always worth talking
to someone else, whether they are a lawyer, another business person,
a cab driver or a civil servant . . . As a matter of routine, in every
jurisdiction in which we have operated worldwide, we talk to
government officials . . . A lawyer can give a lot of insight, but it
never hurts to hear from someone in government and have them
explain practically what to expect.'

Committee member Patricia Ferguson, Labour MSP for Maryhill,
was sceptical about the contribution the First Minister could make.

Patricia Ferguson: I just wondered whether you wanted to illuminate
which areas Mr Salmond was able to help you with and at what point
it was decided that a conversation had to take place with the Chief
Planner to augment what Mr Salmond could tell you.

George Sorial: We discussed the procedural aspects – that is really
all that I can say. I requested a meeting with the Chief Planner because
I wanted more information. I was advised that it was fully within
my rights to do so, so why would I not take advantage of a situation
like that?

Ferguson: My original question was – given that a channel of communication had already been opened up with the Chief Planner,

why did you not just avail yourself of the opportunity to perhaps telephone him directly?

Sorial: I think that it was just a matter of circumstances. We were all in the room when the request was made. Perhaps you are right that I could have done that, but you have to put yourself in the situation. At the time, a lot was going on – I had been in literally dozens of meetings. It is easy to sit here months later and reflect, but at the time the situation was difficult. I do not know why I did not think of calling the Chief Planner myself. I do not think that it really matters.

Sorial turned the question around and said, 'If a chief planner is not ready at a moment's notice when they might lose a £1 billion investment for their country, what are they doing occupying that position?'

In his own testimony, Jim Mackinnon agreed, telling the committee it was not the first time he had given advice to the private sector:

People do not ask us about dormer extensions in Greenock or hot food shops in Macduff; that is not what we get involved in . . . It was not a question of a private tutorial; I made myself available to clarify the process and procedures that were available, in a confusing situation, for a potential £1 billion investment in Scotland. I did not think that that was in any way untoward or improper, because I was not discussing with the Trump Organization the merits of the case.

Mackinnon was uneasy about what an appeal might hold when the indications were that councillors were going to endorse the plan on 12 December. 'If Aberdeenshire Council had supported the development, despite having rejected the application, the appeal procedure would have been a strange thing,' he mused. In his testimony John

Swinney concurred: 'It was possible that, at an appeal hearing, the Trump Organization would turn up to argue in favour of the application, and that Aberdeenshire Council would also turn up to argue in favour of the application.' He worried that such a piece of surrealist theatre would bring the whole planning system into disrepute.

The First Minister, the committee learned, had been taking a keen interest in council proceedings. He had called the council's Chief Executive, Alan Campbell, on the day of the ISC meeting to see how it went, telling his cross-examiners he thought it 'unusual that a decision of such importance would be taken by a committee'. The Marcliffe rendezvous, he said, 'dwelt largely on the possibilities of Aberdeenshire Council being able to consider the application at a full meeting of the council'. He added:

> I had telephoned the Chief Executive of the council that afternoon to ask him for the latest information on the council's deliberations on the matter. I was able to update my constituency interest with the latest information that I had on that possibility. However, the issue of appeal was also discussed at that meeting. It is true that one of the Trump Organization representatives said that they were adverse to appeal. The reason that they gave was reputational damage . . . However, the question of call-in was never discussed at that meeting. The reason why it was not discussed is that I was not aware that it was an option. Incidentally, I suspect that the vast majority of people in Scotland were not aware that it was an option, either. I thought that the options were either that the council could find a way to consider the matter or that the matter could be pursued by appeal. Those were the options that I discussed.

During cross-examination, former Conservative leader David McLetchie, who had proposed holding the inquiry, adopted a rhetorical mode:

David McLetchie: Is it not slightly odd that the Chief Planner, when briefing you on the situation, did not say to you, 'Well, obviously, Mr Trump can reapply,' or, 'Obviously, Mr Trump can appeal,' or, 'There's this wizard wheeze – as long as they haven't signed the decision letter, we can call it in'? Do you not find it slightly surprising that the Chief Planner did not tell you in simple terms that that was an option?

First Minister: No. When Jim Mackinnon gave evidence at last week's meeting, I think he argued that he thought about the matter over the weekend, so perhaps it is not surprising that he did not refer to the call-in option on 29 and 30 November, as that was before the weekend. After that, why did Jim Mackinnon not say that to me either in the phone call that I made to him on 3 December or, indeed, in the courtesy phone call that he made to me on 4 December? I suspect that he deliberately did not say it because at that stage he was forming in his mind what the advice was going to be to the Minister, and he did not consider it appropriate to tell me or to give me advance warning of what that advice was going to be.

McLetchie: On the people who knew that call-in was an option, Mr Swinney claimed in his evidence last week that he knew about the option in advance of his two five-minute telephone conversations with Mr Mackinnon before he took the decision. We also learned from Mr Mackinnon's evidence last week that the Trump Organization had engaged a very expert planning lawyer from Dundas & Wilson and Mr Mackinnon assured us that the Trump Organization's legal representatives certainly knew that call-in was an option. You might not have known that it was an option, but two crucial people certainly did know that it was, yet it was apparently not part of your conversation.

McLetchie also pushed Salmond on whether he had ever denied the engagement took place. The *Evening Express* had been tipped off about the meeting, but our source said it took place on the Tuesday, not the Monday. My parliamentary colleague drew a blank from the Scottish Government when he put the date to Salmond's people. When I chased the story, Salmond volunteered the meeting had taken place on the Monday. In a letter to the committee, he said:

> *A phone call came in to my spokesperson on Wednesday, 5 December, from the* Evening Express *asking, inter alia, if I had met the Trump Organization on Tuesday, 4 December, at the Marcliffe. Ms Dempsie replied that she had no knowledge of that, which is correct since she speaks for me as the First Minister. On Thursday morning, the question was repeated by David Ewan [sic] of the same paper – again asking about Tuesday, 4 December – and Ms Dempsie consulted me. The strict factual answer to that question would have been 'no'. However, I determined that that could be seen as misleading and therefore instructed Ms Dempsie instead to reply making the distinction between my role as constituency MSP and that of First Minister.*

The committee never thought to ask Salmond who else he had *spoken* to during the Marcliffe meeting. The answer? Trump himself, on the phone from New York. He too had heard Salmond's thoughts on procedure and the possibility of Aberdeenshire Council overruling the ISC and saving the day.

As for the meeting at Victoria Quay, Mackinnon called Council Chief Alan Campbell, who asked Sorial and Hobday to leave the room before explaining it was becoming increasingly clear 'the council would be unable to resolve it in a way that was unchallengeable'. According to Campbell, the Chief Planner phoned again and said, 'Look, we're thinking about call-in here.' Campbell told the committee: 'That was the first time that call-in had been mentioned, and it came as a bit of a surprise.' Two hours after the first call, Mackinnon phoned to say the plan was going to be handled by John Swinney, Cabinet Secretary for Finance and Sustainable Growth, who said he had 'enormous confidence in the quality' of advice offered by the Chief Planner.

The parliamentary committee produced its findings on 13 March 2008. It said it believed the 'true purpose' of the Trump Organization's meetings with Alex Salmond and the Chief Planner was 'not to seek advice from either of them about legal processes' but to 'emphasize' the Trump Organization's position following the ISC vote – that it might not appeal:

> Alex Salmond said that, during the meeting, the Trump Organization was uncertain about the routes ahead. The bulk of the meeting was taken up by his (Alex Salmond's) opinion on what he detected about Aberdeenshire Council's wish to revisit the decision that the Infrastructure Services Committee had made. They spoke about the appeal process. Alex Salmond said in his oral evidence that he thought that the Trump representatives were uncertain about the process of appeals. However, in oral evidence to the Committee, George A. Sorial confirmed that the Trump Organization had a wide spectrum of advice on any issues that might conceivably arise. He said – 'There was never any issue relating to our not understanding our options.'

The committee did not accept Salmond had been 'duty bounden' to meet the Trump people as a constituency MSP, and it thought it 'extremely unwise' – but not improper – for the First Minister to act as a hotline to the Chief Planner:

> It seems astonishing to accept that the First Minister did not perceive there might be a risk in his actions, that his actions might be open to question and that as a consequence the decision might be open to legal action. The Committee believes that, far from taking a pre-cautionary approach, the First Minister was cavalier in his actions and displayed, at best, exceptionally poor judgment and a worrying lack of awareness about the consequence of his actions.

The committee also criticized John Swinney for making the call-in on the 'back of two short telephone conversations with the Chief Planner' and was 'very concerned' he did not first 'obtain legal advice nor official advice in written form'. But as with Salmond, the concern was not that his behaviour had been underhand, rather that it might have 'tainted' the process or 'imperilled' the project at a later stage.

None of the committee findings contained an explicit criticism of the ISC's decision. In his testimony, Alistair Stark, of the Royal Town Planning Institute in Scotland, said: 'There was a substantial body of opinion – particularly in the written press – that the planning authority in the instance that we are talking about should have reached a decision that reflected majority opinion in the area. That is not an acceptable way to take a planning decision. One must listen to, evaluate and take into account public opinion, but public opinion can never be the sole criterion when taking a planning decision.'

The trouble was that politics kept getting in the way. MSPs could barely move without being accused of pandering to Trump.

Swinney was rounded on for attending a VisitScotland reception at Westchester for members of the GlobalScot network – the meeting of 2 December. According to the Government, a commercial fee was paid for the venue and no members of the Trump Organization were present. Salmond was grilled for meeting people who were looking to launch a multi-million business in his constituency. The committee, which took the view that the application had been called in to 'retain the potential for the substantial investment', accepted Scotland's planning laws had put Salmond in an invidious position:

> The Scottish Government quite properly attaches great importance to economic development and the Trump Organization's proposal for a major development on this scale in the North-east was clearly of interest to it as it was to the previous administration . . . It can be difficult to reconcile these goals with the operation of the planning system in which Ministers are required to perform a quasi-judicial role.

People who take planning decisions are like a jury in court. They are expected to have lived in a vacuum prior to turning up, to have heard or said nothing pertaining to the application. Salmond *had* passed opinion on the Trump proposal, at a public hustings in the Aberdeenshire town of Inverurie during the election campaign. He told the committee: 'All the candidates were asked about the issue and I answered the question. I said that I was in favour of the development with certain caveats.' However, on becoming First Minister he had to suddenly stay schtum and everyone had to somehow forget the hustings had ever taken place.

The prissiness was touched upon by Jim Mackinnon in his testimony:

> I found it quite amazing to hear Ian Paisley, the First Minister of Northern Ireland, who almost hotfooted to the Trump Organization, say, 'We want you to come to Northern Ireland.' That seems to be quite acceptable. It is interesting that the First Minister of Northern Ireland is responsible for the planning service. The planning service in Northern Ireland is an agency of central Government, and local government is basically responsible for, I think, bogs, bins and burials. So the Northern Ireland First Minister is saying, 'Come to Northern Ireland; we will help you through the process,' while our position seems to be that contacts between Ministers, senior civil servants and potential investors comes under public scrutiny and is in some way improper. I think that, as a Government, we need to reflect on that.

The Trump Organization had tried its damndest to make sure the emergency meeting went its way. Two forceful letters were sent out the day Salmond met George Sorial and Neil Hobday at the Marcliffe.

The Trump Organization's Scottish solicitor Ann Faulds wrote to the council suggesting that public opposition formed a 'new material consideration', necessitating a review of the ISC ruling. She warned the council her client would 'take all necessary steps' to ensure the council exercised all its power in reaching a 'reasonable and appropriate' decision. In New York, Trump's assistant Kelley Stengele sent Salmond an email. 'I have attached some articles that Mr Trump would like you to read,' she said. The attachments were media reports of his interest in Ireland.

The deadline for that deal was now extended by six months. 'We're looking at multiple sites through Northern Ireland, Europe and all over the world,' said Trump. 'It's not something that's particular to what's going on in Scotland. People come to us every day with offers and I would not read any more into it than that.'

An email appeared on the government website, posted in response to a Freedom of Information request. Sent by former First Minister Jack McConnell to Trump in November 2005, it thanked Trump for meeting him in New York. McConnell added: 'I am confident Scotland can offer you a stable high quality business environment.'

McConnell's replacement had been denounced for trying to do his job and Trump's plan had meantime languished in a drawer for eighty-four days. During the wait, he was even threatened with court action under a seventeenth-century law for failing to register a coat of arms used as a promotional crest for Menie. George Sorial tartly noted: 'The committee has not found any evidence for the claims that were made both against Mr Salmond and the Trump Organization because there were none. We are bitterly disappointed we had to go through this entire process which has been a major distraction for all concerned.'

Aberdeen solicitor Peter Macari believed everyone, including the committee, had missed what he called 'the white elephant in the room': the precept around which the call-in pivoted. Ministers couldn't call in an application *after* it had been rejected, and planning law deemed rejection to be the date the applicant received *written* notice of the decision. Scotland prides itself on the rigour of its legal processes. Writing in *The Journal of the Law Society of Scotland*, Macari challenged that conceit:

It is suggested that the fact that the Trump application was verbally refused, and advertised as refused on the council website, is sufficient factual evidence of the determination of the application. Of course it cannot be said to have an 'effective date', because it is not reduced to writing, but the application is logically and rationally determined. You simply cannot ignore this white elephant in the room! In such a controversial situation the matter could surely be put beyond doubt by the Solicitor General on behalf of the Scottish Government giving chapter and verse as to why the call-in is perfectly acceptable. The question remains, at what point are the Scottish Ministers excluded or prohibited from calling in? A call-in after a verbal decision has been made but before it is issued in writing supports the suggestion that the Scottish Ministers may lack the necessary impartiality which should be a feature of all planning applications. Applications should be dealt with on their merits, rather than by mob rule or popular demand. The legal profession has been strangely silent, but there is no precedent either in case law or in any textbook which supports what the Scottish Ministers have done. What ministers have succeeded in doing is sending out a message to the effect that if they don't like something, they are going to change it, and if necessary they will shelve the rule of law so that they can deal with it in any manner they see fit. In conclusion therefore we appear to be faced with a rather sordid state of affairs, and an attempt to shoehorn the required decision into a planning inquiry procedure which is flawed and illegal. It is a lawyer's duty to protect the public from the excesses of government, and at the same time ensure that the rule of law is upheld at all times. To allow such behaviour by the Scottish Ministers to go unchecked and without complaint, and to cloak the present circumstances with a bald 'competent, albeit unprecedented', is simply not good enough.

The way was finally clear to rule on Trump's scheme.

Just a few weeks after the committee report, I met Philip Riddle, Chief Executive of VisitScotland, who described the need for a national investment plan. 'One thing that has disappointed me about the Trump incident is that we've come across as not knowing what we want,' he said. 'One minute we say "this is fantastic" then there are some concerns about the environment, then we go to an inquiry. That sends a very bad message out as a country. Most developers accept there are restrictions, but they have investment opportunities all over the world, and they want to know quickly – is this or isn't this going to go? There are parts of the world where you can go from a blank piece of paper to something on the ground within twelve months, and that's what we've got to compete with.'

Riddle, in Aberdeen for a promotional event, added, 'This is not about relaxing standards but about being much more upfront about what we want and don't want.' He said if a balance could be struck between safeguarding the environment – 'the backbone of our product' – and finding room to build, the country could be in the cash.

There were three ways the government could handle the Trump plan. Do it on the basis of written submissions; through a public hearing where people could present the case for or against; or hold a public local inquiry (PLI) where there would be the opportunity for opposing sides to cross-examine witnesses. Finance Minister John Swinney, who would eventually rule on the plan, opted for the PLI. He said: 'Given the nature of this major and controversial application and the considerable public interest, it is important that the process to examine the issues is as efficient, transparent and inclusive as possible. I am determined that there should be no unnecessary delay in considering this application and will make my decision within twenty-eight days of receiving the Department of Planning and Environment Appeals report.'

Swinney couldn't, however, hasten the DPEA report, and that could take a year to produce.

Trump was ambivalent. 'A year's a long time,' he said. 'I would hope that it would go a lot quicker than that. This is so well supported. There are so many people who want this to happen. At some point I'll leave. I don't know what that point is but at some point I have to leave the beautiful shores of Scotland.'

Chapter 5

JUST JAMMIN'

Hey handsome, do you have money for a hotdog?

In New York, even the bag ladies have a certain chutzpah.

I'm on my way to meet George Sorial, who lives within a few blocks of the Waldorf-Astoria Hotel. It's Saturday morning in Manhattan, 9am but already warm. The Pope happens to be in town and the pavements have been prettified and perfumed with boxes of flowers. There's a lot of security – roads blocked off, sirens whooping, fat cops chomping cigars in doorways – but nothing to spook the tourist. The papal melee adds to the general frisson. This is, after all, the most pulsating piece of real estate on the planet. You find yourself propelled through the streets, energized by the thrum of the traffic. Lights change, horns sound, people move. New Yorkers are primed to go. The city's lack of inertia is invigorating.

Sorial greets me in the foyer of Trump World Tower with a hand-shake and welcome-to-my-town kind of smile. Diplomats live there, as do actors and athletes. Trump, he mentions, takes a big interest in buildings bearing his name.

'One morning I found Mr Trump just sitting here at eight o'clock,' he says, gesturing to the couch next to the entry desk. 'He said we needed to change the décor.'

A concierge takes Sorial's Audi S4 convertible up from the under-ground garage. The roof stays up, talking being more important than a suntan: this is a business trip for both of us. The brief is to check out two Trump courses near New York. The visit has taken some negotiating – the Trump Organization and the *Evening Express* being wary of doing anything that could be construed as currying favour. A cut-price stay at Trump Tower wasn't an option.

We stop for petrol then travel west out of the city. As ever the conversation is about real estate. Trump, Sorial reveals, is planning to remediate a municipal dump on the edge of New York city; to vent noxious gases, drain toxic slurry, bring a dead soil back to life, and in its place build a golf course. It sounds like an Old Testament miracle. *And lo, there were eighteen holes of golf, and much rejoicing.* The real water-into-wine part is, however, the promise of 100,000 homes. 'Trump Crystal City,' says Sorial without a beat.

The roads narrow and the countryside starts to throw up some bosomy farmland.

We're heading for Bedminster where Trump's wife Melania, a former Slovenian model who studied design, spends her summer. Trump usually visits at weekends, Sorial explains, driving there in a white Rolls Royce. Bedminster has its own wedding chapel, which Trump plans to convert into a mausoleum for himself and his family. It's a fair assumption that Bedminster has some sentimental value.

Trump bought the 526-acre estate from carmaker John DeLorean, who died a year after the course opened in 2004. DeLorean was a US motor industry executive who moved to Northern Ireland to make his own car, the one in the film *Back to the Future*. It didn't sell as well as he had hoped and within a year of trading the DeLorean Motor Company was poised for collapse. Ever enterprising, DeLorean started shipping industrial quantities of cocaine around the world hidden in his vehicles. The Feds swooped but failed to make the case stick, but then the trafficking idea had been theirs. The court dismissed their unorthodox business rescue plan, punted to DeLorean by an undercover agent, as entrapment.

We're met at Bedminster by one of DeLorean's former tenants, Ed Russo. Ed looks too ruddy to have wintered in New Jersey. It turns out that he lives in Key West in Florida.

He introduces himself as Bedminster's 'resident tree-hugger

and dirt-kisser'. His wife, Ed explains, used to run a horse centre on the estate after they sold a printing business. Ed became an amateur environmentalist and chaired the planning board in Bedminster, overseeing the drafting of tough regulations for potential developers. When Trump took an interest in DeLorean's estate, Ed introduced more tangible obstacles to building a golf course there. Out in the fields he buried a fire engine, a Volkswagen Camper, 'all kinds of stuff'. When I suggest that doesn't sound like the actions of an avowed tree-hugger and dirt-kisser, Ed defends the booby-trapping as a bargaining chip, as a statement of intent.

'I told Trump, "We're going to spend the next fifty years fighting you unless you're going to provide environmental enhancements, unless you respect the culture and the water quality."' says Ed. 'He invited me to his office and I said, "How can you guarantee you're going to look after the environment?" He said, "I'm going to put you in charge." I was like a kid in a candy store. This place had leaking oil tanks, septic tanks that didn't work. Suddenly there was money to clean up the 526 acres of neglected farmland at Bedminster.'

We get into a golf cart and take off across the course to say hello to the owner himself, who is playing with three others in a competition to mark the season's start.

Trump, flushed but smiling, shakes my hand and immediately tells me how great Bedminster is, how it's been ranked one of the best new courses in the world.

He looks like a man who genuinely enjoys golf – the simple physical pleasure of striking the ball well, the mechanical satisfaction of working levers – precisely because he appears to break off so easily from the game, one that can knot people physically and mentally. Trump often swings a club in his office, a way of de-stressing, of emptying his head of problems and coming at them afresh. When he returns to the ball there is no elaborate pre-shot routine, no careful laying of hands on club and club on ground, no tight-buttocked shuffling on the spot. He just steps up to the ball, hitting it to within a few feet of the pin.

The course was designed by Tom Fazio, whose nephew produced the first layout for Menie. The grass is too green to have been grown without chemicals. The challenge of using fertiliser, Ed explains, is managing the water carrying it off the land. Bedminster's is filtered naturally by a mat of fibrous vegetation. Ed, a former president of the Upper Raritan Watershed Association, is proud of the organic retention basins, proud too of the eight miles of public horse trails. He takes us to an area named 'the big red' by farmers because the clayey soil stained the streams. It doesn't happen now and Ed is adamant no one is complaining about changes to the ecology, least of all the wildlife. 'Fish didn't like it, frogs didn't like it, snakes didn't like it . . .' he says. Ed encouraged scrub to grow, and birds such as the bobolink to nest.

'I tell people, go out and you'll see bobolink. They don't believe me. But clap your hands and five will fly up,' he says.

He wants to do the same with skylarks at Menie, which he has visited twice. Ed calls the dynamic dunes 'a natural disaster . . . like the Grand Canyon, silting up the ocean'. Suddenly he is panning his own country's greatest natural wonder. Here's what Trump faced in his office: an irreverent antagonist, crackling with opinion. 'It's broken but people say, let's not fix it, let's study it,' Ed continues, still majoring on why the Grand Canyon is rubbish. 'Scientists will always say that because that's what they do – study things. But you don't protect a dune by doing nothing. It will go. The North Sea will see to that.'

He wants to see Trump build a golf course in Scotland because 'it's like making wine in France' and is incredulous people should want to preserve Menie as a shooting estate. 'They want to protect birds by shooting them and spreading lead all over the place. It's like a Monty Python sketch, it's just too perverse.'

Before returning to the clubhouse we visit Ed's former home, a big old-fashioned wooden building, painted yellow and white, which now houses estate offices. 'I could have been a curmudgeon and stayed,' he says. He doesn't sound remotely wistful.

Tour over, we return to the Trump National Golf Club. Two convertibles are parked outside, a Ferrari 430 and a Lamborghini Gallardo, roofs opened up like petals in the spring sunshine.

Pictures of other Trump courses line the club's walls. The gallery includes the Trump International Golf Links Scotland, an aerial shot of the Menie dunes, sand and grass edged by the frothy North Sea. The restaurant serves an Aberdeen Angus Beefburger. A Trump Angus Beefburger, that is. You can order Trump Vodka from the bar. We settle for coffee and Ed finds us a drawing room with big armchairs where we await the arrival of three nearby residents. Two of them, I'm assured, viewed Trump's golf course plans with trepidation, at least to start with.

The first witness for the defence is Erik Sketland. His family has lived at Bedminster for eleven generations. He understands what it is to be attached to a place, but as a developer of 'commercial properties' he also understands the 'pressure of progress'.

'I'm very aware of the development process and how it tends to square off in an adversarial relationship rather than in a collaborative relationship,' he says. 'People fear change, and they react. But because of the concept we wanted to be helpful.' There's a pause. 'Of course I may have a different view because of the business I'm in.' Erik praises the readiness of Trump to listen to concerns, to ensure access roads were retained. 'He was very sensitive to the disruption to our lives. Now, if there's a problem or concern, very prompt attention is paid to it.' I have visions of Trump arriving at Erik's house in his Rolls Royce in the middle of the night to fix a broken drainage water pipe.

Sally Rubin's next up. As the boss of the Great Swamp Watership Association, and a member of Bedminster township committee, she put hydrologists on Trump's case. So far, the reports have been good: the club picked up an award for environmental stewardship, scoring top marks for water quality among other things. Sally says: 'The community at large would prefer no changes, to keep it like it was fifty years ago. There were concerns, that he'd come in with money and steamroller over us.' And? 'He hasn't steamrollered us. They've been very even-handed. And he is scrutinised more because his name is Trump.'

Dr Mark Caccavale joins us in the drawing room. He says he 'wishes' he could be a member of Bedminster but even his surgeon's salary won't stretch to the $250,000 joining fee. He doesn't resent Trump's success. 'No one can begrudge people from making money. He's out there, he's hard-edged, aggressive, but I think his heart is in the right spot.' He talks about the anarchy that prevailed under DeLorean, about teenagers driving recklessly on the dirt roads around the farm that eventually became the golf course. 'It would have been safer to let my kids play stick ball in the streets of Brooklyn than let them outside here,' he adds.

He saw the golf plan as a 'better solution than forty or fifty homes'. I mention that Trump's Menie plan includes 500 houses. Sally blanches at the prospect.

'There is no way it would have happened here,' she says. 'This section is rural.'

'I'd have put a "for sale" sign on my house,' says Erik. Sorial, to his credit, resists registering an objection.

The membership model – a $20,000 annual subscription – works at Bedminster because New York and its environs provide plenty of wealthy patrons. In the North-east of Scotland, Trump needs the housing to cover his costs and help turn a profit, not that he sees the housing as a negative. He reckons his 'beautiful homes' will help satisfy the strategic plans to grow the region.

Bedminster has not escaped the burgeoning ambition of developers. The Far Hills, a neighbouring town of 6,000 people, has appeared in the last twenty years. It happens to be home to the US Golfers' Association, the body that decides where major golfing events are held, including the US Open. Trump would *love* Bedminster to host the US Open and has pledged it will happen, even if he's 'an old man, being wheeled around' or resting in his mausoleum nearby.

Trump's relationship with the sport's ruling body has been fractious. Three months before my visit, *USA Today* published a front-page story describing Trump's ambition. Trump was quoted as saying that David Fay, the USGA's Executive Director, had a locker near his own at Bedminster. Fay wasn't thrilled by this chummy image. He claimed he knew nothing about the locker and reportedly resigned his honorary membership.

At Westchester, where we visit after lunch, it is the locker names that get your attention: Clint Eastwood; Jack Nicholson; American football hero Tom Brady; Joe Torre, owner of the Yankees and the Dodgers; and Rudolph Giuliani, the major who helped steady New York's nerve after the Twin Towers attack. The first locker belongs to the owner, Donald J. Trump. Former US president Bill Clinton also has a berth.

'Clinton plays two or three times a week,' explains general manager Dan Scavino. 'He comes up in the evening with eight secret service guys. We've got to know them pretty well.' He reckons such luminaries will be queuing up to play the Menie course. 'It's going to be awesome, just awesome.'

The car park is full of Porsches; they look like pool cars. Westchester has Trump flourishes – a $130,000 chandelier hanging in the entrance, marble from Italy and on the roof, a billowing American flag that looks big enough to get the clubhouse airborne. 'Yeah, the planners said we had to cut it down in size,' says Dan. And, again, a picture of the Menie Links. I'm shown a new function suite. The Aberdeen room.

'It's jammin', just jammin',' Dan says as we set off for a tour of the busy course and an insight into the way Trump does business.

The grass is as uniform as carpet, the bunkers like snowy corries – everything spick except for an incongruous tangle of trees and scrub on an island. 'The Department of Environmental Protection wants it left,' says Dan. And would Dan like to chop it down? 'Absolutely – but it won't happen,' he shoots back. We stop at a railing, which carries a whiff of fresh paint. 'Mr Trump noticed a dent last time he was out,' says Dan. Again I have visions of Trump in a boiler suit, paintbrush in hand.

Trump had been hoping to build a course on a nearby estate that once belonged to newspaper magnate Eugene Meyer. In 2001, Trump told *The New York Times*: 'Here is the option. Either I build 100 houses or I build a beautiful, scenic golf course. It's very simple.' The course got blown out, however, over worries that pesticides and fertilizers would have contaminated a lake that supplied drinking water to local towns.

Instead, Trump bought Westchester for $7.5 million when it went into bankruptcy in 2002. He spent a further $60 million reshaping the course, the biggest earth-moving project the county had known. Another $7 million went on improving one of the shortest holes, where the green is backdropped by a waterfall. The rock face used to support the tee area but Trump wanted things switched around.

'We pump the water back up . . . 5,000 gallons a minute,' says Dan.

Trump likes flowing water; constant forward moment. Trump Tower in New York has an 80ft waterfall in the foyer. When we stop for a bottle of water, Trump's image stares back from the label. Trump argues the merchandising reflects his self-belief, that pride is a commodity to be shared. But make no mistake – Westchester is a business, not a vanity project. The joining fee is $350,000 and annual subscriptions are $18,000. For that price, you might expect dent-free railings.

Trump also built fifteen mansions, which line the driveway to the clubhouse. The homes are worth around $3 million and some are used solely for holidays.

Dan introduces us to the owner of one, Gregg Marks. 'I'm too poor to have two homes,' says Gregg. He's kidding. You can tell from the Ferrari 599 in the garage. And the Aston Martin racked above it. Then there's the Bentley convertible in the driveway. And if you're still in any doubt about this man's ability to afford a second home, you might consider the two sports Mercedes sitting outside.

The homes are not especially grand (hence the need for a racking system) but are worth a lot because of their proximity to the course. Dan tells me that local property on the perimeter has doubled in value. Gregg, who made his money in 'women's apparel . . . trying to figure how to keep them happy', tries to persuade me members' money flows back into the community, that Westchester is no gated community. 'We're dining out tonight,' he says. 'Not at the clubhouse . . . at a restaurant thirty minutes away.'

Dan says Trump is looking to build another seventy-two homes, but not just at the moment. 'The members have had enough of dirt.'

One of Trump's regular playing partners stops his buggy next to Dan's and asks him to caution another player for some imaginary infraction, just for fun. 'This guy owns an oil company and now I've got to go and bust his chops . . .' Dan says, rolling his eyes. Dan approaches the golfer and ribs him for a bit but can't bring himself to put serious heat on a mogul. Joke over, they chat. The player tells Dan where the price of petrol is heading and what his mark-up will be. 'You can see why he's rich,' says Dan, re-taking the wheel.

The local town of Briarcliff is not especially wealthy – men in working boots walk the streets – but the residents aren't left to stand with their noses pressed against the window of Westchester. In winter the rolling grassland is opened up for sledging and cross-country skiing. Dan explained that locals can play Westchester for $75 a round (regular price, $500) for one day every October, an arrangement that manages to sound both generous and mean. 'We could just say it's private, you're not getting on,' says Dan.

The Trump National Golf Club at Westchester provides 150 full-time jobs. 'We like to keep it local and within the community,' says Dan, explaining how the club supports local organisations.

University and high school kids enjoy study placements; the club hosts charity fund-raising events and donates four-ball rounds and lessons with the professional as raffle prizes. Dan recounts his confusion when Trump sent divers into the course's ponds. The thousands of balls collected were sold at Trump Tower for charity.

It also makes good business sense to get on with a community. Trump can't cut down a tree at Westchester without the okay from the townsfolk but decisions that once took months now take a few weeks because of the level of co-operation and trust established.

We return to the clubhouse to meet the man who looks after the illustrious lockers. Jim Flynn, fifty-eight, packed in a job as a linen salesman to join the club, where he now polishes the famous name plates. 'It wasn't going anywhere,' he says. 'I wanted to get in and work for the Trump Organization.' Employees can sound like religious converts. Pro shop manager Marie Siani says, 'It's very important to local people, the value the club brings to their own activities, the excitement of having Mr Trump here.' On the shelves there are copies of Tiger Woods' book about how to play golf. I ask Dan if Trump's friendly with Tiger.

'Yeah,' he says, 'he talks with Tiger. But then there are very few people Mr Trump isn't connected with.'

We meet Allan Klein, who plays almost every day. He doesn't mind the design tweaks, the dirt. 'Mr Trump wants to make sure you are rewarded for good shots, and not rewarded for bad shots,' he says.

It could be another Trump edict.

It's Monday morning and Donald Trump is at his desk in Trump Tower.

He has enjoyed a short commute – an elevator ride from his $50m home on the top three floors down to his twenty-sixth floor office. There are views of Central Park, vast and verdant among the teeming New York skyscrapers, like a big green swimming pool.

This is his domain – Manhattan – but all he wants to talk about is Menie. He's keen to know what *I* think about his tactics. At first I wonder if he's trying to flatter me, to disarm me, but by the third or fourth question – about the mindset of Aberdeenshire Council, the perception among residents – I realise that he does want to hear the answers, that garnering local knowledge is part of the way he operates. Like every good communicator, he is firstly a good listener. On Trump's last trip to Aberdeen he spent four hours driving around the streets, studying the buildings, trying to fathom the city's psyche.

His office is crammed with trophies and prized sports memorabilia gifted to him. The stuff sits on the floor and on the windowsills. A big wrap-around desk, with three red chairs out front, is covered by papers. Trump doesn't use email or an intercom. If he needs anything, he yells down the corridor.

Trump Tower is one of New York's most popular tourist destinations. Thousands pass through its doors each week to gaze at the waterfall, to shop, to eat. It is easy to forget that Trump is upstairs *working*. It is easy to think about the celebrity not the builder, to expect a grand, pristine office rather than something utilitarian. Workstations around the world are personalised with pictures of families, silly Christmas presents, mugs decorated like t-shirts; wee reflections of who we are. Trump's is no different. Framed magazine front covers hang from the walls. 'There's me with President Reagan,' he says. 'And on the front cover of *Playboy*.'

There is a boyish enthusiasm about Trump, an evangelizing zeal. He talks about the 'pride' he takes in his developments, how he enjoys spending time at them, and how much he looks forward to spending time at Menie. He says it's 'inconceivable' the Scottish Government will reject his plans, given the public enthusiasm.

Sorial introduces me to the 'kids' – Don Junior, Ivanka and Eric. They all work at Trump Tower, a floor down from Dad. It's a surprisingly small set-up, just the family and a handful of loyal staff.

Eric recently brokered a deal to build a course in Puerto Rico, which, like the Balmedie plan, included 500 homes. 'The Government came to us,' he says, seated in his office below Dad's. A tournament at the course recently drew 75,000 people, ten times what might have otherwise been expected. 'That was attributable to the Trump name,' he says. Eric is polite about the length and restrictive nature of the Scottish planning process. 'There's been a lot of red tape. The plan's a novel thing, a bit of a grey area.' Don talks about what the family can do for Scotland, daughter Ivanka about what they're doing for Turkey. The answer is always the same – providing 'quality' places for people to live, work and play.

Not everyone agrees they are needed, of course. Nearby, objectors to a forty-six-storey project for the historic Soho district have branded it as out of keeping with the neighbourhood, and have dismissed the hotel element as a way of circumventing restrictions on new homes.

High above Manhattan, you sense the scale of Trump's business operation and wonder why he is bothering with Menie at all. However, that is to underestimate his abiding passion for the game. Yes, he wants to turn a buck on Menie – that's what sustainability means to him – but it's also about winning. He mentions Bedminster's accolade again and then predicts Menie will 'blow it away'. As for the competition on Saturday, Trump's team triumphed.

'By eleven strokes,' Trump says. 'And I won nearest the pin. Two feet, one inch.' Is he allowed to win at his own course? 'Sure,' he says.

I see Trump one more time before leaving, while travelling back to JFK airport. His face looms above a building on a billboard promoting his TV show *The Apprentice*. He's the size of King Kong. The gaze is narrow, focused, but a little too earnest to take seriously. There's a kind of playful pugnacity to Trump, evident when posing for pictures. I ask the taxi driver if Trump is well liked in New York.

'Yeah, he's a source of a lot of jobs,' he says. 'He builds a lot of high-rises. All rich people are liked.'

Perhaps in America, a less hierarchical society than Britain's, they are more inclined to take the view that you have earned it. The driver tells me I could have walked into the Waldorf-Astoria Hotel 'naked except for a cowboy hat' because 'this is America'. If you can pay, you can play.

Chapter 6

HALF-ASSED

When Mary Anne MacLeod arrived in New York in 1930, the iconic city was already starting to take shape. The Chrysler Building, then the world's tallest at 1,047 feet, had just opened and the Empire State Building, which would surpass it in stature a year later, was climbing towards the sky. Mary, then eighteen, had sailed from the Isle of Lewis, off the North-west of Scotland, a flat, bouldery island, frayed by the Atlantic Ocean and pummelled into sandy bays. Mary was born in Tong – known in the native Gaelic as Druim-beag – to crofters Malcolm and Mary MacLeod, who already had six children. Islanders tried to cultivate the land, carrying stones away in fishing creels, men, women and children, indefatigable to the last, but nothing came easy. The bitter soil would support only sheep. The seas were bounteous but murderous.

The islanders themselves were resilient but meek. They deferred to the past, to tradition, crofter begetting crofter.

Mary's sisters had visited New York before her. When it was Mary's turn to make the journey, the teenager met twenty-four-year-old Fred Trump, the son of a German immigrant who made some money running a hotel in the Yukon during the Alaskan gold rush. Fred had shown the same blend of enterprise and prudence as his father. At fifteen he started building garages, somewhere to house the new-fangled automobile. His mother, also from Germany, signed company cheques for her schoolboy son. When Mary met Fred, he had already built thousands of family homes for rent in Queens and Brooklyn – sturdy brick apartments clustered around pocket parks

– and one of the first self-service supermarkets in the world, an innovation that helped keep prices down during the Depression.

Mary returned to Lewis. The romance, however, continued by post and she married Fred in New York in 1936.

They had two daughters and three sons. Donald, the fourth child, followed his father into the real estate business. He too shaped the city where he was born, building towering residential blocks bearing his name. He helped his father amass a fortune of $400m and made an even bigger one of his own. When Mary died in 2000, her son was one of the most famous people on the planet. Seventy-eight years after his mother first travelled to New York, Donald returned to Tong.

Trump has not forsaken the beautiful shores of Scotland. On a blustery Monday morning, his Boeing 727 descends towards the Isle of Lewis, shimmying above the blue-green waters and white beaches. Aboard, his elder sister Maryanne takes her brother's hand and tells him, 'We're home.'

Trump is stopping at Stornoway on the way to Aberdeen, where he will be the first witness at the public inquiry. He says he is persevering only because of the 'tremendous support' of the people. Trump 'respects' the need for an inquiry but doesn't want it to drag on ('no wonder people aren't investing in Scotland'). He figures he can be a star turn: 'I want the public to hear my plans and share my enthusiasm for them. I am confident I will be able to demonstrate my passion for this site.'

But first Trump and Maryanne, a US federal appeals judge, are making a pilgrimage to house number 3, Tong.

The straggling village lies four miles from Stornoway Airport across Broad Bay. A Maybach, the customised Mercedes limousine Trump uses in the United States, is hard to come by on Lewis. Someone has borrowed a black Porsche Cayenne (an equally imposing vehicle) from a local businessman. The Cayenne forms part of a four-car cavalcade.

Lewis's population has almost halved since Trump's mother lived there, falling to 22,000, the result of the decline of indigenous industries like fishing and tweed making. Abandoned windowless crofts dot the Western Isles, like skulls placed to ward off visitors. But 3 Tong is still inhabited – by Trump's cousins Willie and Alasdair Murray. The two-storey house has a little moss on the roof and a garage window is broken, but it is tidy enough. The grass has been cut.

'Morning, everybody. Windy, huh?' says Trump, who has flown six hours from Boston, where he attended an Elton John concert.

Trump poses for photographs with Willie and Alasdair, and Calum Murray and Chrissie MacLeod, two other cousins who live nearby. Calum Murray, sixty, a retired school technician, says the family is 'absolutely delighted' by the visit. Willie and Alasdair show Trump into the house. He reappears within two minutes and leaves them all with a gift: signed copies of his books, including *How to Get Rich*.

From there the party moves to the grounds of Lews Castle. In a visitor centre, Trump and Maryanne settle in a corner to answer questions about their mother's homeland. While Maryanne has visited two dozen times, Trump had been just once before, as a very young boy.

'I haven't been back since because I was busy having some fun in New York, let's put it that way,' he says. Fun is doing business. He mentions seventy-three projects worldwide. 'We're building all over the world, and now we are just happy to be back here.' he says. 'I love seeing it. I've been hearing about it all my life. I think I do feel Scottish. You get to a point in life when you like to think about where you came from, where your parents came from.'

Someone asks Trump about the zippy visit to his mother's house.

'I didn't want to interrupt, people live in the house. And I don't feel it's my place to go and check every drawer. I've got two wonderful relatives who live in the house but I don't think it's appropriate for me to go and make an inspection.'

'My mother would be so proud to see Donald here today,' says Maryanne protectively. 'He's never forgotten where he comes from . . . This is a man I revere. He's a nice guy and he's funny too.'

Questions turn to Menie and the PLI.

'It's possible that had my mother not been born in Scotland I wouldn't have started and I would have probably walked away,' Trump says of his golf resort and the protracted planning process. 'I think Scotland is special – and I wanted to do something for Scotland. The people want this to happen. If it doesn't get accepted it will send a very bad signal to the world. I hope for the best.'

Twenty minutes later, it's back to the convoy.

Trump has offered me a lift back to Aberdeen on the Boeing. We're waved through a gate at the far side of the airport, straight to the plane. The steps hang down from the fuselage at the rear. The aircraft, built originally for American Airlines, has been re-configured to seat two dozen people instead of the original 134. I settle at a big wooden table, which is ringed with cream leather seats: an airborne boardroom. The safety belt buckles are gold-plated. There are Waterford crystal lamps, and a Renoir in a gilded frame. Turbulence, I figure, must be fun.

Trump's quarters, a double bed and en suite bathroom, are to the front of the plane.

'Does anyone want a Coke?' says Trump, standing next to a drinks cabinet as we taxi on to the runway. I'm not expecting a safety briefing. He warns us, with a smile, that the pilots (full-time) are going to have to gun the jet down the short runway. The thought of this concerted burst of energy pleases him.

A minute later we're in the air, banking away from the Isle of Lewis, biggest of the Outer Hebrides, swinging towards the main-land, Scotland's beautiful shores flickering beneath the clouds.

Trump's demeanour is solemn, purposeful. Lips pursed, shoulders back, he strides into the Aberdeen Exhibition and Conference

Centre like a boxer about to enter the ring. An employee waggishly asks a colleague where the *Rocky* music is: you expect to see George Sorial carrying a towel and gum shield. 'You don't get people like Trump coming along every day,' whispers Jim Gillies in the public seats. Jim, who lives in Balmedie and runs a home-improvement business, is rooting for Trump: 'It's good for the area, for employment.' Stewart Milne is near the front. Martin Ford has entered with a cycle helmet under his arm.

The PLI is taking place in a 1,200-seater hall, hung with black drapes. Inquiry chairman James McCulloch is seated in front of hundreds of files, flanked by fellow reporters Karen Heywood and Michael Cunliffe. The inquiry is scheduled to run from 10 June to 4 July. At a pre-meeting to set the timetable, McCulloch has cautioned that 'the identity of the developer is not a material consideration'. Today he reminds everyone there will be no 'point-scoring or tit-for-tat'.

Trump is optimistic – at least according to the magazine *Vanity Fair*. In the May edition, Trump reportedly compared building on the SSSI to 'ripping down a landmark building in New York'. He predicted he would get planning permission because of who he was, which was a 'fucking genius', adding: 'If Jack Nicklaus tried to do this, he'd have zero chance, but they like what I've done, and because I am who I am and my mother is Scottish. I'm going to get it.' Sorial said the comments showed 'confidence not arrogance'.

For the PLI, Trump has enlisted the services of The Right Honourable Lord Boyd of Duncansby QC. As a former Lord Advocate, Colin Boyd brought the prosecution case over the Lockerbie Pan-Am terrorist bombing, which killed 259 people in the skies above Scotland in 1988 and a further eleven on the ground. Town planner David Tyldesley will lead the cross-examination for the RSBP and Scottish Wildlife Trust, and solicitors David and Louise Cockburn, father and daughter, are acting for Scottish Natural Heritage.

'My name is Donald J. Trump and I am a real estate developer and investor from New York City.'

Trump, in a slate blue suit, white shirt, and blue and white striped tie, begins by reading from his precognition, a document framing the arguments for the scheme.

'I very much enjoy playing golf, but even more so enjoy building great courses and developments . . . While my primary business is in the development of buildings in New York City and elsewhere, I greatly enjoy the artistry of creating championship golf courses . . . I know that if I am to build the best golf course in the world it has to be in Scotland . . . It has to look and feel Scottish and be sympathetic to the setting and landscape.'

He addresses with disarming honesty the principal objections – building the course on the SSSI and 500 houses in the countryside: 'The bottom line is that if we were to be refused permission to develop on the southern end of the SSSI, I would withdraw because it would not, and could not, fulfill my vision of doing something outstanding. I have always believed that if you cannot do it well, you should not do it all. I am at a point in my career that if it is not going to be the best, I would not want to build it . . . Golf courses, alone, do not make a fair return on your investment. Without the funding from the construction of homes the economics are far below your acceptable return on investment.'

He admits to finding the planning process 'frustrating' and to wondering 'whether the investment in time, human resources and money has been worth it'. But Trump says he is here today because of the 'great many people who have urged us to keep pursuing this dream, both for myself and for Scotland as a whole'.

Trump's bluntness about the loss of vitality in the dunes and the need to make a profit turns into a pre-emptive strike.

During cross-examination, David Morris of the Ramblers' Association in Scotland is left to ask Trump if families would be allowed to watch the golf from the dunes. Trump wonders why people would want to risk being 'smashed in the face' by a ball and suggests the dunes were 'pretty desolate' before he took an interest in them. When Morris asks how far he would compromise on the location of the course, Trump calmly repeats his position, but in more direct language.

'I'm going to do the greatest golf course or I'm not,' he says, now off-script. 'If you want what we're doing, which will be truly a wonderful thing, let's do it properly. Let's not do it . . . we've an expression in the United States . . . half-assed.'

David Tyldesley, for the RSPB, suggests that Mr Trump's original vision had been to create a 'world-class course' but not necessarily the world's best.

'Let me make it clear so we can perhaps save some time,' says Trump, fully warmed up. 'I am looking to build the finest golf course in the world if given the chance to do it.'

'I don't doubt that it's an aspiration,' says Tyldesley, 'but can I put it to you that it is only a recent aspiration in order to justify the use of SSSI?'

Trump is adamant: 'That is absolutely false. The moment I saw the site I thought it had the potential to be the greatest golf course in the world.'

Under further questioning, Trump does admit he has read none of the environment reports compiled by his experts but counters with a claim he is 'an environmentalist in the true sense of the word', citing awards made to his US courses for sound custodianship of the land. Someone in the public gallery guffaws. McCulloch is onto it immediately and warns people against calling out.

Martin Ford enters the fray. He suggests that Trump has 'little understanding' of the Menie Estate.

'You know, it's interesting, nobody's ever told me that I don't know how to buy property before,' says Trump with a drawl. 'You're the first one. I've done very well buying property. Thanks for the advice.'

Ford says he was 'a bit surprised' Trump had seemed unsure the dunes were designated as an SSSI when he bought the land.

'I know every inch of the site, I know the site, for example, far better than you do,' says Trump with a hint of irritation. 'Details come later. You don't say, "Let me spend a couple of years studying it." It doesn't work that way.'

Ford presses him on the need for 500 houses.

'The housing allows the course to happen,' says Trump sweetly. 'It makes the economics work. But my primary goal is to build the greatest golf course in the world . . . If we got approved today we'd start this afternoon. I want to see it before I get too old.'

Ford quotes a member of the R&A who has reportedly said Trump would never get the Open.

'Over the years people have said things were never going to happen, but they happened, and people are happy,' says Trump. He predicts the course will be better than Carnoustie or St Andrews. 'At one point they were new courses also. Other than the legacy factor, we have a superior piece of land.'

Jab, parry, jab, parry, jab, parry.

Eight hours later, he's done.

A meeting is convened for the media in a small room upstairs, where Trump wedges himself behind a table to face a second inquisition. He reckons the three ringside judges will have marked him ahead on points: 'I think the answers were all 100 per cent. Everybody's telling me we really knocked it out of the box. I listened to the questions from the few opponents we had, and honestly, the questions weren't very good.'

He sounds disappointed.

Trump believes people tried to put him on the ropes because of his fame: 'I think if somebody else had applied they would have gotten it a lot easier than me. I think all the celebrity and craziness is probably a liability for me but it's an asset for the area and for Scotland. Frankly, they are talking about this all over the world . . . Often I find that great things take more time, and I think this is one of those examples.'

*

The next day everyone but Trump – back in New York, where he would receive daily updates – returned to the AECC. The inquiry shifted to a smaller hall.

A succession of witnesses appeared for the organisation (accountants, scientists, architects) to offer a dispassionate analysis of Trump's plans, to quantify the benefits and rebut criticism.

Accountants Johnston Carmichael put construction costs for the resort and village at £1,069 million. Chartered accountant Iain Webster said the addition of housing would convert a projected £20.7 million loss into a £35.5 million profit, and was a necessary enticement for 'investors and lenders'. He said Trump would use £25 million of his own money for the golf course. The price of a single round used in the analysis was £150 for visitors and half-price for locals. Economist Stewart Dunlop of the University of Strathclyde said that once up and running the resort would support 1,418 jobs and generate up to £33.5 million a year for the local economy.

Planning boss Christine Gore also appeared as a witness for Trump. She told the inquiry that the 'sheer scale and unique circumstances' justified a policy departure. Indeed, she saw the housing as a bonus: 'If we're going to achieve our aspirations for growth in the region then the 500 houses are a very small proportion. In context of the future Structure Plan then we would be looking for that number. If we didn't have them here we would be looking to allocate them elsewhere.'

Geoff Runcie became possibly the first Chamber of Commerce boss to appear at a public inquiry. The Aberdeen and Grampian Chamber of Commerce Chief Executive said business tourism was worth an annual £150 million to the North-east and noted the 'potential for expansion is huge', claiming the region had lost out on £11.5 million the year before because it didn't have enough hotel space to host major conferences.

Geomorphology, a study of the way the land is shaped, became an unlikely buzzword.

Professor Bill Ritchie – first seen at the Forsyth Hall in Belhevie

– told the inquiry Menie shared the same formative processes as the dunes of Balmedie, Foveran, and Sands of Forvie (chosen ahead of Menie for inclusion in the Geological Conservation Review). Ritchie, a former chairman of the advisory committee for SSSIs, was nevertheless candid about the threat posed by a golf course: 'Rightly, interest has focused on the golf course architect's need to stabilise the open, un-vegetated sand dome and contiguous areas. If this is done, then a major element in the reason for site design-ation – dynamic and relatively rapid but variable movement in a generally northwards direction – would cease. This . . . crystallises the question whether or not sufficient geomorphological interest remains in this North Menie area to continue to justify the appellation SSSI.'

Dr Dargie, a member of the Institute of Ecology and Environmental Management, had admitted his original advice to Trump had been to avoid the SSSI. 'I understand that similar advice had been given to the applicant from other members of the environmental team,' he confessed. 'I had no communication with Mr Trump as part of this decision. The actual decision to ignore my advice and move towards development within the dunes on the site was already underway. At that point I had two choices – walk away or continue to offer my expertise.'

Dargie also outlined a plan to re-establish vegetation on the SSSI or nearby. Drawing on his own attempts to translocate bog, the ecologist admitted there was no hard evidence it would work with dune habitat but said: 'I feel there must be a relatively high chance of success. I would argue that blanket bog is harder to restore than dunes.' He added: 'I show that sufficient ground is available within and outwith Foveran Links SSSI to re-establish all habitats likely to be lost to development.'

Under cross-examination, Martin Hawtree was too modest to call his design the world's best and too rationalist to defend an unmade course against accusations it might not be, but that didn't mean Hawtree thought Trump was all talk. When asked to name the best golf course in the world, he picked as the benchmark Royal Birkdale, which his grandfather helped turn into an Open venue. He said the Menie course could be better than Royal Birkdale. 'As nearly as it is possible to do, I would guarantee the world class status of this course,' he said. 'I could not do so for any other arrangement or location. The site is the most exciting piece of links land I have seen in my working life.'

In the second week, it was the turn of the objectors to put their case.

Martin Ford said the principle of a golf resort at Menie had been welcomed by the ISC – but the co-opting of an SSSI and the inclusion of housing 'on land not allocated by the development plan for this purpose, and in an inappropriate location' was not acceptable. A golf resort drawing visitors from around the world, Ford said, did not satisfy a policy of economic development that sought to reduce the use of fuels and carbon dioxide emissions. Naturally, he stood by the ISC's decision to reject the plan: 'I thought that the committee was as well equipped, and as an appropriate body as there could possibly be, to take the decision on this planning application. I in no sense felt that the committee's decision was unsafe. The easy option for councillors was to grant the application, but the better option was refusal. The decision to refuse should be seen as a negotiating position by the council.'

In Dr Jim Hansom, Scottish Natural Heritage had found a fearless and spirited witness who spoke with bracing directness. He was careful to distinguish between the destruction of the dunes – demonstrably not the intention – and of the processes giving rise to them. When asked about Trump's claim that the dunes could blow away in a storm, he replied: 'Rubbish.' He was equally contemptuous of Hawtree's professed affinity for the landscape: 'This golf course does not fit in with its surrounding. In some locations there are biblical amounts of sand to be shifted around.' Hansom, a reader at Glasgow University, argued that the sand's redistribution should be left to the wind.

Afterwards George Sorial berated Hansom for his emotive language. 'A famine is a biblical disaster,' he commented, 'not shifting sand around.'

Other arguments smouldered outside the AECC.

Sorial called on Scottish Wildlife Trust policy manager Jonathan Hughes to resign. Hughes had argued the development would break up the 'subtle mosaic of the dune' and be an act of 'ecological vandalism'. More inflammatory was his written statement, the assertion that Scotland 'will happily set aside democratically agreed policy and legislation, so long as the development comes with a big enough economic carrot'.

Sorial said: 'This represents a narrow view of the public local inquiry process and how democracy works. It demonstrates a complete lack of respect for all the reporters' and relevant parties' contributions. He should have focused on the protection of wildlife, not on challenging a legal process he has demonstrated a lack of understanding for. For the good of himself and the public, he should resign.'

Scottish Natural Heritage got slated too. Policy manager Stewart Angus told the inquiry the course would 'fragment and disrupt ecological processes over the golf course's entire footprint on the dunes' and that 'overall biological interest will be very seriously compromised'. What, however, enraged Sorial was the warning that SNH would 'have to consider the denotification' of the SSSI if the Government approved the scheme, and Angus's refusal to commit to offering help and advice in that event: 'We would really have to look very closely at the value gained by getting involved. All I'm committing SNH to do is review the situation in regards to its SSSI status should approval be granted.'

To Sorial, Angus's intransigence represented a potential dereliction of duty, if not overt blackmail. SNH's website states: 'Much of our work is done in partnership with others – local authorities, Government bodies, businesses, community groups, farmers and other land managers, and a wide range of representative bodies.'

Sorial said: 'To say they are not willing to commit to working with any developer is outrageous. They are a public-funded body that has an obligation to. We have agreed to disagree on some issues, but it is for Ministers to decide what happens with the plan. When it comes down to it, we all have to live with it.'

Chapter 7

AN AUDACIOUS PROPOSAL

They gather like kids on a school outing – excitedly, expectantly, checking their water bottles, pulling on rucksacks, happily liberated from their desks. The sombre suits and dresses occasioned by the PLI's court-like setting are gone. Uniforms have been replaced by cargo pants, t-shirts and fleeces: play clothes. People are chatting openly, differences temporarily forgotten, but scrutinizing each other too. The objectors are in greens, browns and khakis, the colours of the landscape. Beneath peaked caps, Trump's team look very much like golfers. Neil Hobday is wearing a polo shirt from Loch Lomond, the Scottish Open venue.

The cars that roll to a halt on the dirt track invite judgment too. Jim McCulloch steps from a shiny black Mercedes estate, tuned by the high-performance company AMG. Not the most propitious sign for objectors. It has to be like this – looking for clues – for insights into McCulloch's value system – because McCulloch can be only so familiar with those around him.

We've come for a day at the beach. It's the official site visit, a chance to walk the Menie Estate – or, as Mickey Foote puts it, 'for the landscape to speak for itself'.

'This will be one of the greatest par-fives anywhere in golf,' says Neil Hobday as he leads the troupe into the long grass.

'We don't want to hear that,' says McCulloch, like a teacher keeping his children in check. 'Just tell us where we are.'

We are in fact walking up the tenth hole, climbing gently, the sea glimmering to the right. According to the Trump Organization's PLI submission, the hole 'sets the tone for a decidedly different feeling course than the first nine'. A wetland lies directly ahead, splitting the putative fairway to provide two lines of approach to the green. You wonder how McCulloch is viewing this landscape, if he is seeing it through the eyes of a golfer, thinking in terms of the shots he would play. You wonder again about the Mercedes, and if the estate provides room for a bag of clubs and an electric trolley rather than, say, a brace of dogs.

The heather and scrub start to peter out. We are entering a world of sand and water and primordial plants: shifting dunes, fixed dunes, slacks and swampy hollows, laced with fescue grass, sand sedge, dune willow and rushes.

The 'green' is back-dropped by a dune, the flanks of which form a natural amphitheatre. The Trump submission has described the setting as 'one of the most memorable sites on the course, rising to a height of 33.5 metres'. It says: 'The magnitude and shape of the dune to the right of the green is so impressionable, it forms an iconic oddity to an otherwise more flat surrounding area'. Everyone *is* impressed by the dune, if not the role envisaged for it.

George Sorial jokes about naming the hole after Martin Ford.

'That would make me feel very uncomfortable,' says the councillor. 'I have no aspiration to be a member.'

Someone asks Sorial if he has seen the green lady at Menie House.

'I don't believe in ghosts,' he replies, smiling.

We climb the Dome. Trump wants to grass over twenty-five acres for the twelfth, thirteenth, fourteenth and seventeenth holes. He argues the use of native fescue will increase habitat for plants and animals. For objectors the Dome itself is alive. Arresting its movement would be like filling a wildlife reserve with stuffed animals.

Martin Ford is on the ground, caressing a minuscule plant: an adder's tongue fern, named after Britain's only poisonous snake.

'Oh goodness, there it is . . . yes. It's thirty years since I've seen that plant,' he says.

Someone spots a golf ball.

'Some lunatic has come out and played golf already,' says Hobday.

'It's a plant,' jokes McCulloch.

Hobday suspects boys from a neighbouring farm have been practising. 'It's better than quad bikes,' he says. Turning south, we plunge between the dunes. The tees and holes are staked out by plastic drainage pipes. Hobday, who attended Sandhurst Military School, leads with ease through the bleached, baking wilderness. He seems as tough as marram grass.

'These could be the greatest closing holes in golf,' he says.

'We're here to observe,' chides McCulloch.

As we start out on the first nine holes, I'm joined by Vic Henderson, who worked at Menie as a dairyman and then as a farm manager, and is still a resident on the estate. Henderson tells me he recently received a package from the international courier FedEx. 'I thought – what have I done?' he says. It was a letter from Donald J. Trump signed in black felt pen, the tall thick letters compacted like New York skyscrapers, thanking him for his support. Trump suggested they might celebrate his 'greatest achievement' – the championship golf course – by 'perhaps playing a few holes'.

'I'm not a very good golfer,' says Henderson, who is surprised to learn that four-handicapper Trump is. 'He'll have to give me a stroke a hole.'

Now seventy-nine, it pains Henderson to see the fields supporting nothing, the demise of agriculture. 'It's amazing, the drift from the land,' he says. 'The course has got to get the go-ahead, for the good of Scotland . . . the wealth it would bring, the jobs.' Henderson takes a functional view of the Dome, which we're leaving behind. 'There was no food for the animals there,' he says. Henderson turns to Jim Hansom.

'Why is the land so special?' he asks.

'It's the process we want to understand,' says Hansom. 'People need to know about the environment.'

'But nobody even knows about the place.'

'That's the problem,' says Hansom.

Henderson looks even more confused.

Hansom believes a storm-torn gap in the coastal dune ridge is migrating northwards, the same gap that allowed sand to be carried inland, gathered up within a moving sheet of glacial residue, and piled on the Menie Dome by the dominant SSW-SE wind. Professor Bill Ritchie believes the gap may have been caused largely by military manoeuvres during the Second World War and subsequent recreational pressure, and that in the absence of human activity it is now closing.

'It's normal academic disagreement,' says Ritchie, shrugging. 'It's a field science, you only say there is a probability of something happening.' I ask Ritchie about his role as a consultant, whether payment puts any pressure on a scientist to find the answers a client wants. I realise immediately that it's an impertinent question. Science compresses opinion, squeezing it out under the weight of empirical fact. Ritchie fields the question graciously, quietly explaining the consultancy contract went through the University of Aberdeen, so guaranteeing impartiality.

We stop at what looks like a shallow grave. Tom Dargie reports that initial attempts to translocate plants from the SSSI have failed. 'It's difficult to believe it's the same vegetation,' says an objector mournfully. Dargie isn't dejected. He reckons that with the 'right lifting gear' (something capable of taking slabs of supporting sand) a ninety-five per cent success rate is possible.

The dunes in Menie's southern half are smaller, grassier and harder-packed: stubble left by the passing sand sheet. At the margins, skylarks and linnets nest in grasses, tits in the willow trees. Orchids flower at Menie in the summer. We disturb a heron. It hauls its body into the air, unfolding its great bowed wings against the blue sky.

Next up, a dead duck. A mallard, the third bird Ford has seen. 'Only 24,997 to go,' he says, referring to Trump's claim that 25,000 were being shot every year on the estate and carcasses left lying. If birds are thin on the ground, so too are people. We've seen just two walkers, accompanied by a spaniel. There is speculation from the Trump camp that the dog belongs to Debra Storr and that the couple have been recruited to convince McCulloch of the popularity of the dunes with ramblers.

We reach the southern end of the site next to the bigger, barer, vertiginous dunes of Balmedie Country Park. A handful of tower-blocks mark the mouth of the River Don in Aberdeen, seven miles away. 'This is what makes the North-east special,' says Ford, looking back to the dome. 'This fabulous wilderness that is available for all to enjoy. I would contend you can't improve on this.'

From where I'm standing, talk of preserving the SSSI for 'all to enjoy' feels disingenuous. You can exalt Menie's intricate network of plant and animal life, you can marvel at the inter-dependency, but what I suspect most people would choose to do in the dunes is run and jump and tumble, shouting 'whey-hey!' as they go. That's what kids and adults do at Balmedie Country Park. Field scientists prod and poke their way towards knowledge; they too leave their mark. To reach that adder fern, our group had trampled other plants and displaced sand. We undid with our feet the baroque work of the wind.

The best way to keep a landscape pristine is to keep people out.

As we arrive, hot and ragged, back at the clubhouse site, Hobday offers everyone an apology.

'Unfortunately there aren't any cold beers,' he says, 'but in a few years, who knows?'

McCulloch says nothing.

How do you measure the worth of the processes that massage the Menie Dome? What additional value attaches to the plants and animals the dunes support? What is a unit of 'environmental capital'? What is the exchange rate? Just what price do you put on an adder's tongue fern?

As the parties gathered at the AECC on 4 July to make their closing arguments, these intractable questions dangled before the public inquiry. In describing what the country purportedly stood to gain, the Trump Organization had the simpler task. Colin Boyd could talk about jobs and tourist spending. Real-number commodities, easily stacked. To plead that the dunes were part of the ecosystem we call the planet and therefore of infinite worth wouldn't do, not within the sober realm of a public inquiry.

Everyone did at least agree on the abacus reporters would be using: National Planning Policy Guidance Rule 14, paragraph 25. This stated that development should be permitted on an SSSI only where:

> The objectives of designation and the overall integrity of the area will not be compromised; or any significant adverse effects on the qualities for which the area has been designated are clearly outweighed by social or economic benefits of national importance.

The guidance didn't, however, express a 'significant' impact as a percentage loss of biodiversity, for example. It didn't define, in terms of gross domestic product or housing provision, what size of social or economic benefit represented one of 'national' importance. As to what 'clearly outweighed' meant, well, that too was open to interpretation. Guidance, of course, is just that, a hint rather than a rule, nothing *too* prescriptive, but beyond allowing for the possibility of building on an SSSI, NPPG 14 presented no specific test, no arbitration.

How could you demonstrate that a significant adverse impact would take place if no definition first existed?

With the public inquiry reaching its conclusion, the audience's eyes were as much on the reporters as on the witnesses. They were being asked to juggle jellies. Blindfolded.

David Tyldesley, summing up on behalf or the RSPB, Scottish Wildlife Trust, and the Botanical Society of the British Isles, said there was 'irrefutable' evidence the SSSI would be compromised, adding that the geomorphology and ecology of the whole system were 'inextricably linked'. He likened a grassed dome to a 'room after a fire has destroyed it'. But what of the second test? Mr Tyldesley reiterated that the Government's goal was 'sustainable' economic development, and thought Trump's plan fell well short:

> I submit that this leisure development, of enormous scale, on a greenfield location, detached from an urban area, relying heavily on high-end tourism and increases in international flights, and which is severely damaging to nationally important natural features, habitats and species, is the epitome of unsustainable development.'

Mr Tyldesley stated that a development 'delivered wholly or primarily in the public interest of the people of Scotland' would be 'much more likely to qualify for the status of national importance, in this context, than a development brought forward wholly or primarily by a private interest'. Building a hospital on an SSSI, it seemed, would be okay. He added that he wasn't 'downplaying' the economic benefit of the Trump proposal, but evidently did not divine any significant social benefit.

In conclusion, he turned on Trump the man:

> Mr Trump's claims are overstated and his aspirations over-ambitious. His answers to my questions indicated to me that he may be in danger of being carried away by his dream, losing sight of the possibility that his scheme may not fulfil its ambitions. He appears to disregard (or deny) the prospect of disappointment, or failure . . . I can understand that Mr Trump does not do detail, but it was worrying to see his lack of appreciation (or to put it another way, his denial) of the harm that his development would cause, even as set out in his own EIS and by his own witnesses. He may have flown the Atlantic to be here, but remarkably, he had not taken the trouble to inform himself about one of the key issues – the adverse impacts on nationally important geomorphological interests, before emphatically telling the inquiry the effects would be beneficial. Mr Trump's concept

of needing to fix the dunes to stop them blowing away is frankly ludicrous.

David Cockburn, summing up for Scottish Natural Heritage, also majored on the fragmentation of the SSSI and the loss of integrity, which he considered both inevitable and irreversible. He didn't accept that genuine mitigation ('measures taken to avoid or reduce negative impacts') was being offered. Plans to translocate turf and soil were characterized instead as 'compensation' – like offering a bloodied boxer a set of false teeth and a box of chocolates rather than a gum shield. Cockburn said there was scant evidence translocation would even work.

Addressing the second test, he opined that because planning director Gore hadn't mentioned NPPG 14 in her precognition it was 'hard to resist the conclusion' that the council had 'not applied its mind to what constitutes a benefit of national importance'. The same observation was made about other Trump witnesses. Cockburn avoided being drawn into the 'national importance' evaluation by putting the onus of proof on the Trump Organization, knowing full well there could be no absolute proof:

> The balancing exercise contained in NPPG 14 . . . is between two elements of 'national importance' but in respect of the SSSI, there is no doubting that its qualification . . . [is] dependent on strict designation criteria . . . By contrast there is no clear test, and certainly no evidence of such before this inquiry for ascertaining whether economic benefits are of national importance, let alone any evidence to prove that such benefits will 'clearly outweigh' the adverse effects.

Colin Boyd's closing submission ran to more than eighty pages. On the morning of 4 July, Sorial seemed especially chipper. Entering the AECC, he said we could expect a 'masterpiece' of exposition from the QC. The night before, Boyd had emailed George Sorial, advocating going on the offensive.

When it comes to oratory, Colin Boyd is no Barack Obama. He seems strangely bashful; there is something of the gangly schoolboy about him. His voice lacks authority and rarely shifts register; he performs with a steady, familiar beat. But the absence of affectation concentrates the mind on *what* is being said, and this is where Boyd earns his money: in cogently building a proposition while systematically dismantling an opponent's case. There is no need for theatrics when you have Boyd's brain and ratiocinative skills. He could sound like Donald Duck and still win cases.

Boyd attested that just eight per cent of the SSSI was needed for the championship course. 'We accept that the Dome will be stabilised and much, though not all, of the geomorphological interest in the North Menie part of the Foveran SSSI will no longer exist,' he said. 'However, North Menie is only a part of the SSSI; the coastal dunes and beach which are critical to the wider geomorphological interest in the area will be retained.' He said biodiversity, which Trump had claimed would be enhanced with his golf course in place, was at least as important as geomorphology.

What he didn't do was dispute that the SSSI's integrity would be compromised. Boyd pointedly explained his position in the language of NPPG 14: 'The applicants accept that the development will have significant adverse effects on the qualities for which the North Menie part of the Foveran SSSI were designated. They argue however those effects are clearly outweighed by social and economic benefits of national importance.'

For Boyd, the development had 'the potential to be a global destination for tourism'. The QC said it was plain wrong to suggest that 'a private company or commercial interest cannot undertake a development of national importance . . . There is a national interest in the provision of a secure energy supply. Yet virtually all energy in the United Kingdom is provided by the private sector.' He rejected as short-sighted the idea that housing could be used only to subsidize the preservation of historic buildings: 'The concept of cross funding is well established in both the private and public sector. It would be decidedly odd to close one's eyes to that reality, especially where it might well mean that a development, which provided the opportunity for substantial economic gains of national importance, might not be able to proceed.'

He dealt with concerns about translocation and Trump's optimism in the same riposte: 'As you might appreciate, in my experience of my client, the word "cannot" does not appear in his dictionary. And for an organisation used to constructing ninety-storey tower blocks, translocation on this scale is not logistically daunting.' And Boyd deftly conflated 'sustaining growth' with 'sustainable growth':

> Sustainability is not just about the environment but includes economic and social elements. Each factor has to be balanced and a judgment reached on the basis of the evidence . . . The development is wholly in line with the strategy and that priority. The development will help promote and sustain economic growth. It will be of a high environmental quality promoting biodiversity and responsibility.

The imprecision of NPPG 14 had allowed Boyd to repackage criticism of his client as a challenge to which Ministers might rise. Only at the very end did sentiment animate his words, Boyd alluding to 'Flower of Scotland', the song adopted as the country's national anthem:

> In the well-ordered world of development planning we try and anticipate the future. We set out our hopes and aspirations and attempt to direct development to our preferred locations. Sometimes, however, an opportunity arises that we have not anticipated, that exceeds our expectations and challenges the cosy assumptions we have made. Seldom however are we presented with such an audacious proposal. You only have to be in the presence of Donald Trump to understand its ambition; or to walk the site to understand its scale; or to stand where the thirteenth tee will be to appreciate its grandeur;

or to listen to Iain Webster to have any idea of the huge sums of money that will be invested and the degree of risk to the developer. As to the benefits, there are plenty of voices to show that this is well understood – from the public outcry following the ISC vote to the near unanimous support of the business community, from the overwhelming support of the council to the thousands of ordinary people who have made representations. But the question is – what is Scotland prepared to invest? What risks do we take? Or are we merely passive players, happy to take the benefits provided they come cost free with no risk? In my submission this truly is a once in a lifetime opportunity. We will not see its like again. It would be a tragedy for Scotland if we let it pass by.

Golf is a game of hope. Perennial optimism prompts lone golfers to roam Scotland's frozen winter fairways, slimmed down bags slung over their shoulders, like nomadic hunters in search of an elusive quarry: the perfect shot. Hope is what keeps golfers punting their ball towards the flag, the possibility of sinking their pitch, their chip, their putt. And it's what had Donald Trump hanging in at Menie: the belief he could deliver the perfect course.

After five years scouring the planet for a site, a year shaping his vision; after spending £6 million on land, and another £1 million assessing, honing, promoting and defending plans for it; after the rollercoaster ride of council committee decisions, a Scottish Government intervention, a parliamentary hearing, and a public inquiry, Donald Trump still believed he could hole out.

Appearing on the *Late Show with David Letterman* a month after the public inquiry, Trump sounded relaxed about his prospects. 'They, I believe – I hope – are going to say yes. And if they do, and I make this statement, it will be the greatest golf course anywhere in the world . . . because the land is the best land that I've ever seen for golf. There also happen to be hotels and other things going up, but it will be a very special place.' When asked if the site was on the west coast, Trump replied, 'More or less.'

Letterman said, 'What do you mean – more or less?!'

Trump extemporised. 'It's such a big area, it covers a lot of territory,' he said.

On 3 November 2008, Cabinet Secretary for Finance and Sustainable Growth John Swinney announced that Trump would be getting his planning permit after all, subject to satisfactory conclusion of legal agreements with Aberdeenshire Council. He said:

> I am content that there has been an efficient, transparent and inclusive process, led by Scotland's Chief Reporter, which has taken account of all of the relevant issues and the views expressed before, during and after the public inquiry. Having given careful consideration to the issues and arguments, I agree with the Reporters' findings and reasoning, and with their recommendation that outline planning permission should be granted, subject to the satisfactory prior conclusion of necessary legal agreements. The Reporters found there was significant economic and social benefit to be gained from this project, which has been a major consideration in my decision to grant outline planning permission.

In their report, McCulloch and his colleagues accepted that 'the dynamism underpinning the designation of the SSSI would, for the majority of the holes in the back nine of the championship course, be halted', adding that 'much, though not all, of the geomorphological interest in that affected part of the SSSI would be compromised'. They were left in 'no doubt' that the economic impact of the development would be 'nationally significant' and 'could thus make a significant contribution to achieving the Government's overarching purpose set by the Economic Strategy'. The reporters said 'full compliance with the development plan was never likely with a complex and unforeseen proposal on this scale' and applying NPPG 14 concluded:

> The economic and social advantages of this prospective development at national, regional and local level are such as to justify, uniquely,

the adverse environmental consequences caused by a development on this scale and in this location.

Their take on Trump?

Mr Trump has been concerned about the environmental effects of the development from the outset, although he acknowledged that he did not know the land was protected when he bought it. He hired the best environmental consultants and has taken their advice and accommodated their concerns within the development. He acknowledged that Dr Dargie advised that the course should be moved inland, but that would not be possible. Dr Dargie is now a big fan of the development. When complete, the land would be environmentally enhanced and better than it was before.

First Minister Alex Salmond was free to endorse Swinney's decision, describing himself as having been 'cup tied', a football expression for playing restrictions in competitions. He said: 'It is great to be able to finally speak my mind. I believe that the economic and social benefits for the North-east of Scotland substantially outweigh any environmental impact, and that this is demonstrated in the evaluation of the three reporters to the public local inquiry.'

During the inquiry, Salmond had popped up at Peterculter Golf Course on the outskirts of Aberdeen to promote Homecoming Scotland 2009, a celebration of Scottish culture in which the diaspora were invited to share. The First Minister was accompanied by Sir Sean Connery, who had been made an honorary member of Trump International Golf Links Scotland (number 007, in recognition of his James Bond role), and was due to drive the first ball at the planned opening in July 2012. Sir Sean admitted he didn't know 'too much about the environmental issues' but he said he hoped they would be resolved to capitalize on the 'fantastic opportunity' presented by Trump's investment.

Those issues had now been settled to the satisfaction of the Scottish Government.

Tom Smith, Chairman of the public-private development organisation Aberdeen City and Shire Economic Future, said: 'Today's decision could be a turning point for our region.' Paul Lawrie, whose own course got the go-ahead after the Scottish Government accepted Aberdeenshire Council's decision to approve it for a green-belt site, said: 'The North-east now truly has the potential to become one of the world's top golfing destinations.'

Objectors felt betrayed by politicians and the planning system. The only potential they saw was for more construction in the countryside. Martin Ford claimed the result set 'a very bad precedent'. Green MSP Patrick Harvie said it demonstrated a 'blatant disregard' for the SSSI designation. Rob Ashlin of Sustainable Aberdeenshire called it a 'damning verdict', and Aedan Smith, head of planning and development at RSPB Scotland, commented it was 'too high a price to pay for the claimed economic benefits from this development'.

Sustainable Aberdeenshire's website struck a sardonic note: 'The decision in Trump's favour is so overwhelming that even the fixers behind the scenes must be feeling a little embarrassed. We are fortunate that Trump is a man of good taste and restraint – if he had asked for a 500ft neon statue of Trump in a kilt that played "Mammie's Heiland Hame" on an electronic bagpipe he would have got it.'

On stage in an Aberdeen pub, city comedian Gordon McPherson joked: 'What do you give a man who's got everything for Christmas? Balmedie.'

The approval, signed off on 16 December, wasn't a green light for Trump to do as he wanted. Reporters had attached forty-six conditions to the permission to ensure construction was 'properly supervised and sensitively executed'. The demands covered everything from the way cut and fill operations would be carried out to the disposal of surface water. Under a draft planning agreement, Trump was to provide ninety-eight affordable homes, a primary school for the area, and £500,000 for community facilities. He would have to offer vocational training and set up and run an environmental management group to advise on caring for the land.

The New Yorker wasn't fazed.

'We are greatly honoured by the positive decision and believe that the people of Scotland will be extremely happy with the final product,' said Trump. 'It will be a tremendous asset and source of pride for both Aberdeenshire and Scotland for many generations.' Trump felt the calibre of the proposal combined with voluminous public support was 'ultimately going to get it approved'. Reflecting on his travails, he paid tribute to Salmond ('a tremendous leader') and to the three reporters. 'They asked hard questions, tough questions, smart questions. It's been a tough experience and a long experience.' Explaining his doggedness, the sixty-two-year-old said his Scottish ancestry had taken this development to 'a higher plateau' and that the backing of people had been 'so important . . . especially in the early stages when I had to make a decision about whether or not to go forward'.

In the end he hadn't let his mother down. All he had to do now was bring forward the detailed plans.

'As soon as we have the planning permissions, we'll start moving,' he promised. 'It will be the greatest golf course in the world because of the height of the dunes and the beautiful topography. Everybody has focused on the golf course but we're also going to build beautiful housing and a beautiful hotel. We're going to do a great job. People are going to come from all over the world.'

A few days later the global money markets imploded. Recession was on its way, and the signs were it was going to be at least as big as the one that had left Trump hung out to dry in 1990.

Chapter 8

I DON'T NEED BANKS

The whole world gets by on tick. People live in houses they haven't paid for. Banks lend them money on the promise it will be repaid from wages. The companies paying the wages also borrow money from banks. They promise to repay it from the sale of goods or services, bought with money borrowed from banks. As we moved into the twenty-first century, banks were borrowing ever more money from other banks and financial institutions to lend ever more money to customers in the hope of making ever more money on the interest. To raise capital they sold on bundles of mortgage debt, which in the financial world counted as an asset.

Money didn't make the world go round. The illusion of wealth did.

As part of the American Dream, President George W. Bush wanted everyone to own their own house, even those who had no real chance of paying for it. Lenders tried to cover their risks in this, the 'sub-prime' mortgage market, by charging above-average interest rates, which was fine, except that US interest rates took off between 2004 and 2006. Suddenly people everywhere started defaulting. Banks had nothing left to lend. All they had were bundles of money owed to other banks, the value of which nobody knew because nobody was buying them.

Towards the end of 2007, when Donald Trump was awaiting a ruling on his Menie proposal, the global financial system had started to unravel as one big confidence trick.

In a twenty-year period borrowing had doubled, taking the average household to the point where it was spending more than it was earning. The desire for immediate gratification saw people falling over themselves to buy flat-screen televisions and mobile phones and laptops, mostly made in China, which was falling over itself to lend the money back to Western governments. Everyone got greedy and reckless, especially banks. Nobody knew what these behemoths were up to any more. Corporate governance was poor, international regulation non-existent. And all the while executives were pulling billions out of the system in bonuses.

So how did governments respond to this profligate behaviour?

By flushing more money into the system, and ordering banks – keen to shore up their own finances – to start lending it out. People were asked to spend, spend, spend.

Whole banks needed saving. Northern Rock was nationalised by the UK Government on 17 February 2008. In the US, Wall Street's fifth biggest bank, Bear Stearns, was taken over by J. P. Morgan Chase, but the government there helped out by taking on $30 billion of mortgage liabilities. The US Government also bought out mortgage lenders Fannie May and Freddie Mac, which had half the country's home loans on their books, many in the sub-prime market.

The US Federal Reserve decided the economy needed a cash injection of $787 billion, described as the 'most sweeping recovery package in our history'. The UK Government's beneficence wasn't finished. It acquired seventy per cent of the Royal Bank of Scotland, Lloyds TSB and HBOS, taking on £150 billion worth of mortgages and pumping in £37 billion. And how was the Government underwriting this? From future tax returns predicated on continuing prosperity.

Towards the end of 2008, the evaporation of credit was hurting the people in a real way. Businesses were closing and jobs going. The Aberdeenshire-based Stewart Milne Group, Scotland's biggest housebuilder, axed forty-four posts after shedding 300 in July – 120 of them in the North-east. Around 100 workers lost their jobs at a fish processing plant in northern Aberdeenshire. The boss blamed a loss of 'confidence in the luxury food sector' and the fact nobody was eating out.

Chancellor Alistair Darling, who decided to tap the retrenched taxpayer for an extra 0.5% national insurance from 2011, warned that the economy was facing its worst crisis for sixty years and that the downturn would be more 'profound and long-lasting' than first feared. Around the time Trump was celebrating the go-ahead for his resort from the Scottish Government, the Office for National Statistics reported that economic growth had fallen by 0.5% from July to September, the first shrinkage in sixteen years. Year-on-year house prices for the quarter fell by 10.2% in Britain and 16.3% in the US.

Jonathan Fair, Chief Executive of Homes for Scotland, which represents companies building ninety-five per cent of new homes, reported that new-build starts were down by almost fifty per cent in the last quarter, with sites 'requiring heavy investment in infrastructure' worst affected. Tony Mackay, an economic consultant based in northern Scotland, had always viewed the Trump plan as an upmarket housing development with a golf course tacked. 'The recent collapse in the housing market throughout Scotland must raise serious doubts over the project or at least the timing,' he said. 'The collapse may be temporary but most housing experts expect it to last for a few years.'

High-end golf developments were not immune to the recession. In Stonehaven, FM Developments went to the wall, and the Jack Nicklaus course with it. In Aberdeen, the city council became nervous about the business case for its Hazlehead course and instead of handing it over to a consortium, left the matter in the hands of a new arm's-length sports trust. The sumptuous Gleneagles Hotel in Perthshire (three courses, four restaurants, up to 700 employees, £1,900-a-night suites, and home to the G8 summit in 2005) offered staff voluntary severance, unpaid leave or reduced hours.

Trump, appearing on *Larry King Live*, was asked who should take the rap for the collapse of the economy. 'Well, there's a lot of greed on Wall Street,' said Trump. 'And a lot of people are making crazy deals and you can blame everybody, even the regular consumer that went out and bought a house and got a mortgage that was ridiculous. You know, we call them exploding mortgages. But you can really blame a lot of people. And I guess you can maybe just blame the times.'

As the crisis deepened, Trump had his own troubles.

A group of lenders led by Deutsche Bank sued him for missing repayments on a $640 million construction loan for the ninety-two-storey Trump International Hotel and Tower in Chicago. This, the world's highest residential building, offered a chance 'to experience the luxury of the Trump lifestyle'. It housed 339 five-star rooms and suites, 486 apartments, a health club, ballrooms, conference rooms, bars, restaurants, and 1,000 parking spaces.

Trump argued he was the victim of extraordinary and unforeseen circumstances that had prevented the bank lending potential buyers money for a mortgage. A 'force majeure' clause allowed payment to be delayed by 'events or circumstances' not 'within the reasonable control of the borrower'. Usually the clause covered floods and labour strikes. An inspired Trump presented the recession as an Act of God. He told *The New York Times*'s Floyd Norris: 'Would you consider the biggest depression we have had in this country since 1929 to be such an event? I would.' Trump counter-sued for $3 billion over the damage to his image. Deutsche Bank took the view that Trump was no 'stranger to overdue debt'.

Such was the faith in the real estate market only a few years before, the construction loan specified a list of *minimum* prices to be charged. Trump, however, wasn't ready to extend to the people who had signed up for condos the same leeway he demanded of Deutsche Bank. 'They don't have a force majeure clause,' he told Norris.

There were grumbles in Mexico, too, where the 526-suite Trump Ocean Resort Baja development was scrapped after construction money couldn't be raised. More than $32 million of deposits were lost. At a sales reception, Trump had assured buyers the site was the 'ideal locale for a premier resort property'. George Sorial said the Trump Organization had only licensed its name to the project. When

I asked him if the company might have been more judicious about its choice of licensees, he stressed the contract had been abruptly terminated after the developer failed to comply with the terms, including a deadline for the start of construction.

Trump Entertainment Resorts filed for Chapter 11 Bankruptcy after missing a bond interest payment of nearly $53.1 million. Trump and daughter Ivanka quit the board first, bemoaning the management's 'wasteful spending'. Trump said his twenty-eight per cent stake was 'substantially less than one per cent' of his net worth and added: 'While the Trump Organization grows and flourishes, Trump Entertainment Resorts, of which I am a stockholder, has languished.' Trump Entertainment Resorts was formed from Trump Entertainment four years earlier under a Chapter 11 Bankruptcy, which protects a company from creditors by allowing it to re-organise. Trump had been Chief Executive.

If anyone knew how to weather a recession, it was Trump. In 1991 he found himself all out of credit after borrowing heavily to prop up businesses. The banks and bondholders agreed to give him extra time to repay loans, more in hope than expectation of recouping at least some of their millions. Within three years, Trump had massively reduced his debt, managing to retain Trump Tower and control of his three casinos in Atlantic City.

When I asked Trump about the economic malaise, he stressed Menie was different from all that had gone before it. The course wasn't being built in partnership with others. He wasn't selling his name. He would be using his own money, around $40 million for the course and facilities. As he put it: 'I don't need banks.'

George Sorial was as bullish as the boss. 'The money is there, ready to be wired at any time,' he said. 'I am not discussing whether it is in a Scottish bank or what, but it is earmarked for this project. If we needed to put the development up tomorrow, we have the cash to do that. It is sitting there in the bank and is ready to go. I don't think Scotland has anything to worry about. As we have said all along, this is a project we have chosen to fund with cash. Mr

Trump has recently increased his cash position and we have no need for a bank loan in respect of the Aberdeenshire project.'

The pound's collapse against the dollar was making the project cheaper. Far from panicking, the director of development was rubbing his hands over the recession and its manifold opportunities. 'There is an economic downturn globally, but we have managed to use that to our advantage,' said Sorial. 'We have bought up projects that are discounted by thirty to forty per cent. Having cash in a downturn like this is a good position to be in. We have a very diverse business range. We are talking about an organisation that has its own TV show, numerous lines of products including clothing, vodka and so on. It is not about one little project.'

Trump had been making cash on the side too. In the summer of 2008, he sold his Florida beachfront mansion for $95 million to a Russian fertiliser oligarch. Trump had picked it up in 2004 for $41 million after its owner went bankrupt. Maison de l'Amitié, with its giant fountain and twenty-four-carat gold bathroom fixtures, became the most expensive house sold in the US. 'I love breaking records,' crowed Trump. 'In an age of so many people getting hurt in real estate, it shows that you can still do well in real estate . . . The world has changed financially and the banks are all in such trouble, but the good news is that we are doing very well as a company and we are in a very, very strong cash position.'

In autumn 2008, another credit crunch was looming and not even Donald Trump could be sanguine about this one.

A report from the WWF, formerly the World Wildlife Fund, predicted that by 2030 we would need two planets to sustain our immodest lifestyles. That's a sizeable shortfall, one whole Earth. You can't produce another one on the back of issuing government bonds. You can't print another planet.

The *Living Planet Report* estimated the burgeoning human population was using more resources than the Earth could replenish every year, that when it came to environmental capital, we had

Down to Business
Donald Trump chats to former airport
boss Andy Flower after landing in
Aberdeen in 2006.

Sharing the Vision
Trump's team, led by Ashley Cooper *(far right)*,
at Belhelvie Village Hall.

Nineteenth Hole
The clubhouse drawing produced when
Trump first arrived in Aberdeen.

Sugar Sands
The Menie Links extending three miles
north to the Dome next to the North Sea.

Laying the Groundwork
Former Project Director Neil Hobday
managed the early plans.

The Chief Negotiator
George Sorial, Trump's International
Development Director, at Menie House.

Making a Point
Trump explaining his thinking to course
designer Dr Martin Hawtree.

Something Beyond
Trump on the site he believes will yield the
world's greatest golf course.

Right: **Victorious**
Alex Salmond is elected MSP for Gordon and becomes the leader of Scotland in May 2007.

Big Decision
Members of the Formartine Area Committee meet to rule on Trump's plan.

Left: **Not for Sale**
Molly Forbes and son Michael at the Mill of Menie – a place called Paradise.

Left: **Home Comforts**
Trump's $50 million apartment occupies the top of his eponymous New York skyscraper.

Kid in a Candy Store
Ed Russo outside his former home, now an office at Trump's Bedminster course.

Aspiring Member
Dr Robert Caccavalle sits in the April sunshine at
the Bedminster clubhouse in New Jersey.

Humble Beginnings
Trump and sister Maryanne *(far left)* with Scottish relatives
at their late mother's home on the Isle of Lewis.

Star Witness
Trump arrives for the first day of the
public inquiry at the Aberdeen Exhibition
and Conference Centre.

Left: **Gearing Up**
Councillor and cyclist Martin
Ford shows his green credentials
at the public inquiry.

Reference Point
Chief Reporter Jim McCulloch flanked by
colleagues Karen Heywood and Michael Cunlisse.

Talking Tactics
QC Colin Boyd *(left)* in discussion with
Dr Martin Hawtree.

Weathering the Storm
Menie Estate boss Sarah Malone and her
1,400-acre office.

The Land Speaks
The rare adder's tongue fern, growing on the Site
of Special Scientific Interest.

Clash of Views
Former record producer Mickey Foote with George
Sorial on the site earmarked for 500 houses.

Day at the Beach
The public inquiry parties get up close and
personal with the dunes.

Traditional Approach
A very rough sketch of the type of hotel
that might appear at the resort.

Home by the Sea
The layout of the village as envisaged in
the masterplan.

Right: **Standing Firm**
Menie Estate resident
David Milne inspects the
masterplan with Molly
Forbes alongside.

Left: **Battleline**
Links Superintendent
Paul O'Connor and
wrecked fencing on the
Menie Estate.

Dogged
Tripping Up Trump member Sue Edwards and a canine
friend await the arrival of Donald Trump in Aberdeen.

Welcome Address
Don Jr, flanked by his father and piper
Bill Hepburn, thanks supporters.

Swinging into Action
Michael O'Leary *(left)*, Sarah Malone,
George Sorial and Martin Hawtree two
days after the construction go ahead.

Turf War
An artist's impression of the fourteenth
hole, which lies within the Site of Special
Scientific Interest.

over-extended ourselves. The WWF reckoned that 2.1 hectares of land should be enough to keep each of us in water, food and fuel. But the average US citizen was reportedly using more than eight hectares to harvest everything from Big Macs to Apple Macs. Britons were marginally less wanton, needing 5.5 hectares. The global average was 2.7 hectares. And the population was on the up.

James Leape, WWF's International Director, wrote:

The recent downturn in the global economy is a stark reminder of the consequences of living beyond our means. But the possibility of financial recession pales in comparison to the looming ecological credit crunch. We have only one planet. Its capacity to support a thriving diversity of species, including humans, is large but fundamentally limited. When human demand on this capacity exceeds what is available – when we surpass ecological limits – we erode the health of the Earth's living systems. Ultimately this loss threatens human well-being.

We weren't just ravaging the planet. We were also purportedly responsible for curdling the climate.

Carbon dioxide (CO_2) is a naturally occurring gas found in the atmosphere. It lets the sun's warming rays pass through to reach the Earth but retains some of the radiated heat (which has a different wavelength). It's what keeps us cosy and makes the planet habitable. But burning coal, oil and gas produces CO_2, and this, coupled with chopping down swathes of jungle, which absorb CO_2, has led to talk of 'global warming'.

While the prospect of growing sugar beet in the garden or spotting a great white shark off the coast might excite some Scots, a mix of droughts, flood and other calamities are predicted for elsewhere (along with war over diminishing natural resources). Using data from earlier warm periods in Earth's history to calculate freaky weather as a function of temperature, researchers at NASA and the Columbia University Earth Institute found an estimated warming of 0.6°C in the past thirty years was 'likely to set in motion dis-integration of the West Antarctic ice sheet and Arctic sea ice'. Lurid as that forecast sounds, science academies from nearly every indus-trialised nation have endorsed the orthodoxy of global warming.

Despite global warming being as plain as a punch on the nose to thousands of scientists, Donald Trump isn't convinced we're cooking the planet. And he's not alone.

Oceanographer Tad Murty, an associate professor of the Carleton's Department of Earth Sciences in Canada, has described global warming as the 'biggest scientific hoax being perpetrated on humanity'. Perhaps its most vociferous critic is John Coleman, a member of the American Meteorological Society and co-founder of The Weather Channel, who brands it 'the greatest scam in history'. As far as he's concerned, the only thing rapidly increasing is the number of scientists opposed to the notion of humans baking the planet. Coleman claims at least 750 have registered an objection with the US Senate Environmental Committee.

Coleman believes global warming is the bogeyman with which the United Nations has tried to scare the world into shape. In the late 1950s, it emerged as a shadowy threat, like communism or flying saucers, only worse for polar bears. The way he tells it, the United Nations' Intergovernmental Panel on Climate Change (IPCC) pulled together research devoted to refining the theory but in doing so perpetuated its erroneous assumptions. The resultant propaganda ensured global warming became a self-fulfilling prophecy.

The concentration of CO_2 in the atmosphere has increased from the 1958 reading of 315 to 385 parts per million in 2008, and most of that still comes from natural processes rather than from the burning of fossil fuels. At the start of the Industrial Revolution, CO_2 was an estimated 280ppm. However, when mammals were shaping up on Earth eighty million years ago the figure was 1,000ppm. Even Ken Caldeira, who contributes to the IPCC and is one of the most respected climate scientists in the world, has conceded a doubling of CO_2 would retain less than two per cent of the outgoing radiation emitted by the Earth.

Supporters of the global warming theory (that is, believers in our culpability) explain that CO_2 is the catalyst for other changes.

As temperature increases so does evaporation from the seas, creating an ever thicker blanket of cloud, which is significantly better at trapping radiated heat than CO_2, and, as the oceans warm, they are less able to hold onto dissolved CO_2, so more enters the atmosphere. But accurately modelling the way these accelerative effects combine is fiendishly difficult. The rise in atmospheric temperature over the last twenty years has not been inexorable: it peaked in 1998. Defenders of global warming say this coincided with a strong El Niño, the periodic drawing of heat from the Pacific Ocean, but no one is quite sure how even that works.

The climate is always changing; the universe is in constant flux. All manner of celestial phenomena affect our planet's weather – the Sun's varying luminosity (thought to be at its strongest for 8,000 years), for example, and the wobbling Earth's distance from the Sun. Forecasting is one enormous and enormously complex fluid dynamics problem, but that hasn't kept the environmental soothsayers from confidently predicting what the weather will be doing twenty or thirty years from now. Ever tried getting a forecast for a week ahead? The real trouble with global warming is that it's not something you want to be complacent about. The consequences of misjudging the situation are rather more serious than dressing for sunshine and getting rain. Carbon dioxide hangs around for millenia.

The North-east of Scotland imagines playing its part in a new industry based on carbon capture and storage, a neat reversal involving sealing emissions in empty oil and gas fields far under the North Sea, but not every country borders a sea with a porous bed.

The UN dreams of legally-binding cuts in greenhouse gas emissions. Britain has pledged to reduce CO_2 production by eighty per cent in 2050. The Institute of Mechanical Engineers estimates the country would need to build thirty nuclear power stations by 2015 to be on course to meet the target. Chief Executive Stephen Tetlow has spoken about having to adopt a 'wartime mentality' towards the consumption of energy.

Nathan Myhrvold and his crew at Intellectual Ventures say we needn't go back to rationing fuel just yet.

Myhrvold isn't a climatologist but by any mark he's a bright guy. He researched quantum cosmology (the biggest brain bender in science) at Cambridge University with Stephen Hawking. In *Superfreakonomics* (by Steven Levitt and Stephen Dubner), Myhrvold observes 'good environmental stewardship' might have inadvertently warmed the planet, cleaning up the sooty atmosphere that acted as a sun shield. Intellectual Ventures has suggested investigating pumping sulphur dioxide into the stratosphere where it could bond with the water vapour and form a protective veil around the planet. It would be the ultimate sun block, a catalytic converter on a planetary scale. We could negate the excessive use of fossil fuels by filling the atmosphere with yet more gas.

Mad? The tactic worked for the financial world. The SO_2 injection could be a kind of quantitative easing.

All of this might seem a long way from a squabble about a golf course in a tiny corner of a tiny country. However, the Menie saga crystallizes a bigger conundrum: how do we square conserving the planet with our base urge to consume it?

In early 2009, the Scottish Government had started implementing what it called a landmark piece of legislation, one for the conflicted twenty-first century.

The Planning Act 2006 aimed to 'create a more efficient process to enable sustainable economic growth for Scotland'. The Government suggested planning had an image of 'being a barrier to development' because of a 'culture that is too regulatory, too reactive, too slow and too technical'. The guidance said planning should be 'more enabling, more facilitating'. It added: 'High quality developments will make successful places that are attractive and efficient for residents, employers, visitors and which will contribute to the Scottish Government's core purpose of sustainable economic growth.'

Sustainable fishing is a concept easily understood – you limit your catch to leave a breeding stock. But what exactly is sustainable development? Is it even tenable?

A report for the UN on population trends admitted 'no human is genuinely carbon neutral' and added that birth control could 'reduce greenhouse gas emissions as much as investments in nuclear or wind energy'. Yet, like all animals, we are driven to prosper and prevail; it's a biological imperative, an economic one too. Propagation is a dirty, grasping business. In rushing to protect the planet, we have embraced noble environmental principles – locally, nationally and internationally – without much thought as to how they might be reconciled with the inflationary nature of growth on the ground.

They entered around 3am. Some were carrying ladders, others plastic golf clubs. On 3 March 2009, the Plane Stupid Open took place – on the runway at Aberdeen Airport. A banner was hung from the terminal roof: 'Nae Trump Games with Climate Change'. Dan Glass, one of the nine intruders, the majority of whom were in their twenties, explained they were protesting against the 'undemocratic decision to allow the airport expansion' and the Trump course. Glass, from Glasgow, said: 'The purpose of this is to highlight the need to combat climate change. Our whole lives we have been told that climate change will define our generation but nothing ever seems to be done. We have filed petitions and lobbied our MPs yet all they seem to do is talk. We need action.'

Chapter 9

A STATE OF LIMBO

It was the perfect pastoral scene. A young couple on a bench beside a pond; mother goose and six goslings waddling past, perhaps destined for their first dip; a street behind bustling in the way villages are supposed to bustle. The light sketches and soft shades gave nothing away about the nature of the shops, but you imagined butchers and bakers and tearooms serving fruit scones. The gentle drawings were redolent of the books of childhood. Another scene showed a toddler playing on a toy tractor. Mum, binoculars in hand, looked towards hummocky dunes where more geese flew overhead in a v-formation.

These images, released in the late summer of 2009, showed how Donald Trump's village and resort might look on the ground. The pond was part of a 'wetland park'. Paths ran down to the beach. One connected with the neighbouring village of Balmedie. It was all very inclusive.

The masterplan was drafted by Gareth Hoskins. His architecture practice had been voted the best in the UK and was ranked top of the Power 100 list by the industry in 2008. Projects led by the firm included the revamp of Edinburgh's National Museum and the capital's £70 million Princes Street Galleries shopping scheme. The practice had also produced plans for a golf resort on the Cowal Peninsula in Argyll and Bute, and a clubhouse for the Gwest development near Gleneagles. Hoskins was an advisor to the Royal Institute of British Architects and on the board of the Scottish Government's watchdog Architecture and Design Scotland.

For Menie, he drew inspiration from towns across the North-east, settlements conceived as a whole and laid out with stern, Presbyterian precision 100 or more years ago. He dismissed contemporary developments as 'a sea of housing' without 'heart or structure', but then few architects were afforded the chance to design a village from scratch. The promotional brochure trumpeted 'a seamless unification with the landscape' to create 'a strong sense of place and belonging'. The brochure concluded: 'Trump International Scotland will be a world-class destination to visit and an inspirational place to live. Synonymous with the Trump brand, all aspects of this development will be built to the very highest architectural and design standards.'

There was only one potential complication with this grand new vision. It included land Trump didn't actually own.

Bizarre as it sounds, under Scottish planning law you can lodge an application for anywhere you fancy. You could put forward a proposal to turn Balmoral Castle into a hotel or to flatten the Scottish Parliament for a shopping complex. You could apply to extend your home all the way into a neighbour's garden – or, if you really wanted to unnerve them, to add a conservatory to theirs.

The new Trump masterplan appropriated four homes: Leyton Cottage, Hermit Point, Mill of Menie and Menie Fishing Station. A field belonging to Pitgersie Farm and a former council-owned car park in the centre of the championship course were also used as part of the blank canvas. Explaining the changes, Hoskins said that after examining the original outline, he told Trump more 'elbow room' was needed, fifty acres or so. 'We took a very objective review of the site planning and our remit to produce a world-class development,' he said. 'The changes allow you to create a more cohesive development. There were practical issues – service access and emergency access.'

Trump didn't just apply to have these five pockets of land (Mill of Menie and Menie Fishing Station were counted as a single plot) included in the 'emerging' masterplan.

He asked the council if it might consider securing the sites with compulsory purchase orders (CPOs).

The power of the state to take private property for public purpose is enshrined in law. Compulsory purchase in Scotland dates back to the 1700s. CPOs were used for large-scale reconstruction at the end of the First World War, and in the 1960s and 70s to support road building. Councils, utility companies, railways and Historic Scotland are all empowered to use CPOs. Trunk road agency Transport Scotland issued orders for the demolition of thirteen houses lying in the way of Aberdeen's bypass (due to be built in 2012). Market value, as determined by the Lands Tribunal, will be paid along with an element of compensation.

Scottish Ministers see economic regeneration and wealth creation as a legitimate 'public purpose'. Elaine Farquharson-Black, a specialist in planning law with Aberdeen solicitors Paull & Williamsons, explained that local authorities are seen as having an 'important role in this regard' – for example, in the event that 'private sector efforts at land assembly are frustrated'. Farquharson Black, who co-wrote (with Jeremy Rowan Robinson) the definitive *Compulsory Purchase and Compensation: The Law in Scotland*, said: 'The use of compulsory powers will quite often follow from the establishment of a partnership, sometimes between different public bodies, but increasingly with the private sector. This is generally because although local authorities have wide powers to undertake the development of land held for planning purposes, they may lack the necessary entrepreneurial skills and may have difficulty accessing the resources necessary to implement a scheme of regeneration.'

When asked about CPOs, George Sorial refrained from reminding everyone of the promised jobs and land for housing and instead focused on the Trump Organization's hopes of reaching a 'fair and amicable' settlement with the landowners. 'Compulsory purchase exists as an option,' he said. 'It's not one that we chose to immediately pursue – it's viewed as an option of last resort. This is something we could have done years ago. The fact that we have chosen to pursue our goals of acquiring these plots peacefully is testament to our nature. We are doing everything in our power and, I think with two exceptions, I am confident that we will have positive and peaceful outcomes.'

Aberdeenshire Council also moved to reassure the public that it was not about to seize residents' homes, and emphasized that any such move would first have to be backed by councillors. A spokesman said: 'Local authorities do have compulsory purchase powers, but whether or not they would be used in this case would be a matter for consideration by the full council. We would expect the applicant to have considered and exhausted every possible opportunity open to them before the council would require to consider using these powers.'

Critics believed it was always Trump's intention that land be forcibly acquired, that you didn't have to be an award-winning architect to spot the advantages of including in a masterplan layout pockets sitting within the Menie Estate or enclosed by it on three sides. Before the public inquiry, some residents had vowed they wouldn't sell to Trump, so invoking CPOs was always a possibility. But back then, Trump was still trying to win permission to build on the SSSI, and that was provocative enough.

Hoskins conceded there were 'a few bits of land' he was 'surprised' hadn't formed part of the original plan. However, he also stressed that the redesign wasn't simply about perfecting the look of the resort or optimizing its operation. Hoskins said that meeting the extensive list of planning conditions imposed by the Scottish Government necessitated finding more space on the ground. 'It allows you to move away from the Site of Special Scientific Interest,' he explained, describing the creation of a buffer zone between the sand dunes and holiday homes.

Letters detailing the planning applications for the five sites were hand-delivered early one morning.

Susan Munro, of Leyton Cottage, didn't find hers until she arrived home from work in the late afternoon. A Menie resident for twenty-six years, she occupied the four-bedroom house with her husband

John and two sons, Murdo and Findlay. 'I was shocked,' said Susan. 'I am upset about the way it has happened. It is an awful thing. My youngest son was born here and Murdo was two when we moved here.' There was bafflement, too, as she recalled a visit from Trump many months earlier. 'He came to my door when he was down and he said, "Susan, you're sitting on a gold mine," and then reassured me he would be a good neighbour and that our house wasn't essential to his plan.' Susan said Trump nevertheless offered £150,000 for the house, later upping his bid to £175,000.

'That wouldn't even buy a two-bedroom flat in Aberdeen,' she added. 'Our intention was to stay here forever. When I saw the yellow envelope, I thought, here we go again.'

The other owners, Mark and Gillian Hewison, and farmer George Moir, refused to comment.

Mickey Foote compared Trump's overtures to the notorious Highland Clearances, which took place in the eighteenth and nineteenth centuries when landowners forced out tenants to make way for sheep.

When I spoke to Foote, he was recovering from an illness. His voice was ragged, his breathing laboured, but the physical struggle amplified the conviction of his commentary. He denounced Trump's 'antics' as 'disgusting'. 'He's being positively feudal in his approach,' said Foote. 'This is not the Scottish way. There is not one good reason why people should sell their homes for the glorification of Mr Trump. He's not satisfied with what he's got. He's going to turn around and squash the little people. This is modern-day clearances.' Foote ended by calling on the council to rule out any such move: 'If Aberdeenshire Council has any grain of self-respect for its fellow countrymen it should squash this notion about compulsory purchase orders without delay.'

It wasn't just Mickey Foote who wanted the council to rule out CPOs. Martin Ford put forward a motion:

Aberdeenshire Council will not use compulsory purchase powers to force Aberdeenshire residents from their own homes on or adjacent to the Menie estate.

Ford had quit the Lib Dems to form the Democratic Independent Group with Paul Johnston, Sam Coull and Debra Storr after a bitter falling out over Trump. Johnston was referred to the Standards Commission over claims the offer of land to Trump for social housing might be perceived as a 'sweetener'. The full council voted to write to the watchdog, describing his comments as a 'serious breach' of the code of conduct. Storr refused to support the proposal, but failed to give due notice to the party leader. She resigned before she was expelled. Johnston – who had been careful not to make an overt accusation – was cleared.

The exodus weakened the ruling Lib Dem-Conservative coalition's grip on power, leaving the administration with just thirty-four members out of sixty-eight councillors and dependent on the vote of Lib Dem Provost Bill Howatson to pass any decisions.

George Sorial condemned Ford's CPO motion as 'a clear breach of protocol, ethics and the law', arguing that Ford was expressing an opinion on a planning matter ahead of it being considered by the committee. He said: 'I am shocked, surprised and disappointed Cllr Ford feels he has a right to flagrantly abuse his power.' Sorial wrote to Aberdeenshire Council asking that Ford along with Debra Storr, Paul Johnston and fellow councillor Sam Coull be debarred from future votes after engaging in a 'pattern of public opposition'. Ford said: 'This is either an attempt to gag us or an attempt at intimidation. Either way, it is going to fail. I don't give in to bullying and intimidation.'

It might have been a greater shock if Martin Ford *hadn't* challenged the threat of CPOs at Menie. This was a councillor who, on the same day, put forward another motion calling on the council to support commitments from the Lib Dems and Tories opposing an additional runway at Heathrow. If he was ready to take a pop at the world's busiest airport, he was ready to go a second round with a man with a Boeing 727 in his garage. Ford's motion was tabled for the next full council meeting, giving the Trump Organization less than two months to strike deals while they still had at least the possibility of CPOs in their back pockets.

Ahead of the push for new land, Trump started marshalling his forces on the ground.

In August 2009, he appointed thirty-four-year-old Sarah Malone as Executive Vice President of Trump International Golf Links Scotland. Malone grew up in the fishing town of Peterhead, twenty miles north of the Menie Estate. She modestly calls herself a Buchan 'quine' (the North-east word for young girl), one who happened to graduate with an honours degree in Fine Art from the Glasgow School of Art and later completed a postgraduate diploma in arts administration. She joined the Gordon Highlanders Regimental Museum in Aberdeen as curator and left as an executive director, having helped oversee the building of a £1.2 million extension.

The job talks had started a year earlier and culminated in a trip to New York. 'I think he is a visionary, a very positive man,' she said of Trump. 'I can't work for someone I don't believe in. I think it's a phenomenal project.' Malone saw it as a chance to get even with Edinburgh and Glasgow, to snare visitors who knew nothing of regimental museums in North-east Scotland. 'There's no question that it will have an immeasurable impact on tourism,' she said. 'It's quite clear it will give us a completely different level of exposure. For too long the Central Belt and the Highlands have stolen the limelight. Everything that makes Scotland wonderful is within a short driving distance around this region.'

She compared great golf courses to great art – 'enticing people back' – and cited her appointment as evidence of Trump's interest in heritage.

When Malone was in charge of the museum she never hesitated to put the most precious pieces on public display. She was ready to risk exposing them to damage because, locked away in a vault, they had for her no context, no meaning, no real-world value. She might have been alluding to the Menie dunes. 'The project is going to create jobs for the generation that's coming up,' she continued. 'It's loud and clear as far as I can hear that people want this development. The objective now is for the people of the North-east to work to make it our own.'

The appointment of Malone was announced outside MacLeod House, as Menie House had been renamed. The mansion was now officially Trump's 'Scottish family residence'. A refurbishment was underway. Red tartan carpet had been laid in the hallway. There was a big-screen television in Trump's bedroom so he could watch sport.

Don Junior, Trump's eldest son, who introduced Malone to the media, said his father was entrusting the project to him as the family representative on the team. 'This is a Trump project in its entirety,' he said. 'It's our capital and we want to build it perfectly. We've spent tens of millions of dollars to get to this point. It's very near and dear to our hearts and we intend to see it through. Frankly, it's the top priority in terms of development around the world.'

Don Jr is the Executive Vice President of Development and Acquisitions, a job he insists he had to work for. 'In my family, kids aren't handed vast sums of money for doing nothing,' he said. 'We knew we had to work if we wanted to earn.' At thirteen he spent a summer working as a dock attendant making minimum wage plus tips ('a great way to learn about good and bad service') and then 'weeks' digging ditches for a landscaper. 'My father told me that if I'm going to tell someone to dig a ditch then I'd need to know how to do it and how long it would take first.'

He tells a story about his dad that sounds like one of Zeno's paradoxes. 'My father spent a lot of time with us and every morning he'd say the same thing: "Don't smoke, don't drink, don't take drugs and never trust anyone." Then he'd say, "But you trust me, right?" If I replied, "Of course, you're my father," he'd joke around and say, "My son's an idiot – he's forgotten everything I taught him!"'

On his first visit to the dunes in 2006, Don Jr immediately phoned his father in New York. 'I told him, "I've never seen anything like this."'

Standing outside MacLeod House, he said the golf course would help preserve the 'beauty' of the dunes. 'It's not New Yorkers coming in to try to do it their way. We try to make something that really fits within the natural environment and the parameters we are given to work with.' But the first thing Don Jr and Malone had to do was wait. The design parameters had yet to be established. Delivering the 'greatest golf resort in the world' was contingent on the Trump Organization winning planning permission for those five extra plots.

'Ah, Mr Trump's number one fan.'

As I settle on the bench next to a protestor, I don't expect much in the way of conversation. He perceives the *Evening Express*, and its reporter, to be resolutely pro-Trump. I've seen him before, outside council meetings and at public exhibitions, always waving a placard opposed to the Trump development.

We're at the Ellon Kirk hall, where the Formartine Area Committee is meeting to consider Trump's outline planning application for the new plots at Menie. Chairman John Loveday has carefully explained what the debate *isn't* about – CPOs – telling everyone they 'don't exist' and are for 'another time'. The protestor, who lives within a few miles of Menie, isn't bound by the Chairman's directive.

'It could be your home, my home, anybody's home,' he says as we sit in the early September sunshine. 'It would mean anyone can apply for CPOs and turf someone out of their home because they want a piece of land. It would set a precedent.'

He believes Trump has duped the people.

'Now we know people's homes are involved. That was not made clear at the outset. They've bought their house, worked on it and they're being driven out by a foreign millionaire. Where's his sense of geography? His mother was born on the west coast. This is the east coast! People are going to lose their homes because he wants to build a golf club. It's not going to benefit anyone locally except for a few old men. We've got a championship course at Murcar, and at Royal Aberdeen . . .'

I repeat Trump's assertion that his will be the 'greatest' anywhere.

'Every golf course he builds is the "world's best",' he says dismissively. 'Everything has to be the biggest. He's full of baloney. He's a victim of the recession, he's having problems in America.'

I say nothing, letting his words carry off in the breeze. It's the first day of September and pleasant enough, but summer has passed. Rowan berries hang from nearby trees like last drops of sacrificial blood.

'I'm sorry,' says the protestor, 'but he's behaving like a spoilt American brat – "I want! I want!" – but he can't do it. This is Scotland.'

I point out that Trump has succeeded so far, and with the blessing of Holyrood. He doesn't argue but says he won't be voting SNP again while Alex Salmond is in charge. Or for the Lib Dems. 'Liberal dictatorship,' he says derisively. 'We didn't elect George Sorial. We didn't elect Donald Trump. There are a few straight councillors and they have been put through the wringer for it.'

We chat some more and the protestor divulges something that partly explains his trenchant opposition, the hours spent cutting and painting wood, the zealous slogans and placard-waving. A family member's home was bulldozed for a block of flats under a CPO in England. He says he's too unhappy to talk about it. 'I still feel pretty sore over that,' he adds.

I leave him to his placard and return inside.

John Loveday is briefing councillors ahead of the debate.

'Land ownership is not a planning matter and certainly has no relevance whatsoever to the planning applications we have in front of us today,' he says. In their report, planners have already recommended approval. Council Officer Sonya Galloway reiterates there is 'no sound land-use reason' for not supporting the applications. She adds that four of the sites lie within the wider development area, with the fifth bounded on three sides by the area to be developed. She deflects concerns about the lack of specific environmental impact studies for the sites, which Scottish Natural Heritage has deemed unnecessary. Four of the five are covered by a wider assessment. None has any special designation.

Gareth Hoskins takes to the floor for a presentation. He says the original masterplan was a 'loose' application and that the challenges of protecting the environment 'were not fully understood' when it was produced. Hoskins stresses to the eleven councillors that the extra pockets are 'essential' if 'the quality of development envisaged can be achieved'.

'It would be the type of world-class destination and place-making that Scotland should have the confidence and ambition to achieve,' he says. 'I feel very confident that what we are seeing is a fairly definite masterplan.'

Hermit Point owner David Milne would see his house, crafted from an old Coastguard Station, expunged. That it lies next to the proposed hotel rather than directly in its way appears more objectionable; the fact that his property should be razed for decorative reasons. Milne argues the application is 'unlawful'. 'No principle of development has been established at those sites,' he tells the committee. Sue Edwards, who has expressed an interest in using the council's plot of land at Menie for a whale and dolphin centre, tearfully implores any councillor with 'soul and compassion' to reject plans that are placing residents under 'heartbreaking' stress.

The deliberations are brief. SNP councillor Allan Hendry says he has received dozens of letters, from the UK and abroad, from people opposed to the development, but only four from local residents. 'Now, I stay in the local area,' he says. 'Local people who stay in the vicinity along the coast are in support of this development, in general.' Fellow SNP member Rob Merson moves to support the recommendations, which are being taken as a whole. Debra Storr puts forward an amendment calling for the submission to be rejected, contesting that 'the applicant has not proved that it would significantly improve the Menie application'.

Loveday recalls being opposed to the original application. 'My reason for that was purely down to the large number of houses that were being forced upon us at the time. We have moved on from that since then. But I look back and wonder why on earth these five plots were not included – it would have made life a lot easier if they had been.' Confirming his support for the motion, he adds: 'This is obviously a very good thing for the whole area. How we move on now from this point is really up to the applicant and not up to us.'

The plans are approved by 9-2.

Outside, Don Jr, shades removed, reflects on a 'great decision'. 'We recognise the sensitivities,' he says. 'However, we also recognise the importance of the land to the development.' When pressed on why the applications weren't included in the original plan, Don Jr replies that 'fifty other things had to be decided' at that time.

No one seriously expected the planning decision to go against Trump, certainly not the residents. Michael Forbes said he didn't bother to attend the committee meeting because he 'knew' what was going to happen. 'I want it to go to compulsory purchase because it will drag on for years,' he commented. 'It's a vengeance thing now, it's become personal to Trump, I think. He wants everybody who went against him all out.' Susan Munro was 'disappointed but not surprised' by the decision, while David Milne said the only way he'd ever leave Hermit Point for good would be 'horizontally in a box'.

The protestor was right. This was all about CPOs. Having approval to build on someone else's land counted for nothing because without that land no plan could be realised. David Milne wrote to councillors asking them to support Ford's motion:

The compulsory purchase of several homes would be devastating to those involved, including myself and my wife, and the responsibility for the emotional turmoil and reputational damage to the area would lie with those that vote in support of the use of compulsory purchase orders . . . The questions you need to be aware of are not just the immediate ones of morals and ethics of the individual councillors who actually cast the votes, but what happens next . . . As developers realise that Aberdeenshire Council is happy to use these powers to make it easier for them to execute commercial developments, the council and councillors will receive increasing numbers of similar requests and be expected to approve them without any qualms.

Sarah Malone responded to the letter with a press release:

We must not allow these short-term difficulties and differences to obscure our vision of the long-term gain. This development not only complements regional and national agendas for tourism and economic development, it also paves the way for future inward investment. With regard to the small group of individuals that propagate their personal views in the name of the people of the North-east, their claims are false and misleading. They do not represent the voice of the people, nor do they care for the future prosperity of the area . . . At a time of deep economic recession, very few developers are in a position to drive forward a £1 billion project with a global vision. The Trump Organization can, and continues to work together with the people of north-east Scotland to deliver this world-class resort.

The political arguments were becoming ever more coarse and polarised. On her website, Debra Storr applauded Rob Merson for being the first SNP councillor to 'come out against the use of CPOs', Merson was, however, irate over what he called a 'complete misrepresentation' of his comments at the Formartine Area Committee. In order to progress consideration of Trump's new planning application in principle, he had suggested members should think of it being brought forward on a 'willing buyer-willing seller' basis, but Storr had failed to include his proviso 'should that not be the case, then that is a matter for discussion and debate at another time'.

He was invited to clarify his position on Storr's website but refused. Instead he chose to outline his position in an email to the *Evening Express*. Merson had reservations about the possible use of CPOs but saw Martin Ford's motion as 'premature':

> It would be entirely wrong for councillors to surrender any legitimate right of recourse which should remain open for their consideration, when they have no knowledge of the evidence or circumstances which might arise in this, or any other application coming before them in the future. I take the view that compulsory purchase orders should only be invoked with great reluctance, and the justification for each request would require to be considered on its individual merits. While such notices are normally associated with public service works and infrastructure projects, they are not exclusively so. In such a major planning application of national importance it is only right that Aberdeenshire Council should be in a position to give full consideration to every option which is legitimately available to it.

Picture again that pastoral scene. The village square, the park, the wholesome shops, the sociable geese. Now imagine having your pick of the 500 houses – a two-bedroom bungalow or a £1 million mansion, whichever you prefer – for seventy per cent of the asking price. If you don't like the house or your neighbours, no worries. You can sell it on and take the profit. Not enough? Well how about free golf as well? Worried about selling your own house? The offer includes the market value of your home plus fifteen per cent.

This was the deal Donald Trump put to residents at Menie four days after winning planning approval for their plots.

Don Jr described it as a 'very generous offer' that reflected the 'level of respect' for his 'neighbours'. His tone was conciliatory. 'We are not trying to banish people,' he said. 'On the contrary, we are saying we want you to stay and be a part of the community in which you have lived in the past. We want them to be part of this project.'

Susan Munro reckoned Trump needed to be more generous still. 'If we put it on the market we could probably get more than Trump's offer because of the location,' she said. 'But I do not think anybody would turn down a good offer.' David Milne complained that Trump's messenger 'slunk off' after delivering the offer without 'so much as an attempt to speak to anyone in my home at that time'. He added: 'The offer for our four-bedroom house, which is for £230,000, is of no interest to us as our home is still not for sale.'

Trump wasn't just bidding afresh for homes. He also asked Aberdeenshire Council to suspend any decision on CPOs to allow more time for negotiations.

There were advantages to letting talks run. To have pushed for CPOs just weeks after making an offer on the homes would have appeared mercenary. Consider, too, that a refusal to sell might be construed as residents holding out for a better deal, as greedy games-manship. For Trump there was certainly more to be lost than gained in councillors voting to support Ford's motion. Ruling out CPOs in principle would have ruled them out in practice, and that would have weakened Trump's negotiating hand considerably.

The CPO issue, however, was not about to be defused. If anything, it was intensifying. The Green Party's Scottish leader Patrick Harvie claimed: 'Trump's move constitutes a cynical and calculated misuse of them. They should not be used for this purpose now or ever. This whole fraught process has seriously undermined the integrity of Scotland's planning process.'

An indication of just how tense the atmosphere in New York was came in an interview Don Jr and George Sorial gave to the *Sunday Herald*. The Glasgow newspaper reported that Ann Faulds, a partner with the Edinburgh law firm Dundas & Wilson, employed by Trump, had previously advised the former Scottish Executive on its compulsory purchase policies. She was a co-author of a 2001 government report that predicted the deployment of CPOs would increase and averred 'it may no longer be appropriate to restrict their use to cases of last resort'.

In the article, David Milne offered an observation rather than a criticism: 'This is indicative of the way the Trump Organization works. They engage people who have worked for government to allow them to understand every wrinkle, loophole and furrow in the legislation.'

Patrick Harvie struck a shriller note: 'This is revolving-door government of the most insidious sort, with influence and power apparently being bought and sold for Trumpton gold.'

Don Jr retorted: 'Should I hire a farmer to act as my legal adviser? Would you hire a truck driver to carry out brain surgery? It's the most asinine argument I've ever heard.' A spokesman for Dundas & Wilson said it was 'commercially naive' to suggest there was anything 'inappropriate' in Trump using the services of Ann Faulds. The Scottish Government called the implication 'ludicrous'. Sorial was more forthright. He was quoted accusing the paper of writing 'shit'.

Two days before the council committee gathered to consider CPOs, the Trump Organization issued a statement in the name of its President and Chief Executive Officer:

> Once again Martin Ford and his few supporters are sending a very clear signal to the world that Aberdeenshire is Closed to Inward Investment and that developers and other business people are not welcome. Given the current economic climate and record-breaking unemployment in the construction industry, one wonders whether Martin Ford has any plans for economic growth . . . He has used the very people he claims to represent to exploit and promote his own misguided agenda at great public expense. The Aberdeenshire Council should not allow a handful of self-serving people to interfere with

our goals of creating a very popular project that will bring pride and thousands of jobs to Aberdeenshire . . . We look forward and are ready to start construction of what will be the world's greatest golf development in November.

Martin Ford was shaving when I phoned his home. His wife asked me to try again in five minutes and when he eventually took the call he sounded as breezily defiant as ever. He said he was not prepared to leave residents in a 'state of limbo' that 'verged on cruelty'. He said supporting his motion would be an act of 'humanity'. 'I mean, your whole life is on hold,' he said, empathizing with the residents. 'I can't imagine how ghastly it must be living with that threat.' He described the 'coercion' as 'grossly offensive' and added: 'It's none of my business, or the council's business, whether these householders sell to Trump. But they also have the right not to sell.' I mention George Sorial's claim that lodging the motion was a violation of planning rules and would be prejudicial to a fair hearing when detailed designs came before the council. 'This is not a planning decision,' said Ford. 'I know he's claimed it but you know it's nonsense.'

He had been ousted as chairman of the ISC and branded a pariah by some. But once again Martin Ford was holding the Menie joker.

Chapter 10

THE SUPPORT OF SIR SEAN

The shopping list had been put together two months in advance:

Golf clubs from Amazon, £30.

Wigs from eBay, including USA shipping, £230.

Rubber face masks, including USA shipping, £300.

Van rental, £50.

Banners (homemade – spray stencils), £10.

An exchange of emails listed 'paper custom' masks as a cheaper alternative to the rubber masks. Ropes, string and ladders came under the heading 'equipment needed', as did a 'team of people'. The props were to be used to dress around a dozen statues in 'Donald Trump Outfits'. On 24 September 2009, the Menie Liberation Front duly struck, photographing their radical re-invention of Robert Burns, Queen Victoria and Lord Byron as a New York real-estate developer at twenty sites in Aberdeen, Edinburgh, Glasgow and Stirling. In an anonymous press release, the MLF said: 'We are dressing up famous Scottish statues as the American tycoon to symbolise the way Trump thinks he can walk over Scotland.'

Impotent though the stunt seemed, it did hint at a renewed militancy among protestors and the potential for resistance on the ground.

Several weeks earlier, Tripping Up Trump (TUT) had held a mass picnic at the Menie dunes, an occupation of sorts. Around fifty people attended what was billed as the Last of the Summer Dunes Picnic. Group co-ordinator Martin Glegg described it as a 'friendly, family day just enjoying the dunes because we might not be able to do so next year'. It wasn't clear how many of the participants were in the habit of regularly 'enjoying' the dunes. The use of signs to direct people to the beach suggested that for some it may have been a first visit. Those attending included Susan Buchan from Luthermuir, near Laurencekirk, fifty miles away. 'It's not just people in the local vicinity who care,' she said.

George Sorial had asked TUT to respect land-access laws, but was otherwise indifferent.

The statue stunt (the props, the costs) was described in a series of emails exchanged between TUT members and leaked to the *Evening Express*. The emails revealed a fraternity among protest groups, and a multiplicity of memberships. The proposer wrote: 'Importantly this will not be a Tripping Up Trump action so as not to discredit the more mainstream movement. Hopefully it will tie in with the announcement of an "airplot" style campaign happening on the affected land.'

Martin Glegg wrote: 'If it was possible to go ahead with this idea we need to think if we should do it in the name of Tripping Up Trump.'

A minute from a TUT meeting on 14 July, sent by semi-retired petroleum engineer Geoff Lamb, showed 'the Trump wig and mask statues plan was deferred' until after the protest picnic at Menie on 26 July. He wrote: 'It's likely to be seen as anti-social, risk of damage to statues, etc. For less damage the hats had better be installed by sticks, and not by leaning ladders.' When I spoke to Lamb he insisted that a 'discussion' of the proposal rather than its planned enactment had been deferred, and that the idea itself was later 'knocked on the head'. TUT, as Martin Glegg stressed, had disassociated itself from the stunt in a press release: 'TUT was not involved in this recent action and can confirm that it will carry on spreading the word through advertising and our petition.'

That wasn't the end of it, though.

The Trump Organization passed the emails to Grampian Police, Sorial calling the correspondence a 'smoking gun'. TUT, meanwhile, asked the police to investigate the leakage. The *Evening Express* hadn't revealed its source when contacting TUT but organisers were evidently of the opinion they had been spied on by Trump. TUT spokeswoman Sue Edwards said: 'This is very sinister. We have contacted the police about the Trump Organization having obtained private emails between TUT members since we do not know how these emails were intercepted . . . The preparedness of the Trump Organization to go to considerable lengths to spy on TUT says far more about them than it does about TUT.' Don Jr told the *Sunday Times* that his father had many 'associates' in Aberdeenshire who shared intelligence about the Menie development.

If the Trump Organization *had* planted a spy in TUT, the Americans weren't alone in trying to infiltrate the ranks of other parties. The TUT correspondent who had advocated supporting the statue stunt suggested in the same email that the group 'should get an imbedded journo' from *The Press and Journal* who they 'wouldn't have to tell anything'. 'It would be a good opportunity to get a tough paper on our side,' the person added.

TUT had in some ways taken over from Sustainable Aberdeenshire, which had lost momentum after the Scottish Government's decision to back Trump. Glegg, twenty-seven, was from Banchory, a town eighteen miles west of Aberdeen, but was based in the Central Belt where he was a teacher. Glasgow man Jonny Agnew, who was arrested over the protest at Aberdeen Airport, was an active member of TUT but said Plane Stupid was 'very separate'. According to a TUT source, two co-accused from Glasgow had also attended TUT events.

Unlike the MLF, Plane Stupid didn't always have to count the cost of paper and string. Cosmetics giant Lush, based in Poole in Dorset, had donated more than £500,000 to radical green and humanitarian activists, which included paying the legal costs incurred by Plane Stupid after its members camped on a runway at Stansted Airport in December of 2008. Lush campaign manager Andrew Butler said: 'We have supported them in the past and may do so in the future. We feel the threat posed by climate change is something that potentially affects all of us.' Butler said that 'unchecked' airport expansion was not compatible with promises to cut aviation emissions, and that social change required 'direct action' as well as new legislation. He added that when Lush flew people overseas for meetings it paid its own 'internal carbon tax'.

Butler didn't view Trump's resort as a 'necessity' and said 'using soap and shampoo is a great deal more a part of our lives than playing eighteen holes of golf'. Daily hygiene requirements accepted, one might question how many people felt a pressing need to reach for Lush's Vanilla in the Mist soap ('as good at waking you up as a freshly brewed cup of java') or Heavenly Bodies cream ('to make you smell like a chocolate orange cheesecake') when showering.

Around 100 people are milling around the entrance of the Aberdeen Exhibition and Conference Centre, many of them wearing TUT badges. The statue stunt seems to have done its job of whipping up interest in the CPO debate: the public inquiry never drew this number of spectators. TUT has a protest petition with 15,000 signatures. People have been photographed signing up outside Trump Tower in New York, but in turning it into a global petition they have rather undermined the impressiveness of the numbers.

Aberdeenshire Council has booked the AECC for the meeting at which Martin Ford's motion is due to be heard, its own public gallery having room for only thirty or so people. As we file into the hall, no one is quite sure what will happen. Ordinarily this kind of decision-making would be informed by an officer's report, one providing a policy context and a recommendation, but this is no ordinary day.

David Milne, who is being allowed to address the councillors, is called to the front first. He is clapped heartily as he walks the length of the hall, past Sarah Malone and Neil Hobday, who are sitting at the front of the public gallery.

Milne takes his place on a podium. The dense dark beard makes him look like a youngish minister searching for gravitas.

He is quick to mention his neighbours, to seed the impression of a community under threat. 'You as a local authority have been asked to use these powers in a way they were never intended to be used, as a threat and bargaining tool by a commercial entity,' he says. 'That commercial entity has been attempting to bargain, even with those who may wish to bargain, whilst waving the loaded weapon of compulsory purchase in full view of the public gaze . . . To delay taking this vote today would make it appear that the local authority was simply taking instruction directly from the developer.'

Only now does Milne get personal: 'I don't know how many of you have even tried to imagine what it is like not knowing if your home will be your home for much longer, not knowing if the next birthday or Christmas will be the last in your own home.' The health and safety consultant is struggling to read his own words; it's as though their import is only just beginning to register. 'It is a horrible situation to be in, not knowing if people who are effectively your neighbours will throw you out of your own home.'

This isn't a speech. It's a sermon. Surely the vote will go the way of the motion.

But Ford isn't invited to speak. After praising Milne for being so succinct, provost and chairman Bill Howatson moves to other council business on the agenda, another presentation, about a proposal to build a civic square in Aberdeen.

A sense of anti-climax settles on the hall. People go for coffee in the reception. It's almost an hour before the committee returns to Ford's motion.

Ford congratulates Milne on his eloquence and says he has nothing to add. Others do, however.

Peter Argyle, who replaced Ford as chairman of the ISC, talks about what it is to lose a home, but Argyle isn't sympathising with Milne. He points out that people are displaced every day for any number of reasons; that, in essence, none of us know which birthday or Christmas might be the 'last in our own home'; that redundancy or divorce or illness or the building of a bypass could divest us of that comfortable certainty. That no one can or should expect life to be predictable.

Some councillors do offer Milne succour. Bryan Stuart says he 'wholeheartedly' supports Trump's project but adds: 'I would find it difficult to vote people out of their homes for the sake of a golf course.' Alastair Ross ventures there is a 'great groundswell' of opinion opposed to the use of CPOs for a private development, and adds: 'I will never vote to remove you or your neighbours from your homes for a golf course, so please be assured of that.'

But today councillors are not being asked to remove Milne or his neighbours from their homes. They are being asked to forever rule out the use of CPOs on the Menie Estate; to keep Milne and his neighbours in their homes by affording them a protection no one else in Aberdeenshire or Scotland enjoys. Joanna Strathdee expresses her 'heartfelt sympathy' for the residents but warns that supporting the motion 'could also impinge on the council's ability to acquire a site for a primary school'.

Martin Kitts-Hayes says ruling out CPOs on the basis of a motion – a 'scurrilous' motion, as he puts it – rather than a 'detailed report' would not stand up to scrutiny and leave the council open to a legal challenge. He puts forward an amendment:

> As a general principle, Aberdeenshire Council will only consider through due process compulsory purchase orders which are for the benefit of the general public interest. Aberdeenshire Council appreciates the uncertainty and concerns which are being felt over the use of compulsory purchase powers, but will take no action on this particular notice of motion as it would be inappropriate to make a decision without a detailed report being available for full and proper consideration.

This is not, you suspect, something he has just come up with: it is too brilliantly equivocal. Kitts-Hayes stresses voting for his amendment is not a vote for CPOs, but no one asks what might pass for 'general public interest'. A project promising more than 1,000 jobs when the region's main industry was in terminal decline? The Scottish Government thought so when granting outline planning permission.

The council votes 55-6 for the amendment.

There are jeers of 'spineless' from the public gallery.

'A wasted morning,' says Michael Forbes as he walks down the corridor. 'There's still a cloud hanging over our heads, a big Trump cloud.' David Milne accuses the council of 'cowardice and collusion'.

People leave with the sound of alarm bells ringing in their ears. Real bells, that is. Someone has set the fire alarm off.

Within a few hours of the decision, Trump was on the phone. He was 'humbled' the council had seen things his way, and let the situation be. All the talk was about starting work on the course in November, about thatching the dunes with marram. He required detailed planning permission, yes, but nothing more: the land was already his. An official statement, issued by him later that day, attempted to ostracize opponents:

> Councillor Ford's motion to debate compulsory purchase was an irresponsible and deliberate attempt to undermine this process and circumvent Scottish law. Aberdeenshire Council's decision shows that a small band of renegades who are only thinking of themselves cannot block a significant investment that the overwhelming majority of people have supported.

In presenting his amendment, Kitts-Hayes had voiced something similar, claiming Ford's motion was being 'used by a small group of people to further their own political ends'. It emerged, via an unnamed source from within the administration, that an alternative amendment had been considered by the ruling group, one worded 'slightly different from Martin's . . . a little bit more precise', but that it was dropped on the strength of legal advice.

Had council lawyers been told a team of Queen's Counsellors in Edinburgh was poised to seek an injunction against the CPO vote?

While the Kitts-Hayes amendment reserved the right to use CPOs in principle, plenty of people at the meeting recoiled at the prospect, enough to make Martin Ford think councillors would have voted against CPOs had it come down to a straight choice. George Sorial wasn't disagreeing but thought Ford's motion was impetuous. He sounded thoroughly exasperated by what he saw as repeated ploys to frustrate the democratic process. Political argument he could take. Attempts to delay decision-making or pre-empt it were much less acceptable.

So too were personal insults. Sorial accused councillor Sam Coull of 'racism' after receiving this email:

> My computer has been deluged with messages asking that I vote against CPOs tomorrow, my mail bag has been full and I have a 12,000 petition online all saying that DT should not be allowed to have people evicted from their homes . . . quite apart from those less than complimentary messages relating to hair styles, Noo Joysee ethics, etc. Frankly, I think you have got it all wrong. I shall be backing Martin Ford's Motion all the way tomorrow, in order that DT can move on to Ireland . . . his next deal or whatever.

Coull rejected the contention he was racist, pointing to his thirty years as a councillor as evidence of his public-spirited disposition. He said his 'phonetic spelling' of New Jersey ('Noo Joysee') was a 'bit of fun'. Sorial wasn't laughing. In a reply to Coull, copied to the council's new Chief Executive Colin Mackenzie and the Standards Commission, he wrote:

> While I understand and respect that our view on the Menie Estate development may differ, I find it unfortunate that you would use

your position on the Aberdeenshire Council to mock my nationality and accent. Racism is never acceptable, and your comments are both unprofessional and inappropriate.

Trump himself was taking a lot of personal stick, having been lampooned and traduced in a way no Scottish developer would have been. But then he wasn't just a developer. He was Donald Trump, host of *The Apprentice* with a star on the Hollywood Walk of Fame, a man who lived like a king at the top of a golden tower bearing his name, who bottled and sold everything from cologne to vodka in honour of his success. His celebrity seemed to encourage, even legitimise, the invective. Did people believe they part-owned Trump, that like every other celebrity he was somehow their creation, theirs to worship or damn as they pleased? Fame had objectified Trump, turned the man himself into a commodity. People were judging him as they might a washing machine: with stark, uncompromising language.

Yes, Trump could be irascible and unsparing. Sometimes he was happy to project a cartoonish image, to use his fame to excite or intimidate. 'I think my persona is tougher than it should necessarily be,' said Trump. 'I have a lot of good friends, I have a lot of good relationships, but people don't necessarily see that in my public persona. Basically I think I'm a much nicer person than my public persona. I'm very loyal to people and places.'

It wasn't just ordinary folk offering an opinion about Trump. Somewhat improbably, Oscar-winning actress Tilda Swinton entered the CPO debate. Swinton, who won her Academy Award for *Michael Clayton* in 2008, lives in the town of Nairn, ninety miles from Menie. The actress was quoted in a TUT press release accusing Trump of 'industrialised bullying' and an 'attempt at a twenty-first century Clearance'. In response, Sorial reiterated that he wanted only to negotiate with landowners, and that compulsory purchase powers resided with the council.

When I put Sorial's point to Swinton in an email, she said she was 'delighted' to hear CPOs weren't on the agenda. She continued: 'It is important that they are aware that it is principally on this matter that the controversy that has arisen rests. Maybe if they could produce hard – inviolable – evidence that this is the case – that they are not, as has been reported, actively seeking to forcibly turn people out of their homes and off their land – many (I suggest many more than 1,000) people local and not so local would rest easier in their beds.'

But that wasn't the end of the exchange. Trump said that in comparing the Menie plan to the Clearances, Swinton's comment had trivialised 'a tragic event in Scottish history ... It's a shame that she would disgrace the thousands of Scots who suffered for her own personal gain'. Trump dismissed Swinton as a bit-player: 'Tilda Swinton, who I don't know and have never heard of, should have spoken up three years ago and obviously is enjoying this publicity stunt at my expense. In any event, I have the support of Sir Sean Connery and this very small group of dissidents have Tilda Swinton. I'll take that deal any day.'

Just when it seemed the wrangling about CPOs had stopped, planning boss Christine Gore was accused of being 'too close' to Trump, something she denied. Spinwatch, a Glasgow-based body that monitored public relations, used the Freedom of Information Act to obtain a letter sent by Gore to Ann Faulds after Trump notified the council in February of his intention to seek CPOs. Gore wrote:

In terms of public relations and management of the inevitable media interest, I would request that we be given at least a week's notice of your intended submission date. Thereafter, close liaison will be required in order that we can have a managed approach to what is inevitably going to be a difficult and emotive reaction.

David Miller, Professor of Sociology at Strathclyde University and head of Spinwatch, said: 'The council is supposed to protect the public interest, not the private interests of a major corporation. These documents suggest Aberdeenshire Council is too close to the Trump Organization.'

Towards the end of October, the CPO debate finally abated – but only because attention was swinging back to the dunes.

27 October 2009. We're in Ellon Kirk hall again, in an upstairs room, for another meeting of the Formartine Area Committee. People are pressed against the walls, brushing against bookcases stacked with Bibles. Someone has under-estimated the interest in agenda item 13C: a request to plant marram grass at Menie.

Marram's roots run deep; its thick, triangular blades are resistant to salt. It's the perfect vegetation for straitjacketing a sand dome. The application involves preparing the ground for the marram, which will be harvested on site. The grass will be hand-planted (sprigged). Fencing will be erected to help corral the shifting sand and re-contour the dunes.

This is the first detailed planning application for the estate submitted by the Trump Organization.

It is, in effect, a request to start work on the championship course.

Planners are recommending approval. In her report, Sonja Galloway has acknowledged the masterplan should have been finished prior to submission of detailed plans, but said the grass planting had been brought forward 'in order to meet this planting season' and to minimize 'any further delay to the project'. The Scottish Wildlife Trust and RSPB see it differently. They have objected on the grounds Trump is trying to 'circumvent the conditions of the outline consent'. Galloway's report says the conditions have been 'addressed for this application'. Should the development not proceed, Trump must provide a financial bond that would pay for the dunes to be restored to their natural state.

Committee chairman John Loveday has called a recess so more chairs can be found. When councillors re-convene, Don Jr and Sorial move from a cramped row near the back of the room to the front. The go-ahead could be just minutes away now, but first the New Yorkers must listen to a report about a planning application for a garden shed. Such is council committee fare.

Even when we get to 13C there is what now feels like an inevitable call to defer.

A reform of national planning law requires applications for two hectares or more of land to be ruled on by a full council after a pre-determination hearing. Debra Storr warns it might be procedurally 'unsafe' for the committee to determine the plan and calls for independent legal advice. A legal officer rejects the concern and confirms an independent opinion has been sought. Christine Gore is confident item 13C – approved in principle by the Scottish Government – doesn't represent a 'significant departure' from the area's planning blueprint; that it can be dealt with, then and there, under the old system. That's the same system that allowed the Infrastructure Services Committee to junk the outline plan.

When the committee rules to carry on, Storr and Paul Johnston refuse to take part in the debate.

Trump's Scottish lawyer Ann Faulds addresses the committee. She says Trump has 'persevered with his plan often at great expense and with a sense of bewilderment'. 'It is by far the most scrutinised project I have seen in over twenty years,' she says. 'Quite simply, Mr Trump wants to start his project.' She calls on the committee to get with the 'new era of planning' designed to encourage 'co-operation and respect', and suggests approval would be a 'vote for common sense in the Scottish planning system'.

David Milne suggests that it would instead represent a 'substantial insult'. He also offers evidence from the British Trust for Conservation Volunteers that winter is not the best time to plant marram grass, repeating the claim from the SWT and RSPB that the application is a 'cynical attempt to bypass' conditions imposed on the development.

We move to the debate.

Talk of 'chestnut pale fencing' makes it sound like we're at a fashion show.

Rob Merson has heard enough and moves to approve, saying, 'Now the time has come to move forward with this.'

Loveday agrees it's time to lead rather than listen. Jim Gifford, however, wants details of the re-instatement bond thrashed out ahead of any permission being granted. Isobel Davidson wonders whether a bond would have any real value, observing that a tree can't be put back after chopping it down. Someone asks if Trump should reimburse the council for time and effort spent dealing with the planning application should the development fail to materialise.

George Sorial is out of his seat, talking to Ann Faulds near the back of the room.

It feels like the plan is slipping away again amid the interminable talk.

Sorial returns to his seat but remains agitated. Any delay now could miss the October-to-March 'window' for planting marram, when vegetation is dormant and water levels are favourable.

Loveday is asking Gifford if he is proposing an amendment.

For two years George Sorial has sat and squirmed through meetings like this, listening to digressions and remonstrations, to arguments sincere and pernicious, to political spats and personal insults. But today he cannot stay silent, not when officers have lost their voice.

'We *have* a bond,' he yells from the floor.

Chapter 11

THE DEBATE WE NEED TO HAVE

In the autumn of 2009, the venue for the Scottish Open Championship was still without a buyer. Loch Lomond Golf Club had been put up for sale in the summer for a rumoured £100 million after its US owner Lyle Anderson failed to renegotiate debts with Halifax Bank of Scotland. The administrators decided to cut fifty staff from the 140-strong workforce. A statement from the club said: 'The decision was made after the club elected to move from a twelve-month operation to a more seasonal one to reflect the variable usage of the club.'

If anything, the plight of Loch Lomond vindicated Trump's stance at the public inquiry, his insistence that housing was needed to make a course viable. Loch Lomond Golf Club, near Luss, in Argyll and Bute, charged a £75,000 joining fee and annual fees of £3,250. Menie would be pay-and-play. Trump had briefly considered buying Loch Lomond, which would have come with the rights to the Scottish Open, but now he had permission to start work on his own creation.

George Sorial's interjection at the Formartine Area Committee did its job. Chairman John Loveday reproached him for interrupting councillors but he succeeded in prompting an officer to confirm talks had indeed taken place with the Trump Organization regarding a bond for the reparation of ground.

The way was open to vote on the marram planting – and support was unanimous.

The next day Don Jr called a press conference at Menie, where he dodged the mud in his Gucci loafers while posing for celebratory photographs.

Hard as it was to imagine people chaining themselves to a sand dune, Grampian Police were nervous about protestors showing up, and patrolled the area in an unmarked car. The Menie project had been keeping them busy, the force having told MSPs that unless the Scottish Government provided extra funding they would have to divert officers from other beats to keep order at the site. Fourteen complaints had been lodged, thirteen from staff. Eight related to vehicles or people being on the land, three to abusive correspondence or phone messages, two to thefts, and one to hare-coursing. Just two of the incidents resulted in crime reports being compiled. One was closed when the complaint was dropped and the other remained 'undetected' as no suspect had been identified.

Earlier in the year, Debra Storr had complained to police that security staff had blocked her car as she tried to leave the Menie Estate after taking a photograph of a locked gate – one meant to stop cars getting in. Storr feared Trump was contravening land access laws and the right to roam. The Trump Organization said it was combating marauding 4x4s and quad bikes: the Land Reform (Scotland) Act 2003 promotes *responsible* access, and excludes vehicles. In an open letter to the councillor, Trump said estate managers had 'never barred the public from our site'. He told Storr she should be 'ashamed' of herself and added: 'It is clear that your intentions are not constructive but are instead designed to harass and discredit our plans.' Storr said the notion of her harassing Trump was 'somewhat bizarre'.

Two local firms were appointed to carry out the preparatory work at Menie. Moray Landscape, from Cullen, would plant the marram, while EnviroCentre from Stonehaven would provide a team of ecological 'clerks', having previously kept watch on the Cairngorms National Park project and the surveying of Aberdeen's bypass route. Aberdeenshire architects Acanthus DF had already been picked to design the clubhouse. Lena Wilson, Chief Executive of Scottish Enterprise, welcomed the contracts as an 'important milestone' on the road to delivering hundreds of jobs.

Cork-based SOL Golf Course Construction, which had carried out modifications on behalf of the R&A at several Open venues, was appointed as the main contractor for the championship course. 'Magical' and 'flawless' were the words chosen by Managing Director Michael O'Leary to describe the Menie landscape and Hawtree's design. Paul O'Connor was offered the role of links superintendent after approaching Trump. His green-keeping team had produced a near-perfectly conditioned course for the 2007 championship at Carnoustie. O'Connor met Trump on the estate prior to taking the job. 'He was very positive, very open,' said O'Connor. 'His heart is in providing a real championship golf course.'

The day after the FAC meeting, a second lifetime membership was handed out. This one went to Marcliffe owner Stewart Spence, who was being tipped to run Trump's hotel, despite having a five-star one of his own.

As Christmas approached, Trump's spirit was generous. He might not have fancied adding Loch Lomond to his gallery of golf clubs but he did instruct aviation firm Avpro to find him a bigger jet. The specification included a bidet and a shower. Again, Trump was capitalising on having hard cash in times of recession. 'A lot of companies have had to give up their private jets,' said Sorial. Trump's 727 (built in 1968 and worth £5 million) was costing £6,000 an hour to maintain and fly, four times as much as more modern planes of comparable size. A newer model promised to be more economical.

Switching to, say, a Boeing 737 would be Trump going green.

While Trump was mulling over his choice of new plane, Martin Ford was calling on the UK Government to show 'strong leadership' at the United Nations Copenhagen Climate Conference. Ford said: 'This is the debate we need to have. We had better get used to it.' Aberdeenshire Council backed his motion but failed to spot the call for collective action. When Ford asked colleagues to welcome 'the decision of BAA not to proceed with work on the additional runway at Heathrow Airport', they rejected his motion, arguing work had only been 'postponed'. Councillor Jill Webster said air links gave the North-east efficient access to world markets, and added: 'Our duty is to represent the best needs of Aberdeenshire.'

The council backed another Ford motion, this one aimed explicitly at Trump's resort.

Ford asked the council to affirm its commitment to upholding the United Nations' Universal Declaration of Human Rights, including Article 17(2) – 'No one shall be arbitrarily deprived of his property'. Ford had asked the Institute for Human Rights and Business if the acquisition of land for a private-sector development was a human rights issue. Executive Director John Morrison referred to an excerpt from a draft paper on land appropriation, which Ford read out:

> Human rights are interdependent, universal, inalienable, and indivis-
> ible. The range of rights involved in the context of land acquisition
> is wide. The realization of many rights is closely associated with land
> ownership and usage, and access to land becomes a pre-requisite for
> certain rights to be realized. Furthermore, to secure those rights,
> certain civil and political rights require protection. While there is
> no specific, codified 'right to land' under human rights law, it is clear
> that 'land' includes a very broad range of rights which the state has
> the primary obligation to protect, and companies have the respon-
> sibility to respect.

Ford said: 'The discussions so far have been about the economic benefit and planning legislation, but this is a human rights question. We need to establish in the minds of those taking decisions on the council, but also in the wider public mind, that they need to see this as a human rights case . . . Any decision by the council to seek to force them out would have to take into account human rights legislation and I want to draw councillors' attention to that.'

He called on colleagues to 'remember' the vote they had made.

The displacement and dispossession of native people was engaging filmmakers too.

Themes explored in the council chamber had made it to the multiplex. Pixar's *Up* showed curmudgeonly Carl Fredricksen resisting attempts to buy his house, which stood in the way of a towering urban development. *Avatar*, from *Titanic* director James Cameron, pitted a militaristic mining corporation against the Na'vi, who lived on a distant planet in a giant tree, under which lay the valuable mineral Unobtanium. The oppressed took to the air, Carl tethering his house to thousands of helium-filled balloons, the Na'vi defending their land on the backs of psychedelic pterosaurs. (Trump probably would have optioned the skies: when he built Trump Tower he spent $5 million on the air space above the neighbouring Tiffany store to preserve the view.)

No one expected to see Michael Forbes's home becoming airborne over the North Sea, or David Milne swooping on Menie House astride a large winged lizard, but both of these hugely successful films had equated taking someone's home with identity theft. The Na'vi's memories resided in the forest, the roots of which acted as a neural network; Carl's were bound to the mailbox he had painted in early adulthood with his late and much-missed wife Elly. Both films posited a relationship between personality and place, and showed how quickly an argument about territory could turn physical.

Labour peer and Oscar-winner Lord David Puttnam exhorted Trump to learn from his production *Local Hero*, in which the oil baron played by Burt Lancaster eventually agreed to build his oil refinery offshore rather than in the midst of a Scottish community. Describing Trump's plans, Puttnam told *The Times*: 'This saga is the real-life version of a film I made more than twenty-five years ago. Thankfully, *Local Hero* had a happy ending when the American developer came to his senses and withdrew with dignity. It would be great if Donald Trump would take the time to watch it.'

Trump, to be fair, was proposing to build a golf course, not an industrial plant. When Martin Ford told the public inquiry the course would be visible from the road, George Sorial commented afterwards, 'You'd think we were talking about a nuclear power station.' An offshore golf course would have certainly been novel, but possibly beyond the means of even Donald Trump to fabricate. As for the R&A, it's a fair bet they would have choked at the very thought of an Open staged above the sea rather than next to it.

On 7 December 2009, the same front page dominated fifty-six leading newspapers across the world. In twenty different languages, including Chinese, Arabic and Russian, the 'profound emergency' confronting humanity was expressed in an editorial penned by the Manchester-based *Guardian*, and printed to coincide with the Copenhagen Climate Change summit. The tone was apocalyptic:

> Unless we combine to take decisive action, climate change will ravage our planet, and with it our prosperity and security. The dangers have been becoming apparent for a generation. Now the facts have started to speak: eleven of the past fourteen years have been the warmest on record, the Arctic ice-cap is melting and last year's inflamed oil and food prices provide a foretaste of future havoc. In scientific journals, the question is no longer whether humans are to blame, but how little time we have got left to limit the damage. The science is complex but the facts are clear. The world needs to take steps to limit temperature rises to 2°C, an aim that will require global emissions to peak and begin falling within the next five to ten years. A bigger rise of 3-4°C – the smallest increase we can prudently expect to follow inaction – would parch continents, turning farmland into desert. Half of all species could become extinct, untold millions of people would be displaced, whole nations drowned by the sea.

The editorial doubted whether Copenhagen could produce 'a fully polished treaty' given the indifference of the US Congress, but hoped targets for cutting emissions could be in place by the UN climate meeting in Bonn in June 2010. It quoted one negotiator as saying, 'We can go into extra time but we can't afford a replay.' The rallying call went out to ordinary folk as well as politicians. Salvation, the editorial said, required us to change our lifestyles: 'The era of flights that cost less than the taxi ride to the airport is drawing to a close. We will have to shop, eat and travel more intelligently. We will have to pay more for our energy, and use less of it.'

As the leaders of 192 countries gathered in the Danish capital for the summit, a return to the Dark Ages seemed but a few years away. 'The clock has ticked down to zero,' said Yvo de Boer, the head of the UN's climate body. 'The time has come to deliver. The time has come to reach out to each other.'

Unfortunately for the UN, it was first presented with a crisis of its own. Someone had apparently reached out to the server at the University of East Anglia's Climate Change Research Unit, which analyzed data for the Meteorological Office and supplied it to the Intergovernmental Panel on Climate Change, and hacked into thousands of emails. One missive, from 1999, appeared to show the director Phil Jones fiddling climate change data to make the case for global warming: 'I've just completed Mike's *Nature* trick of adding in the real temps ... to hide the decline.' Certain increasingly sceptical sections of the media were left frothing at the mouth.

The 'decline' didn't relate to temperature but to tree growth. The spacing between annular rings was routinely used to estimate temperatures from hundreds of years ago when the Met Office didn't exist. The technique produced a graph showing warming trends spanning centuries. Trouble was, in the second half of the twentieth century, tree growth hadn't accelerated while temperatures had reportedly risen. Rather than rejecting the correlation as unreliable, Jones did what Mike Mann recommended in the journal *Nature*: he simply superimposed actual temperature readings from the 1950s onwards over the figures predicted by tree rings.

He saw nothing inconsistent in the approach and said the word 'trick' was used here colloquially as in a 'clever thing to do'. He said it was 'ludicrous' to infer anything 'untoward'.

Some of the Copenhagen delegates thought otherwise. Mohammed al-Sabban, Chief Negotiator for Saudi Arabia, told the conference: 'The level of trust is definitely shaken.' Of course, as the representative of a major oil producer, he may well have been quite pleased to have his trust shaken.

Two nations moved to unite and lead forward a divided, dithering world.

Scotland and the Maldives didn't carry quite the political influence of, say, the United States and China, but they did have a joint statement to galvanize delegates and renew resolve. They pledged to work together to 'communicate the urgency of global action to tackle climate change and for agreement at Copenhagen'. Scotland vowed to cut its emissions against the 1990 level by forty-two per cent in 2020 and eighty per cent by 2050, among the most ambitious targets on the planet. The Maldives, meanwhile, aimed to be 'carbon neutral' within ten years. How this feat would be achieved, President Mohamed Nasheed didn't say. Allowing his country to vanish under the Indian Ocean amid the rising seas forecast by global warming would have done the trick, but might have seemed defeatist.

The Copenhagen Accord, when it came, was brokered by US President Barack Obama and Chinese Premier Wen Jiabao. The three-page document 'recognized' the scientific case – skinny tree rings not withstanding – for keeping temperature rise to no more than 2°C but contained no agreements about the hows and whens. Meantime, carbon trading would continue, allowing rich countries to buy their way out of emission cuts by providing poorer countries with the technology to deliver theirs. It was rather like allowing a criminal to escape prosecution because he offered to pay for another felon's rehabilitation. This insidious practice had spawned a multi-billion-dollar carbon brokerage industry.

Back in Scotland, Salmond's attempt to style himself as a world statesman drew predictable opprobrium. He was derided as self-important and starry-eyed, as a political leader singularly uninterested in domestic policy because, critics scoffed, he had none. The SNP, the argument went, had been rumbled as a single-issue campaign group, pathologically obsessed with constitutional reform and defined only by its antipathy towards the Union, desperate to wrest power from Westminster but clueless about what to do with it. Scotland's relationship with England was portrayed as that of a teenager trapped resentfully in the parental home: frantic to leave but lacking the wherewithal, and forced to accept beer money in the meantime.

More embarrassment accrued when it emerged that £61 billion of loans were needed to keep the country solvent at the height of the financial crisis, and that Scottish banknotes didn't have the same legal protection as English notes. Lord George Foulkes, who helped push through new regulations underwriting Scottish currency, was quoted in *The Scotsman* as saying: 'We came within twenty-four hours of a Scottish bank collapse. There was a very real risk of actual notes in your wallet becoming worthless.'

The First Minister was struggling to retain power in his own country too after the SNP lost Glasgow North-east to Labour in a by-election.

None of this must have played well to Trump, who had been served well by Salmond's Government.

Some people thought Salmond should be trying to save Scotland's jobs rather than the Earth from a nebulous threat of global warming. Salmond, no dummy when it came to economics, reasoned he could do both.

The First Minister aired his solution when he was in Aberdeen to address a youth summit about the future of the North-east. I spoke to Salmond beforehand about a proposal to build a new £140 million square in the centre of Aberdeen. Energy tycoon Sir Ian Wood had offered £50 million to help raise to street level a Victorian park, already earmarked as a new base for a local arts group. The group had been offered a home in the square but were worried a £4.3 million grant from the Scottish Arts Council would not be transferable. While local councillors were terrified of derailing the planning process by speaking out, Salmond was typically forthright. 'One way or another, the arts project will be funded,' he said.

Out front with the youngsters, Salmond was at his engaging best – droll, self-deprecating, imperturbable. He asked the audience of senior school pupils and university students how many of them imagined remaining in the area. Not many hands went up. One young man said he wanted to be First Minister, then Prime Minister.

'So you're planning to work your way down?' said Salmond.

A journalism student suggested opportunities for her career didn't exist in the city where she had studied.

'Well, of course, there are some folk here from Aberdeen Journals . . . who might well agree with you,' said Salmond. He laughed. Everybody laughed. Salmond's disposition acted like a thermostat.

'Aberdeen is a pretty lively journalistic centre but maybe you're specializing. What kind of journalism are you thinking of going into?'

'Arabic.'

More laughter.

'Yeah, right. Okay, okay . . .' Salmond rolled his eyes. 'Then with respect to Aberdeen Journals, the opportunities are reasonably limited.'

Salmond explained he had been European correspondent for the *Emirates News*, the newspaper for the Gulf states. He spoke about the expectation North Sea oil and gas would dry up in the 1980s, and segued into his real theme of the day.

'There's maybe forty years of significant oil and gas to be extracted round the waters of Scotland,' he said. 'If you wanted, you could start your career and finish your career in these waters. One hundred and sixty thousand people work in the oil and gas industry in Scotland. But, you know, there is another industry which is about to emerge, which in my estimation is going to be as large . . . a big second win on the energy lottery . . . That's going to happen first in wind energy, then it's going to happen in tidal, then it's going to happen in wave energy. The waters round Scotland have about a quarter of Europe's resource. I tell you within ten years we will have 20,000 jobs within that industry in Scotland. And that will just be the start.'

Salmond guided his digression back down to its starting point, seeking out the gaze of the journalism student, relaxing again.

'I don't think this will mean that there will be a demand for Arabic specialists . . . but nevertheless it opens up a whole range of opportunities.'

During the session, tourism wasn't mentioned. Salmond did talk about golf, when he touched upon Scotland's Active Nation campaign during our interview. 'I'll dedicate myself to making sure, come what may, I have my round of golf every week instead of occasionally,' he said.

Shop, eat and travel more intelligently.

Where did that leave the North-east and its vision of tourists flying in from around the world, driving from golf course to castle to whisky distillery and back, partaking of lavish dinners every night, and flying home with an armful of souvenirs? Donald Trump could put solar panels on the roof of his hotel but he couldn't bring guests in by glider, not all the way from the United States or Japan.

The push for carbon emission reductions was unremitting. It was presented as the 'central concern' of Aberdeenshire Council's new development plan in a committee report. The UK Government wanted the aviation industry to peg emissions by 2050 at 2005 levels. The Committee on Climate Change – a public watchdog – advised that while it would still be possible to build a third runway at Heathrow and stay within limits, expansion at regional airports would have to be curbed.

In the meantime, there was every possibility the perceived political inaction would intensify opposition and trigger further protests at Aberdeen Airport and on the beaches of Menie.

It should have been straightforward. Putting posts in the ground, throwing some netting over the dunes, adding the marram. But at

Menie nothing was proving straightforward. Objectors were never going to stand by and watch sprigs of grass stuck into the sand like American flags. As the battle for the dunes moved into a decisive stage, an unlikely general surfaced to lead the resistance movement. Molly Forbes, Michael's eighty-five-year-old mother.

She moved to Menie from Aberdeen after her husband, a fisherman, died. As her portable home was being put together one summer day, she came up with the name *Paradise*, which is carved on a wooden salmon outside her door. Forbes, who grew up in Belhelvie, loves the stillness of Menie, the sight of deer flitting between the rushes or a heron moving serenely above a burn. The links has a strange, ethereal quality to it. On a summer evening, when the haar rolls in from the sea like ghostly breakers, enfolding the vast dunes, and the air fills with plaintive bird cries, you could be on another planet.

Molly Forbes cannot understand why, if Trump thinks Menie is so beautiful, he should ever want to change it.

In a bid to stop him, she asked the Court of Session to halt grass planting and preparatory work on the estate ahead of a full judicial review of the granting of planning consent. She also petitioned law lords over the inclusion of her home and the other sites in the new masterplan.

In a statement, Forbes said:

This is a major development by anyone's standards, including the formal standards set by the local authority, and as such they were obliged to refer decisions to the full council. They have failed in this obligation, and in their rush to allow the project to go ahead they have grievously let down local residents. I never expected in my life to face eviction from my home, let alone for a golf course. This is not a battle I would ever have sought, but Mr Trump and Aberdeenshire Council should know that I will never give up, and I urge them to think again.

Forbes was represented by Frances McCartney, who thought the application should have been submitted with an environmental impact statement. Ms McCartney ran the Environmental Law Centre Scotland, a non-profit organisation based in Paisley that aimed to 'help community groups, individuals and the voluntary sector to protect the environment'. McCartney was also TUT's lawyer.

George Sorial didn't want to comment on the legal challenge – led by QC Aidan O'Neill – because he didn't want to give it any credence.

In New York, however, the boss was all out of lip to bite.

Trump didn't care for dissembling. Michael Forbes had already hinted he might sell his home if Trump retracted the derogatory remarks made about its condition. I asked Sorial if Trump had considered finding a form of words that would appease Forbes without capitulating; that would deliver Mill of Menie. Sorial said there was 'no way' Trump would countenance apologizing. There sounded to be more chance of Trump allowing Forbes to live at Trump Tower. If Forbes was principled, so too was Trump. Some North-east folk thought Trump a 'phoney' because, like a lot of Americans, he was courteous and enthusiastic (as opposed to sullen and cynical). Well, now he was almightily pissed. He issued a bruising riposte, tantamount to a declaration of war:

It is tragic that an elderly woman is being exploited to further the personal vendetta of Michael Forbes and his few supporters. Over the years, my representatives and I have often seen Mr Forbes and he has always been dirty, sloppy and unkempt in his personal appearance and demeanour. While he is a terrible representative for Scotland, whenever the cameras are rolling, he parades in front of the press looking groomed and wearing a kilt – he truly enjoys the attention that he would have never received without Donald Trump.

In a recent television interview that was broadcast in the United States, Mr Forbes made Scotland and its people look terrible. He is a loser who is seriously damaging the image of both Aberdeenshire and his great country.

His property is a disgusting blight on the community and an environmental hazard, with leaking oil containers, rusted shacks and abandoned vehicles dumped everywhere. It is a very poor image and representation for the world to see of Scotland. Instead of wasting the Court's resources, he should spend time cleaning up his land so it does not look like a slum – and a low level slum at that! Perhaps he thinks that by creating an 'eyesore' I will pay more for his land.

The claims asserted today against our project are misguided and not based upon fact. We have always respected all planning and legal procedures and have satisfied the rigorous requirements of government ministers, planning officials and statutory consultees. Our applications have been the most scrutinized submissions in Scottish planning history and I am sure that the Aberdeenshire Council, which voted almost unanimously in support of them, is proud of their actions. It will also bring a great and positive acclaim to Scotland, unlike the image portrayed by Mr Forbes.

Many polls have shown that ninety-three per cent of the people of Aberdeenshire and Scotland are in favour of this development. My representatives and I have always treated Mr Forbes with respect (even though it is obvious to me that many people in his life have not) but I have now instructed my people never to deal with him again. If Aberdeenshire wants to remove this blight and environmental hazard from what will be one of the greatest developments on Earth, they should do so without our involvement. If the environmentalists were true to their cause, they would also act to have him removed or forced to clean up the terrible condition of his property.

We have commenced construction on what will be the world's greatest golf course and leisure community, creating thousands of jobs and generating millions of pounds of revenue for Aberdeenshire and Scotland during these difficult economic times. The marram grass operation, which has already started and is employing many local people, can only be done (transplanted) from November 1st through February, an already tight schedule. If this application were rejected, which it fortunately was not, the project, which everyone is clamouring for, would have been delayed for at least one year. Many jobs would be lost.

We will not be distracted by the rants of the local village idiot and intend to vigorously defend any challenge to our project. As far as Mr Forbes' mother is concerned, it's too bad she is being used like this and we wish her the best – but I guarantee that my mother, Mary MacLeod, would have sternly told her son to 'clean up this mess!'

It was hard to imagine the chief executive of Shell or BP dictating a letter like this.

Forbes, who rejected the claims, was unbowed. He told *The Scotsman*: 'If I am the village idiot, he must be the New York clown. He is just a child that's never grown up. I don't understand why he is getting his nappy all in a knot.' Martin Ford called the statement 'the standard reaction from Mr Trump to anyone who stands up to him'. I spoke to Molly on the phone shortly afterwards. She prickled at Trump's claim that she was somehow her son's puppet. 'I have a mind of my own,' she said. 'I came out here from Aberdeen to live in peace. That's all Michael and I want.'

As Lady Smith, who would rule on Mrs Forbes' challenge, retired to consider her verdict, Trump was taking his traditional festive break at his Mar-a-Lago Club in Palm Beach, Florida.

The former estate of food magnate Marjorie Merriweather Post (once the richest woman in the United States) had been turned into a private club and spa. According to the Trump Organization, it paired 'the sophistication of the Trump name and the lavish Palm Beach lifestyle'. One employee works full-time on the original tiles. 36,000 of them, some hundreds of years old, imported from Spain. Trump believes you have to be 'insane' about detail to keep an enterprise from failing. He spent eight months choosing chairs for the Mar-a-Lago ballroom. Trump had always wanted to turn

Mar-a-Lago into a private club but figured he'd never get permission. When the local council wrongly stopped him from breaking it into fourteen plots, he filed a $100 million lawsuit. They rushed to offer him the plots, but that was no longer good enough. He demanded and successfully attained zoning for the club.

For Trump, who thinks if you look forward to holidays you're in the wrong job, the stay at Mar-a-Lago was a chance to indulge his twin loves: family and work. 'I play golf daily and since it's my golf course, I'm checking it out at the same time for improvements and refinements,' he said. 'It's a great way to know things are in the best shape possible and the same for the Mar-a-Lago Club. Since I love my work, I find it relaxing in itself and being with my family makes everything great.' Don Jr was there too, looking forward to spending 'some great time at the beach' before celebrating his thirty-second birthday on Hogmanay: 'I get to wake up in the New Year a year older, which is never a great start once you break the age of about twenty-five.'

Florida neighbour Tiger Woods was facing a torrid Christmas. The world's number one golfer had been hospitalised after crashing into a fire hydrant outside his Miami home in the middle of the night. Woods was reportedly escaping his angry wife, Elin. In the days that followed he admitted on his website to 'transgressions' before promptly disappearing from public view. Celebrity gossip columnist Perez Hilton quoted Trump as saying Tiger needed to 'get back on the course and start winning tournaments'. Trump added: 'He'll do that. He's just the best golfer. He's a really talented person and he's a really good person . . . He's going to be just fine . . . mark my words.'

Trump was used to playing the long game.

I asked Sarah Malone if Trump might be offering Tiger sanctuary at Mar-a-Lago. 'Don't even go there,' she said.

Trump treated himself to a spectacular Christmas present – two new golf courses. He bought the 400-acre Branton Woods Golf Club in the Hudson Valley in New York state and the 365-acre Pine Hill Course in New Jersey. Trump wouldn't say what he paid for them but was happy to explain they had cost £25 million each to build and had been given planning breaks inconceivable today. 'These two courses are each considered among the finest in the country and I am proud to add them to my growing list of clubs,' he said. 'Today, they would be virtually impossible to replicate from the standpoint of receiving governmental and environmental approval or from the standpoint of cost.' Both courses were to be operated as 'high-end ultra-luxury private clubs'.

Trump had recently added the 850-acre Lowes Island course, lying on the Potomac River near Washington DC, to his list.

Architect Gareth Hoskins received a Christmas gift from the Queen when he was made an Officer of the British Empire – but only just. The invite was sent to the wrong address and Hoskins only learned of the decoration when the Cabinet Office called to find out why he hadn't replied.

Aberdeen got a present from the Scottish Government – the go-ahead for a city bypass. Martin Ford, who had opposed the road at a public inquiry, condemned the decision as 'a ghastly strategic mistake'. Ford said: 'Last week, Alex Salmond was so concerned about climate change he gate-crashed the Copenhagen conference. This week, his Government is actively undermining its own climate change promises by approving the Aberdeen Western Peripheral Route. Approving the construction of this road makes no sense at all in the context of the legislation committing Scotland to reducing carbon emissions.'

Lady Smith delivered her opinion on 6 January. She did not accept that the application to plant marram should be treated as a 'separate, stand-alone' application: 'The matters for which approval was sought in the application in respect of the marram grass works were not a change to or extension of the development for which outline permission was granted. It is plain . . . such work was always envisaged.'

Molly Forbes' counsel argued her client had 'an enforceable

legitimate expectation' that a pre-determination hearing would take place. Lady Smith took the view that even if that were so, Forbes should have spoken out when the plan first went in: 'Since she did not submit representations to the planning authority in respect of that application, she does not fall within the category of persons entitled to attend such a hearing.'

Lady Smith also rejected the claim that a new environmental impact assessment was needed: 'It is not the rule, even in the case of a development for which an EIA is required, that a separate one has to be prepared at each stage of the process.' Nor did Lady Smith accept Molly Forbes was entitled to 'justice in environmental matters' under European law: 'That submission appears . . . to ignore that this petition is brought by the petitioner as an individual, not as representing any group or organisation and as occupier not of adjoining property, but of a mobile home situated about a kilometre away from the work.'

The judge concluded:

> I have serious reservations as to whether or not the petitioner has established a *prima facie* case. It is, for the reasons I have explained, highly doubtful that she has the requisite title and interest; I am not persuaded that her present averments demonstrate that she has, even when viewed in the light of the oral submissions made on her behalf. Further, her case on the merits is, for the reasons I have explained, a distinctly weak one . . . It is not as if there has been no assessment of the likely environmental effect of the work on the dunes. They were assessed in some detail as part of the work that went into the grant of outline planning permission and, as I have explained, the planning permission for the marram grass works does not relate to a change or extension of the original work.

Trump was 'honoured' by the ruling and reasserted: 'We are now starting construction on what will soon be the greatest golf course anywhere in the world.'

An obdurate Molly Forbes reminded everyone the battle wasn't over:

> I am disappointed by the court's decision and have asked my lawyers to advise me on the prospects of appealing the ruling. It is important to note that this interim order does not stop me from proceeding with the action in relation to the other planning permissions granted, including one which would allow Mr Trump to develop Mill of Menie, where I stay, against my will.

David Milne, who had promoted the same arguments at the Formartine Area Committee, found the judgment 'laughable'. 'Molly had been under the impression that her son's objection would also cover her and so it should,' he said. Milne had 'no doubt' her appeal would be successful and added: 'In the meantime I have the misfortune to be able to look out on the main sand dome where I can see the handful of non-local labourers struggling to work in the wind and cold that is part and parcel of the Menie Estate.'

Milne had a point about the weather. The whole of Britain was under snow. It had been falling more or less every day since 17 December. Temperatures in the North-east dipped as low -18°C, the same as a domestic freezer. Molly Forbes had failed to scupper work at Menie but an Arctic air stream did the job for her. The Menie Dome looked like a polar ice cap. And the marram-planting season had only two months to run.

Donald Trump didn't need anybody's house for his championship golf course. Not Molly Forbes's, not her son's, not David Milne's. However, when it came to delivering an immaculate product, there was one piece of land not yet in his ownership that held a key design advantage. It was barely a third of an acre but sat in the centre of what was to be the championship course, next to the clubhouse site, between the outward and inward nine holes.

The grassy area, bought by the former regional council for £35 in

1976, had functioned as a public car park for the Menie Links before Balmedie Country Park opened. On some days, up to eighty cars would converge on the beach. Residents were forced to erect a sign 'no access to the beach' to dissuade drivers from blocking a private farm track. Aberdeenshire Council now deemed the car park surplus to requirements. The council couldn't sell the land to just anyone, however. A local authority was by law obligated to deliver 'best value', which usually meant getting the highest price for any asset.

Half-a-dozen noted interests were on the table. Former Northeast Green MSP Shiona Baird wanted to buy the land to donate it to the Scottish Wildlife Trust. David Milne was after it too, claiming his was a 'genuine attempt to preserve part of the environmental heritage' rather than a bid to block Trump.

What else might be done with a bit of scrub? One possibility was to break the land into hundreds of parcels and sell it on to climate change protestors around the world, a move that would lengthen the compulsory purchase process and delay development. The tactic had been employed to protect rainforests – and was being readied against Heathrow Airport.

Actress Emma Thompson, comedian Alistair McGowan, and Greenpeace Executive Director John Sauven were part of a group that bought a one-acre plot of land needed for a third runway. Explaining their purchase (they had pretended it was for a donkey sanctuary) in January 2009, Thompson said: 'I don't understand how any government remotely serious about committing to reversing climate change can even consider these ridiculous plans. It's laughably hypocritical.'

It might have been Martin Ford talking.

McGowan said: 'BAA were so confident of getting the Government's go ahead, but we have cunningly bought the land they need to build their runway. Now that we own it, we'll never sell it to them and we're confident that we'll be joined by people from all over the world who will help us defend it.'

John Sauven trilled: 'We've thrown a massive spanner in the engine driving Heathrow expansion. As the new owners of the land where the Government wants to build the runway, we'll resist all attempts at compulsory purchase.'

Trump was caught in a pincer movement. Pinned down by the snow, he was also confronted by the prospect of objectors annexing strategic land at Menie.

Chapter 12

A GLOBAL SUPERBRAND

On 19 January 2010, Trump's first wife appeared as a life model on British television. Stretched out on a chaise lounge, she cupped her head coquettishly in her hands; another woman posed next to her, standing against a pillar, rump pushed out. Ivana Trump wasn't actually nude but in flesh-coloured knickers and bra. She had wanted to wear her own hosiery, not the garments provided, worrying that her 'boobs' would never fill the bra. The organisers let her pick stockings from her own wardrobe but nothing else.

Behind a row of easels stood the artists. They included footballer turned actor Vinnie Jones; actor turned lay preacher Steven Baldwin; Alex Reid, there for having had sex with best-selling writer Katie Price (aka Jordan); Dane Bower, who had also had sex with Katie Price; and actress Stephanie Beecham, who told everyone she had been offered £40,000 to have sex with an unnamed admirer (we could rule out Katie Price – Beecham was talking about a man).

Such were the contrivances of *Celebrity Big Brother*.

Ivana Trump had emerged from a magician's box ('Surprise, surprise!') part-way through the seventh series, which was being touted as the last. The format had remained largely unchanged. Contestants were incarcerated in a house stuffed with hidden cameras and microphones, set silly tasks, invited to nominate one another for eviction, and then dispatched by the public vote. *Big Brother* (a repository for exhibitionists masquerading as members of the public) had devalued celebrity by producing counterfeits; television became a looking glass through which anyone could step. *Big Brother* and *Celebrity Big Brother* had converged incestuously: Jade Goody, a *Big*

Brother contestant, re-entered the house as a celebrity contestant in the fifth series.

Ivana (track-suited, heavy Slovakian accent, catchphrase 'it is what it is') seemed game enough for the show, rolling up her sleeves to wash dishes and rolling down her joggers to model. She regaled housemates with stories of time spent aboard private yachts and planes, of singing down the phone to her dog (*'Tiger, Tiger, doopsee, doopsee'*), of the brazen women who passed their phone numbers to her ex-husband Donald while she was sitting next to him, and of their eventual parting ('the trust was gone'). Ivana pocketed $20 million and a $14 million Connecticut estate from the divorce but ended up with a more valuable asset – the Trump name.

Branding provides the perfect default choice for a risk-averse, time-pressured society. Homogeneity makes life predictable; it removes the anxiety of decision-making and possible disappointment. A famous American name goes a long way. People in Aberdeen will queue in chain restaurants for food and coffee even when the only guarantee they are getting is of something expensive and insipid. Local shops daren't be too different.

Trump was very much a franchise and doing well out of reality television (the fancy new name for a fly-on-the-wall documentary).

According to *Forbes* magazine, he made £31.25 million to the year ending in June from *The Apprentice*, which he owned with producer Mark Burnett. Only Simon Cowell (*X Factor, Britain's Got Talent, American Idol*) pulled in more at £46.9 million. *The Apprentice*, in which competitors audition to join the company, had been syndicated in Britain (anchored by Lord Sugar), Italy, France and South America. A new season of *Celebrity Apprentice*, played for charity, was to premiere in the United States in March, and the regular show had been recommissioned. Paul Telegdy, Executive Vice President of Alternative Programming at NBC, said: '*The Apprentice* is a proven brand, and we believe its return is more relevant than ever since it will provide new hope for many Americans struggling in this difficult job market.'

Trump talks about possessing a 'global superbrand'. Reputation is something he defends ferociously, especially when it comes to what he's worth.

His estimate of his wealth, a court learned, could vary between $4 billion and $6 billion depending on how he was feeling. Trump's casual approach to domestic accountancy was revealed after he slapped Tim O'Brien with a defamation suit for claiming in *TrumpNation: The Art of Being the Donald* that the mogul had $250 million at most. In a deposition to defence lawyers, Trump said: 'My net worth fluctuates, and it goes up and down with markets and with attitudes and with feelings, even my own feeling.'

When asked whether he had ever exaggerated about the success of his properties, he said 'not beyond reason' and added: 'I think everybody does. Would you like me to say, oh, gee, the building is not doing well, blah, blah, blah. Nobody talks that way. Who would ever talk that way?' Bedminster had recorded a net loss of $4.6 million in 2005 but Trump was unfazed, reasoning he'd profit in the long-term. When lawyers showed Trump had wrongly claimed ownership of a hotel and condo in Hawaii, Trump retorted that a strong licensing agreement was 'a form of ownership'.

A New Jersey judge dismissed Trump's case, not because he agreed with O'Brien, but because Trump had failed to demonstrate 'clear and convincing evidence to establish malice' needed to make a defamation case stick.

Trump remained a symbol of riches, filming a cameo for *Wall Street 2: Money Never Sleeps*.

The UK economy was waking up, at least according to the beleaguered Prime Minister Gordon Brown. In his New Year message, he said: 'We have already seen off the worst of the recession . . . 2010 is when we will get Britain moving forward again.'

On 4 January, the world's highest building officially opened – 169 floors, 2,683ft, 10°C cooler at the top. The Burj Dubai had shops, restaurants, a nightclub, a gym and a Giorgio Armani-designed hotel. The brief, in what sounded like the premise for a science-fiction dystopia, was that none of the residents should ever have to leave (there was no mention of an Armani-styled crematorium). Built by developer Emaar Properties and Dubai's ruler Sheikh Mohammed bin Rashid al-Maktoum, the Burj was to be a monument to economic might, but at the time of opening, none of the thirty-seven floors of office space was occupied. Dubai's riches had been exposed as something of a mirage.

Two months earlier, Dubai World – a state-sponsored construction company – fell behind with its credit repayment and the government couldn't help bail it out. The Trump International Hotel and Tower (Trump had licensed his name to another Dubai developer) was axed in the summer. One wonders where the real wealth resided in Dubai's business model, if property speculation and tourism could ever match oil – of which the emirate has comparatively little – as a primary economic driver.

Is it because he is rich? Is it because he is American?

Sue Edwards is forlorn. She is standing in the corridor of Ellon Kirk hall, wondering aloud about the fate of the council car park. Aberdeenshire Council's legal team has recommended that the Formartine Area Committee, meeting in private upstairs, should award Trump 'special purchase status'; that is, one 'with an existing interest in another asset that has economic, legal or geographic association with the asset being valued'. The report valued the land at £1,000 but consultants said the council should accept nothing less than £10,000 for the site.

Debra Storr and Paul Johnston are first downstairs. The committee has agreed on the recommendation and instructed officers to enter exclusive negotiations with Trump and report back. Storr wanted the site put on the open market 'The council should use an open process for the sale of this land to get the maximum financial return,' she says in the corridor. 'I would expect that to be the Trump Organization, but it seems the council is content to offer the Trump Organization a sweet deal.'

Might there be an appeal?

'Too soon for me to say.'

Paul Johnston is confounded. 'I think the public should have concern about the way in which this was done,' he says. 'I think they have headed down the road of providing a sweet deal for the Trump Organization . . . At times their logic for their decisions beats me. There was one justification there in the meeting which I was just gobsmacked at. Basically, they might end up selling the land for too high a price and then have to agree to a CPO to buy it back. I mean, the logic of that astounds me, but we're in a kind of fairytale existence with this development.'

Council leader Anne Robertson appears. She refuses to talk about a confidential meeting. Chairman Loveday is next. There is no sweet deal, he stresses, because no deal has been done. Yet, 'It is a special case . . . It is sitting right in the middle of the proposed golf development . . . We need to move this on. We're certainly going to get good value from the land compared to what it is currently worth.'

'It was inevitable,' says Sue Edwards, hearing that her whale and dolphin centre plan will not be entertained. 'The council is hell-bent on processing the application through as quickly as possible.'

The Intergovernmental Panel on Climate Change (IPCC) had mucked up. Glaciers were not melting at the rate predicted by a seminal report in 2007 on climate change. Nothing like it, in fact. The claim there was a 'very high' (that is, more than ninety per cent) chance that thousands of feet of Himalayan ice would be gone by 2035 was, it turned out, taken from a 2005 campaigning report from the World Wide Fund for Nature. The WWF had seized upon a 1999 magazine article featuring glaciologist Dr Syed Hasnain, who was simply speculating. IPCC report author Dr Murari Lal told the *Mail on Sunday* he had included Dr Hasnain's stupefying but unverified claim to encourage politicians 'to take some concrete action'.

The disquiet among global warming sceptics was best captured by Peter Taylor, a former policy advisor to the UK Government, the

European Commission and UN Organizations, who said: 'We're being fatally led up the wrong garden path by green businesses, politicians, the IPCC and their computer geeks with their doctored spreadsheets and forecasts. They need to get out more and study the real world, not their virtual reality, because, like the asset bubbles of the financial crisis, the global warming bubble is about to burst.'

In *Chill* (published in December 2009), Taylor, who had studied science at Oxford University, amplified a theory first put forward by Danish astrophysicist Henrik Svensmark. Taylor warned we were on the cusp of an 'episode of cooling potentially comparable to the Little Ice Age'. That's the chilly spell that lasted seventy years from 1645 to 1715 and featured The Great Frost, which froze the River Thames in London. Temperatures in Scotland were 1.5°C to 2°C down on today's, enough to shrink the growing season and devastate yields.

Taylor saw climate change as very much a cosmic phenomenon. The Earth is bombarded by atomic particles from exploding stars deep in space. If the Sun's magnetic field – which oscillates over hundreds of years – is strong, they are deflected. If it is weak, they hit us. Taylor believed these particles were seeding, through the condensation of water vapour, thick low-level clouds that stopped the Sun's rays reaching the Earth (unlike the thin high-level clouds that trap radiated heat).

When I contacted Taylor, he was touring climate research laboratories in the US. 'There are other mechanisms at work related to the solar magnetic field,' he said. 'Ultimately, however, it is cloud changes that drive the natural cycles of change.'

When it came to Trump and the deleterious lifestyle he was accused of encouraging, Taylor thought it a mistake to 'over emphasise the carbon issue'. 'The whole story may unravel over the next few years,' he said. Taylor saw no evidence of global warming in the North-east: 'I have discussed Scottish ecology at length with specialists on Cairngorm ecology and they see no changes attributable to "global warming". Highland species have not suffered declines. I expect the warming cycle – 1980-2005 – now to shift to a cooling cycle with colder winters.'

It seemed all you had to do for proof was look out of your window. Scotland was experiencing its coldest winter for a generation, along with parts of North America and Eurasia. But in Canada, North Africa, the Mediterranean and parts of Asia it was warmer than usual. And while Greenland and Antarctica were losing ice, according to some reports, the Himalayan glaciers in the Karakoram Range were getting bigger. People couldn't even agree on how best to monitor the patient. Some climatologists said the sea was the best place to take the Earth's temperature, and put the record air temperatures of 1998 down to the esoteric El Niño phenomenon that caused heat transfer from the Pacific Ocean to the atmosphere.

Taylor had got one prediction bang on: the Climate Change Conference would yield no result. The accord was not formally adopted and contained no target for emission reductions, and few countries were rushing to produce an action plan. To Taylor's mind, politicians had no hope of agreeing a consensus when scientists couldn't offer one. Professor Jeffrey Kargel, from the US Geological Survey, who was involved in exposing the Himalayan glacier error, said that overall, the IPCC's fourth report on climate change impacts was otherwise 'very solid and very accurate'. He said: 'This is a self-correcting system, that's what happened, that's what science is.'

Paul Hardaker, Chief Executive of the Royal Meteorological Society, moved to defend not just the system but the results it produced. Writing in the *Guardian*, which continued to lead on climate change, he said:

Good science by its nature should always be transparent and robust, that's how it works. Scientists collaborate by sharing information with each other and comparing results. It is through this comparison that we understand where the uncertainty lies and how we can focus our efforts to improve knowledge and understanding. The important thing about the problems surrounding the University of East Anglia, and the questions it has raised in people's minds about climate science, is that lots of groups around the world have done similar things to the scientists there, and they've all been showing similar results.

You dig a hole, put the grass in, and cover the hole.

A boy is describing planting marram grass on the Menie Dome. He and seven classmates from Balmedie Primary School are on their hands and knees but having fun. It's 29 January. The snow has receded and the frost has released its grip on the sand. The planting is back on schedule, helped by a concerted effort made before the snow arrived. Half of the 3.5 acres requiring stabilisation has been completed. The fifteenth hole is done. Work on the fourteenth's tees, the seventeenth green, and the eighteenth's tees is progressing.

The kids, in green hard hats and fluorescent jackets, are out on the thirteenth hole. Two of them are clinging to one of the steeper slopes like climbers on a final pitch. 'Cute,' says Sarah Malone as she stops her Land Rover. It's been a spirited mile-long journey from Menie House, the vehicle slewing sideways in the mud and using all of its suspension travelling over the ruts and potholes. The Land Rover is one of several new vehicles. Malone tells me they're washed every day.

Bamboo canes mark where the sprigging should take place. Fences are used to encourage a build-up of sand. Some have been vandalised, the wiring cut and the posts knocked over. To keep the sand put, netting has been laid over flatter parts of the dunes. The marram strands, taken from denser patches on the site, are patted into place with a little collar of sand. The grass is being planted in a grid pattern. It looks like the Dome is having a hair transplant.

There are a dozen workers in all on site, some of whom have been with Moray Lanscapes for thirty years. But today is about the two girls and six boys from Primary 5, in the field as part of a project on conservation.

'We're planting marram,' says another pupil. 'To keep the sand dunes stable for Mr Trump.'

Malone says the collaboration is about creating a 'greater sense of ownership' for the next generation, for the ones who may live, work or play here.

The deputy head teacher sees it as a chance for children to 'better understand their heritage' and how crofters tried to make something of the sand. I ask if any parents have refused to let their kids learn from Trump. 'I'm not going to go into that,' she says. 'I don't want it to be political.' Malone tells me the parents are well up for it.

Trump has established ties with the school, having provided a climbing frame and new football strips, one of several donations to local organisations, including the local leisure centre, a part-time fire station, a pipe band, and a charity supporting injured service personnel and their families.

In the United States he has been involved with philanthropic work for cerebral palsy sufferers and Vietnam veterans. In *Think Like a Billionaire*, Trump writes that 'wealth carries social responsibility' and that 'some portion of personal wealth must be used to help those who are in need, to reward good work, and to encourage better work and higher productivity in the greater community'.

I climb to the top of the dome.

To the north, Buchan seems to merge with the North Sea under the grey sky. Over centuries, people built walls where trees wouldn't stand, fortified the earth, raised cattle and crops. The North-east was made by people going where no human really belonged: into the mutinous North Sea with their nets, down to its depth with their drills, refusing always to give up.

The bracken below the escarpment where David Milne's house sits (and where the hotel and holiday homes are to go) looks black, as though it has been burned. Against the pallid sky, Aberdeen rises like Mordor across the Dead Marshes.

I walk back to Balmedie Country Park by the coast, passing Michael Forbes' home. There are cars, a snowplough, a tractor and a curious red cone. It looks like the nose of a ballistic missile.

I slither through the dunes towards the beach. The embankment of a burn has broken away, revealing the marram's roots, six feet long and as thick as cord. Tenacious and resilient, the grass might be a symbol for the endeavours of farmers and fishers.

No one's on the beach. A dead sperm whale came ashore here just before Christmas. Today a group of sandpipers pick in the surf. Helicopters thrum overhead every quarter of an hour; a half-dozen supply ships straddle the horizon. For the moment, Aberdeen is still very much about oil.

On 19 February, the world of golf conjured what was easily one of sport's most transfixing spectacles. Tiger Woods said sorry. It was a bizarre show of contrition, beamed across the world like a presidential address.

Woods, statement in hand, emerged from between shimmering curtains like a compère at a holiday camp show. The setting, however, was reminiscent of a chapel. The world's most famous adulterer took his place at a lectern before a small, select audience – business associates, friends, his mum, seated and curved towards him like mourners – and spent fourteen minutes flagellating himself: 'I want to say to each of you, simply and directly, I am deeply sorry for my irresponsible and selfish behaviour I engaged in . . . I was unfaithful. I had affairs, I cheated . . . I felt that I had worked hard my entire life and deserved to enjoy all the temptations around me.'

He stuttered, he wept. He clasped his hand to his bosom.

That so private a man (that is, when he wasn't dropping his pants in a church car park, if reports were to be believed) should repent so publicly made for hypnotic viewing. If Woods sounded less than sincere, that was because it was hard for *us* to connect with *him*. Circling, nagging, was the question – just who was this all for? The clue, perhaps, was the venue: the PGA Tour headquarters in Florida. You could imagine a penitent Woods explaining himself to his mother, but to do so while abasing himself before millions of television viewers reduced Tilda Woods to a prop; a replacement for the absent wife and kids who had once bolstered Tiger's whole-some family image.

What did he say? 'Mom, I've something to tell you . . . here's a pass for the PGA.'

Had this been a press conference we might have got an answer to the question most people at home wanted to ask. Not – 'How's Elin doing?' Not – 'Why should we accept your insistence you've never taken performance-enhancing drugs when you've just admitted lying to those you hold dearest?' Not – 'Would you recommend Ambien to couples who have to work in the morning?' But – 'When are you going to play again?' Woods said his priority was further therapy, adding: 'I do plan to return to golf one day. I just don't know when that day will be. I don't rule out that it will be this year.'

Perhaps he did have a date in mind. To have been specific might have appeared unseemly or calculating, like turning up for his PGA confessional in a Nike cap.

The biblical tenor of Woods' delivery made him sound like a fallen angel rather than a two-bit cheat. Maybe that was the intention. Only a demigod could tumble so far. Only the once-pure could sin so much.

Donald Trump, appearing on US television, offered a bracingly pragmatic perspective.

'Tiger's a friend of mine and I have a lot of respect for Tiger as an amazing athlete, but this whole thing has got totally out of hand,' he said. 'I have a whole question as to whether they should even get back together. It's so damaged and if the reports are just half true I would recommend Tiger call it a bad experience, say bye-bye, go out and be a wonderful playboy and win tournaments and have a good life.'

Trump had come close to writing off Menie as a bad experience. And now, what he hoped would be the world's best ever course was unveiled in its final specification, all 7,474 yards of it. The detailed tee-to-green layout was submitted to the council along with the new masterplan showing the scale and location of the buildings. Martin Hawtree, not a man given to bombast, called the course 'close to ideal'. 'The golf course will lack for nothing,' he said. 'There is nothing missing and the layout as conceived would contain no weak holes. It will produce simply the most dramatic, stimulating, invigorating stretch of golf anywhere I have seen in my career.'

Trump reminded people he had helped map out every hole with Hawtree, who praised Trump's perspicacity and readiness to 'walk for hours over the site'. 'They are all going to be hard,' said Trump of the holes. 'It has been a lot of work to get here, but when people look back in years to come they are going to be proud of what will be without doubt the best golf course in the world. Every single architect I have spoken to has said that this is the best piece of land they have seen for a golf course. Once this is built I will be there a lot. I have a tremendous amount of money invested in this project and I don't have a mortgage on it – it's all coming out of my pocket.'

The Masterplan Design Statement ran to 271 pages. It particularised everything from the degree of shelter afforded by trees (expressed as wind speed attenuation) to the predicted energy usage and carbon dioxide emissions of the buildings.

The village, to the south of the site, radiated from a central square bordered by cafes, a pub and playgrounds. It curled north in a crescent, looking like a giant inverted comma around the golf course. There was mention of a small supermarket, a hairdresser, a hall with a nursery, and a GP and dental surgery. No site was identified for a primary school or affordable housing; they would be built elsewhere. The village would be accessible by foot or bike, or by car or bus from a new road connected to the trunk road running north of Aberdeen. Gawping at Menie House would be discouraged. 'The setting of the house will be strengthened through the introduction of a new tree planting to reinforce a sense of separation and enclosure,' said the statement.

An accommodation block for 400 staff was missing from the

masterplan. Sarah Malone said the Trump Organization was reacting to concerns about jobs going to transient workers. 'We are committed to providing local people with jobs when they become available,' she said. 'We need to make provision for staff on site, but we will integrate that into the residential village.' The number of holiday homes was reduced from 950 to 600. The number of buildings, however, would stay the same. There were now 186 golf villas next to the village, not thirty-six. And 200 'residential units' (ranging from one- to three-bedroom apartments) would sit alongside the 500 'residential houses' (two-bedroom terraced houses to six-bedroom detached houses) in the village. The statement said:

> An integral and important catalyst of the design development was TIGLS [Trump International Golf Links Scotland's] proposal to move 200 apartments from the resort development area into the residential village. This move was encouraged by the planners and Architecture and Design Scotland as it benefits the development twofold. Firstly it will reduce the pressure on the sensitive landscape to the north of and adjacent to the Site of Special Scientific Interest and secondly it will help create a development with a sensible and healthy mix of housing types and densities that can support the community facilities that the planning authority and TIGLS envisage and aspire to have, enabling the creation of a much more sustainable community than the construction of 500 detached private houses, which the Indicative Layout would have provided.

This seemed to suggest Trump was looking to build 700 *homes* at Menie. Malone said it hadn't been decided whether to sell these 200 apartments as time-shares or as private residences because the Trump Organization needed to retain 'flexibility' as the project progressed. She conceded the descriptor 'residential unit' may appear to some confusing, but added: 'The bottom line is that we have planning permission for 500 homes and 950 holiday homes.'

Detailed architectural drawings of the buildings would come

forward in due course, the hotel and holiday accommodation followed by the housing. The sketches at this stage were suitably bland, dazzlingly so. The hotel – grey and rectilinear – didn't even have windows; it looked like a Stalinist prison. Trump favoured a baronial confection of stone and wood, something to suggest the course had been there for long time, but Architecture and Design Scotland, whose seal of approval would smooth the planning process, wanted to see a more progressive design of steel and glass (as did Hoskins). Its report on the new masterplan said:

> At the last review the panel were not convinced by the quality of the designs for the hotel and felt that some of the historical precedents referred to were entirely inappropriate for this context. Though still of the opinion that a landmark building could work well on the site, we feel strongly that a prominent building on such a very sensitive site should reflect Scotland as a modern and vibrant nation, rather than try to recreate historical pastiche . . . We understand that detailed designs for the hotel will come forward as part of a separate development brief and application. However, the design concept for the hotel will become enshrined within the masterplan and we do not yet feel that the designs for the hotel have been sufficiently developed for us to feel confident that a satisfactory solution will be arrived at.

Overall, however, they were satisfied with Gareth Hoskins' work, commending the masterplan's 'light touch':

> The sensitive response to the site and its wider landscape, the overall landscape strategy, the distribution of buildings across the site, and the quality of linking spaces between them successfully achieves the broader ambitions for the designs set out by the project team.

The Trump Organization's commitment to nurturing North-east talent saw it invite three design students from the Robert Gordon

University in Aberdeen to come up with a Trump Tartan. The group at Gray's School of Art were asked to produce corporate colours for Trump International – Scotland, for possible use in the clubhouse and hotel. It wasn't a commission as such but Trump was keen to give the kids first crack at the job.

Donald Trump has never concocted anything so fantastical – a putting surface made from green icing and bunkers filled with brown sugar. The cake is carried into a function suite next to the Udny Arms Hotel in Newburgh. A message is piped across it: *A Vision for the Future*.

Edith Murdoch, retail manager with bakery Murdoch and Allan, has come bearing a gift for Trump's team at a public exhibition for the masterplan and course layout. The bakery, which employs more than eighty people in the North-east, is hoping to take a place in the Menie village.

Edith explains that staff on training courses are told a cautionary story of how an elephant chained from birth remains stationary even when freed. 'It just needs to see a bit of chain,' she says. Edith believes all of the North-east can learn from the parable. 'Do we want to standstill for the next thirty-five or forty years?' she says.

More baking arrives. Cupcakes, with a blob of green icing. A paper flag reads: 'For the token quine employed by Trump.' It's a gift to Sarah Malone from Tripping Up Trump, placed on a table used to display information about the resort. Malone is not enamoured with the offering and clears the cakes away.

The protestors pore over maps with magnifying glasses while media photographers click away and cameras run. The stunt is called 'the mystery of the missing houses', the point being that the masterplan does not show the properties Trump must acquire before being able to build the resort he wants. A protestor places a Monopoly-style house on a map. Malone leaves it put.

Molly Forbes is here, wearing a blood red jacket and equally vivid lipstick. Sue Edwards too. David Milne arrives. Protestors flutter around him: Milne has acquired a sheen of celebrity. He is a kent face.

Milne engages a consultant in a discussion, questioning whether the stabilisation of the dunes can survive the spring storms. People stop moving and listen. Malone looks caught between allowing Milne to interrogate her team member and risking the consultant becoming a foil. Meantime, another visitor complains to me that he's unable to see the exhibition because of the protestors.

Project Director Neil Hobday, standing at the other end of the table from Milne, has seen and heard enough.

'This is here for the public to come and have a look at what we're doing,' he says. 'Pick your own platform, pay for it somewhere else, invite the media, and do it there. Just clear off, clear off.'

Malone winces.

'Neil, I was invited here by yourselves and I am not telling these people anything they don't know,' says Milne.

'You were not invited here to hold court. You are trying to hijack the whole show.'

'I am asking questions. I am not hijacking the show, as you say.'

'This is an exhibition. This is a public exhibition, not the David Milne show.'

Hobday challenges Milne on his assertions that the resort will fail.

'It's a twenty-year-old business model of conspicuous consumption that has failed in numerous other locations worldwide,' says Milne.

'Grow up David, just grow up,' says Hobday.

The Project Director walks away. Malone is aghast. It's hard to believe life at the Gordon Highlanders' Museum was ever like this.

Five minutes later, she's ready to offer a view and concedes 'passions and emotions' were running 'high'. Malone suggests Milne's method of providing feedback was 'inappropriate'. 'He is talking about matters that we don't believe he is well-informed on,' she says. 'If this happens again he will be asked to leave.'

*

Donald Trump is planning a luxury golf resort which his company says would bring jobs to Aberdeenshire, but his plans would require evicting local residents who do not wish to sell, and building on protected land. Do you support this project?

This was the question put to the Scottish public in a poll commissioned by the Scottish Green Party. Of the 1,001 adults surveyed, sixty-four per cent answered no. The results were released by MSP Patrick Harvie during a visit to Molly Forbes' home. He took the opportunity to call on Trump to rule out the use of CPOs. 'Increasingly, people are taking a very simple view on this,' said Harvie. 'They see a bullying billionaire bent on throwing vulnerable local residents from their own homes and on trashing this extraordinary environment.'

Opinion polls were everywhere – a General Election for the UK Government had been called for May 6. Sue Edwards was Scottish Green Party candidate for Gordon, running on a compulsory purchase ticket. CPOs were not strictly a green issue but here was the link to the Copenhagen summit and opposition to Heathrow's third runway and fears over Himalayan glaciers going the way of an ice lolly dropped in the street on a summer's day. The broader battle was about the right to clean air and fresh water in years to come, about the need for compassionate environmental custodianship of the planet. In their eyes, Trump was out to pillage the Earth. And all that mattered was stopping him or slowing him to the point where he could no longer endure the inertia.

The Independent Democrats accused Aberdeenshire Council of making the task ever harder after the administration ruled out motions on climate change and airport expansion. As part of a move towards 'modernisation', new rules required councillors to 'make a robust case' for a motion being 'relevant to the council's business'. Martin Ford said democracy had been replaced by the 'tyranny of the majority'. George Sorial said it sounded like Ford was confusing council business with the American Civil War.

David Milne demanded a full, unreserved apology from Malone

and Hobday for claims he had been spreading 'misinformation' at the Udny Arms exhibition.

Milne couched his ultimatum in legal speak, defying the Trump Organization to prove 'beyond reasonable doubt' that he had lied. He was brassy enough to risk slandering Malone, rubbishing as 'patently untrue' her insistence that negotiations with residents were ongoing. Milne wasn't to know just who Malone was chatting with but she wasn't about to start playing semantics. Her attitude had hardened noticeably in response to the personalised attacks. She was far from an ornamental presence. Buchan quines are as steely as the men who fish the seas.

Sorial said he would have welcomed a lawsuit from Milne. Only the worry of appearing heavy-handed had kept the Trump Organization from taking legal action against detractors. 'If it had been the States we'd have had fifty suits,' said Sorial, who believed the Trump Organization had been repeatedly maligned.

Maybe they reasoned they were setting the dunes free, that tearing out 10,000sq ft of hand-planted marram grass and smashing 400ft of fencing around the fifteenth green was an act of emancipation.

No one was calling it sabotage but vandalism was rarely this precise. Two diggers were trashed – doors prised open, electrical wiring ripped out, batteries taken, sand poured into the engines. Sugar was added to 3,000 litres of diesel kept in tanks. Sarah Malone conceded the perpetrators were unlikely to have been kids on a weekend rampage. 'It is a disgrace that there are people around us who are prepared to stoop to such callous acts of vandalism and the destruction of our environment,' she said. 'Our aim is to enhance and develop the site, while others now evidently seem intent upon destroying it.' Replanting the marram was likely to take several weeks. The total repair was estimated at £50,000.

Malone pledged to up security, which was just as well. Trump was to carry out a site inspection on site within a month – and bare sand, broken fences and idle diggers were not what he was expecting to see. First, Trump had to make it across the Atlantic Ocean. The anarchy of spring 2010 wasn't confined to Menie. An Icelandic volcano had erupted, spewing forth clouds of vitreous ash. Eyjafjallajökull succeeded where the Copenhangen Summit had failed, curbing air travel at a stroke. The turbine-glazing plumes halted flying across Europe. Malone didn't think Trump would be put off visiting by the rumbling volcano, by a mere cataclysm. 'He'll be here,' she said. 'Even if he has to come by canoe.'

Chapter 13

THE GREAT DUNES

A man is polishing a Range Rover, buffing the alloy wheels, wiping down the windscreen for a second time. The vehicle is one of four black Range Rovers – line-topping Autobiography Sport models – reverse-parked at a former flying club terminal on the eastern side of Aberdeen Airport, pointed at the exit. There's another shiny black car stopped, a Jaguar, transport for Aberdeen's Lord Provost. Across Farburn Terrace, Sue Edwards is standing with her dog and some friends. The collie is wearing a fluorescent jacket on which someone has penned: 'Don't hound these people out of their homes.'

Donald Trump is on his way.

Just after 10am, his Boeing 727 lands: the canoe wasn't needed. The plane stops at the training base, far from the main terminal. It's the same aircraft Trump had when he first visited four years ago, a new purchase having yet to be made. A black golf bag with gold trim – matching the colours of the jet – is transferred to a waiting Range Rover. Trump is in his usual sartorial combo: black Cashmere coat, dark suit, white shirt, vibrant tie.

Runway greetings over, Trump enters a room where the media are waiting. He seems surprised by the throng of photographers and journalists. 'Wow, this is a big thing here, we'll maybe have some fun,' he says, stepping between cabling and camera stands. 'I hope my hair didn't blow too hard out there.' He sits behind a table with Don Jr and explains his mission: 'We've started on the golf course and it's moving along nicely. I'm here to meet with Martin Hawtree and the team and make sure it's just right.'

Trump enthuses about the land he will be inspecting later in the day.

'I've seen nothing comparable to these dunes. I am henceforth – I own the land – going to name them the Great Dunes of Scotland.'

Trump has called them this before, when interviewed by *Vanity Fair* in 2007, but back then he thought this was how everyone referred to them.

'I think it's more appropriate, a bigger name, a better name, and I think it's a name people can really understand and relate to in Scotland.' Trump doesn't think he is being presumptuous. 'The "Menie dunes" doesn't mean anything. They're the biggest dunes in the world, the tallest, the most spectacular. I think we should name them after Scotland . . . Arrogant would be if I called them the Donald J. Trump Special Dunes.'

Colin Wight from the BBC comments that the 'dunes in Namibia are a lot bigger than the dunes at Menie'.

'Okay, well . . .' says Trump, shrugging off the dissent. Nothing is going to spoil his excitement today.

'We're travelling with the Golf Channel, in the world of golf the biggest thing there is, highest demographic . . .' He points out he's on the front of *Golf Magazine* in the US, and that the winner of *The Apprentice* graces *People* magazine. He asks one of his entourage to bring him a copy of *People*, which he shows to the media.

Trump says he has now spent more than $60 million on the Menie project and is estimating a final price tag of well over £750 million.

'It has got a little bit less expensive because the dollar has gone up and the pound has gone down. Call me lucky or call me a genius.' European banks, he says, are phoning him up, 'begging' to lend him money. 'I don't even have a mortgage on the property. I think I do that in honour of my mother. I think so much of this project that I have decided just not to finance it. At some point when we build the hotel and everything we'll probably do a little financing but it will be very conservative.'

'The one advantage I have is that no matter where I go in the world people want me.'

Even when questions turn to Michael Forbes and the prospect of compulsory purchase, Trump remains resolutely upbeat.

'If we build a $300 million or $400 million hotel, I don't think you want the windows looking down into a slum. In the US if he was stopping a hotel, and the hotel produced hundreds and hundreds of jobs, they would say, "We are sorry but we will condemn and we'll pay you money, you'll get fair value for the land . . ." This isn't a man so in love with his land that he can't see straight. I've had that over the years, people that were truly in love with their house . . . Forbes made a deal with us twice to sell and then he broke the deal and then he went round saying what a bad person I am. Story of my life.'

'There were two handshakes then we gave up,' he claims.

It has just been revealed that Forbes *has* sold his land, or rather an acre of it. Tripping Up Trump has persuaded sixty people to take a share. Trump isn't fussed.

'Somebody said that he sold a little piece of his land to people who don't even live in the area in order to trip up Trump. I think they call it Tripping Up Trump. It's a little late to trip me up because, honestly, we're under construction. I'm a very substantial guy . . . I think he was stupid to do it because he lost control of his own property. Now, I'm not going to make a deal with him until I make a deal with these other people. I wouldn't have done what he did especially when I think he really wants to sell, he just wants much more than the property's worth.'

Trump figures it will be 'awfully hard' to build a hotel with Forbes there, but notes that it's for the council to judge whether he should be shifted.

'It's sad that his property is in such poor condition. My mother, she was so meticulous. If I dropped a little piece of paper on the floor as a baby she'd say, "Pick up that paper!" She was immaculate. The people of Scotland are that way. His place is a pigsty . . . Maybe his heritage is somewhere other than Scotland. If he cleaned up his property, I'd feel a lot different, but he should clean up his property, not for Trump but for himself. Okay, enough of that.'

More than thirty minutes have passed and much of the talk has been about Forbes.

'He's not a thorn in my side,' says Trump softly. 'I met him twice. He was a very nice person.'

'We're here to put the finishing touches,' says Don Jr. 'The last little minute details, moving the holes a little bit so that we can secure what will be the great work that we're putting together.'

Trump winds up the press conference much in the same way he did four years earlier.

'The people coming to the resort will be golfers. These are people from all over the world and they are going to be spending money in your stores, staying in your hotels, and spending money in your restaurants. Aberdeen is going to be very happy. When they come to Scotland, they will play here, they will play St Andrews, they will play Royal Aberdeen and lots of other courses. But we will be the one that brings them here more than anyone else – and that's a big statement.'

Three hours later, Trump's in the dunes. Now he's the one asking questions as he follows the route of the championship course, starting at the tenth. He's accompanied by Martin Hawtree, Don Jr, George Sorial, Sarah Malone, Gareth Hoskins and personnel from SOL Golf Course Ltd. Some of his US executives are here too. Though detailed plans for the course are already with the council, minor tweaks are permitted. These will be the final brush strokes.

'What do you think, Martin?'

Trump wants to move the championship tee for the eighteenth to near the top of the coastal dune ridge, to have it 'hanging out over the sea'. Hawtree concurs and a surveyor records Trump's wishes to the nearest centimetre. 'People will come up to the tee just to take pictures,' says Trump. 'Nobody's ever seen a hole like this.'

That is, until we move to the fourteenth, which plunges between the shaggy dunes.

'People are going to die when they see that hole,' says Trump. 'It's possibly the most spectacular hole we've seen in golf.' He turns to the construction team. 'I really want it done the way I want, so please don't fuck me up.' He's laughing, but the point is made. We stand and stare into the canyon, the fairway delineated by the dunes, funnelling towards what will become the green. 'I think I should cut SOL's contract,' says Trump. 'They're not going to be doing anything.'

The fifteenth also heads north in parallel with the beach. Hawtree and his team have made conspicious sense of this confused but exhilarating landscape. It feels like the course is there already, beneath a dusting of sand, nudging the surface like a fossilized skeleton; the fairways simply await excavation. 'All we're really having to do on this hole is put down grass,' says Trump. 'It's that good.'

Squalls blow across the dunes as we move to the opening nine holes. The group stretches as people stop to put up umbrellas. Trump and Hawtree remain together. Trump is maybe a foot taller. His voice booms, Hawtree's is whispered. They could be an old music hall double act.

The very first hole is troubling Trump, a long par-four into the prevailing wind that could spoil a player's score before they've reached the second tee. With Hawtree's blessing, he asks Don Jr to check out the view of the green from a dune across a valley. Don Jr wades through the wet grass and scrabbles up sand. He reports that play doesn't look any easier from the alternative tee position. 'How about that dune?' shouts Trump, gesturing further towards the sea. 'Yeah, try that one, Don,' says one of the New York team, fanning the joke. Don raises a finger, descends and rejoins the group.

Trump wants the course to be user-friendly. This is not vainglorious creation, ego as edifice. He cares about the distance between holes and the amount of climbing people have to do – 'We're not getting any younger, Martin,' – or seem to do: he likes the seventeenth fairway's linear rise towards the highest point on the course. 'If people are playing, they don't know they're climbing.' There is an appreciation of real-world constraints. Money isn't the issue – Trump never asks 'how much' when discussing design changes – but accommodating golfers of varying standards and fitness is. Maybe it's the businessman thinking about repeat custom.

After an assurance from Hawtree that the first green is big enough to tempt big hitters on their second shot, Trump elects to lengthen the par-four into a par-five. The extra yardage will allow the tee to be moved back, closer to the clubhouse, bringing more cohesion to the layout. 'The most important holes are the first and the last,' says Trump. 'That's what people remember.' The ninth will change from a par-five to par-four, keeping the course par just where the R&A likes it.

A burn at the back of the third green has coiled towards the course, undercutting the friable banks. Chunks of Trump's green are no more, reclaimed by the sea. 'It's a different hole, Martin,' he says. Don Jr takes to another dune and Trump and Hawtree go with his recommendation to bring the tee around a little, allowing them to move the green away from the avaricious burn. Concrete blocks straddle the gap where the burn splits the dune ridge: a barrier to repel German tanks during the Second World War. 'Do you think they needed an environmental impact assessment for those?' says Trump, deadpan. Someone explains the spurs are classified as a historical monument and must stay put. 'I don't want to move them . . . The Scots were great fighters.'

Dan Scavino has seen these dunes many times before, in the photograph that hangs on the wall of the Westchester club he manages for Trump, but this is his first visit to Menie. 'The American courses are great but this is unbelievable,' he says. 'It's mind-blowing.' Trump starts talking about *Citizen Kane*, how director Orson Welles never bettered the picture. He speculates Menie might be Hawtree's *Citizen Kane*, his too. Standing there in the rain, Trump sounds mournful rather than blustering. A dream dies the moment it comes true. There is an ineluctable sense of loss – a loss of purpose, of motive force, of faith even; and, for two men in their sixties, the presumption of time to come.

After five hours, Trump is done. His team goes to fetch the Range Rovers. Trump and Hawtree walk back together, umbrellas at their sides, Trump bending to hear the architect's words. If Menie was to be their *Citizen Kane*, it would also represent Trump's apogee: he was all out of superlatives. Trump and Hawtree are the last to depart the dunes, to leave the mortal embrace of the sands.

The following morning the lugubrious rain clouds have gone. The sun is shining over the Menie Estate, where a reception has been arranged for around fifty business leaders, media bosses, and civic dignitaries. Trump is back in a suit and tie, ready to meet his guests in a marquee among the dunes. An hour before, he greets me with a handshake in Menie Lodge, brimming with enthusiasm. He believes this is a big day for everyone in the North-east. 'We'll be giving Aberdeen and Scotland tremendous public relations because they are talking about this development all over the world,' he says.

Rumination isn't Trump's thing.

'There was a point when we got that very unexpected negative vote – it was totally unexpected – when I did say maybe it's time to pack it in,' says Trump of the council's decision to reject the plan. 'But, you know, I just don't give up. For some reason in my life, I've just never given up. The economy is tough, there are lots of places you can spend money today, and I did question that for a while. But I felt that the land is so amazing, and I do have my heart in Scotland because of my mother, that I wanted to go on.'

The amazing land. Scotland. My mother.

Sometimes it feels like you're pulling a string in Trump's back.

This, however, is the art of abstraction. Trump has found his riff and is happy to leave you to change the chords underneath, to give his answer a new context. We've ended up with the rhetorical equivalent of a dance loop. *The amazing land. Scotland. My mother.* It has started to feel like Mary MacLeod is still alive, that she might show up on the estate and thrust a broom into the hands of Michael Forbes. Out on the course Trump had asked if the 'lakes' (ponds below the Menie Dome) were being kept. It wasn't a request, more a casual inquiry. Trump, remember, prefers waves and waterfalls: perpetual motion.

'We've hired many people from the area,' he says. 'Employees are ready to go and we will be creating many jobs in the long term.'

Before I leave, Trump does a piece to camera for the *Evening Express*'s Aberdeen Champions, an annual celebration of people who have served their community, overcome adversity, or shone in sports. The Trump Organization has sponsored one of the categories. I hand Trump a quarter-page of script. He studies it for a minute, asks some questions, then falls silent. He sits. And sits. I'm wondering if he needs a prompt when he launches into, 'I'm Donald Trump . . .' He wings it, mentioning his ancestry, telling people they're all winners.

'It's much better if you can get it on the first take,' he says, pleased with his impromptu performance. Trump stands and straightens his jacket. 'That'll be a million dollars.'

Down on the estate, guests are starting to arrive. A security guard is posted on a dune, one of dozens of people on protection detail. Music is played across the sands: Wagner's 'Ride of Valkyries'. It puts you in mind of *Apocalypse Now* and Lieutenant Colonel Bill Kilgore's Tannoy-armed helicopter. Will Trump turn up musing, 'I love the smell of herbicide in the morning'? Probably not, but it does feel like we're at an outpost, on the fringe of a war zone awaiting the arrival of a heavily-guarded commander.

When Trump steps from a Range Rover he is greeted by the more genial sound of two pipers. He's in his Cashmere coat, serious again. After privately welcoming guests, he steps onto a podium with Aberdeen's Lord Provost and Don Jr, who makes the welcome address.

'It has been a long time in the making and we are really here to get going,' says Don Jr. 'It was spectacular for me to be able to walk a final version of the course with my father, to say this is now what we're doing, this is what will be etched into this land forever.'

The Lord Provost is next. 'Even as non-golfer, I can say that the excitement in this is absolutely outstandingly wonderful.'

Absolutely outstandingly wonderful. Even Trump would struggle to match that kind of hyperbole.

'I would like today, to these two gentlemen, to present them with the City Council plaque, which would perhaps indicate the support that they've had and will continue to receive from the City Council.'

As civic honours go, it's a bizarre one.

'I would say to them both, thank you for coming to Scotland in the first place and proceeding with your development. Not without its difficulties, I would have to say, but proceeding with great heart.'

The difficulty, in this case, being the manner in which Aberdeenshire Council discharged its democratic duty.

Trump moves to the mike. 'Well, I'd to thank everybody for being here, but much more importantly for their tremendous support. We have so many friends in the audience and they've been here right from the beginning. I also want to thank George Sorial and Sarah Malone and all of my staff. They've been amazing. A man who is one of the great architects of the world – in the world of golf – Martin Hawtree, is with us. Where is Martin . . . Come on up here, Martin . . . You have to be up here.'

Hawtree looks as though he would rather be back in the dunes.

Trump talks about meeting R&A Chief Executive Peter Dawson.

'I said, "Peter, I'd like a reference. Who would be the best architect for what we want to do, environmentally speaking and from the golf standpoint?" And he said, "I recommend strongly Martin Hawtree." I said, "Well, what happens if I don't get Martin, who would you recommend second?" He said, "My second recommendation would also be Martin Hawtree." So I had no choice, I had to get Martin Hawtree. And I got him.'

Trump explains where Menie will fit into his golfing portfolio.

'We have twelve world-ranked golf clubs right now. I have one on the Pacific Ocean, I have one on the Atlantic, I have one in Palm Beach. You know, I have great stuff, but this is something that is really beyond . . . We think that when we have our next meeting of this group we'll be cutting a ribbon, Martin, and that won't be in too long, probably in less than eighteen months. And we'll have created hopefully a masterpiece, a masterpiece that Aberdeen and Scotland can be really proud of.'

To finish, Trump invites some questions from the media, corralled in a separate part of the marquee. 'Some nice ones,' he adds hopefully. Trump is asked what he would say to people who believe he has 'ridden roughshod over planning legislation'.

'There really is little controversy,' says Trump. 'There's tremendous support for this project. One of the papers had a headline saying, "Trump met by protestors as he gets off his plane". So I figured I'd have thousands of people. There were two people and a dog, and the dog looked more vicious than the people. They were nice people – they were waving to me – I said, "Are they on my side?"'

Forbes denied he had reneged on any land deal with Trump – that there had been any handshakes. 'It doesn't bother me what he says,' he stated.

Even as late as spring 2010, the Trump Organization believed it might strike a deal with Michael Forbes, that the boss's criticism could somehow be modulated and a peace treaty produced. Now the talk was of building an equipment hangar next to Mill of Menie.

George Sorial wanted the council to consider using the new Housing (Scotland) Act to serve a maintenance order on Forbes. 'Obviously, anyone who sees that property realises that it's a complete disaster and an environmental embarrassment that cannot be left the way it is,' he said. 'If ever there was a situation to implement these laws, then this is it.'

Forbes was bemused. 'I think local authority people around the country will have to tell an awful lot of farmers and other folk to clean up their properties,' he said.

Tripping Up Trump had called the one-acre plot, bought from Forbes, The Bunker. The owners included Lord Puttnam, Sue Edwards, Martin Glegg, David Milne. 'Compulsory purchase for this kind of project would set a very dangerous precedent for all of Scotland,' said Puttnam.

'The reason we are doing this is to defend the families threatened by a compulsory purchase,' said Glegg.

Martin Ford saw the purchase as a linking of arms to 'defend the basic human rights of others against a bullying developer and a spineless council'. 'In these new circumstances, it would also be suicidal for the council to go down the compulsory purchase route, since that now comes with a guarantee of involvement in a lengthy legal battle with residents from across Aberdeenshire and beyond,' he said.

Ford may have been right about the ramifications, but the number of owners was not a material planning consideration.

According to lawyer Elaine Farquharson-Black, what mattered was whether the plots were needed 'to fulfill the best planning objectives for the land'. The fact Trump stood to make a profit was also an irrelevance. More than a dozen homes were due to be demolished for Aberdeen's bypass, which had been promoted by the trunk road agency because the dual carriageway would help speed goods to market, people to places of employment, service new industrial sites, and encourage tourism. Aberdeen City Council had reached for CPOs to help turn a former college into an oil company office. CPOs cleared the titles on parts of land site in unknown ownership, allowing transfer to the developer.

Land doesn't have to be 'indispensable' to justify the use of CPOs: case law has determined it is enough for land to be 'required' by a developer, and a salubrious view from a hotel window was certainly something Donald Trump required. Bob Reid, a former Aberdeen City Council planning director and now one of Scotland's most respected planning consultants, said: 'The legislation concerning CPOs is most often used to facilitate access to land-locked sites. The classic defence is to show that another access arrangement is equally or better suited to servicing that land. The defence that any land-owner would mount would be that his or her land was not required for the development because other eminently practical arrangements exist.'

Martin Ford fervently believed homes should not be sacrificed for the 'convenience' of a developer. He had a hunch colleagues lacked the nerve to back CPOs, and was determined to end what he saw as procrastination. Ford tabled a question asking the provost (chairman of the council) and committee heads to reassure Menie residents they would not support CPOs. 'It's an issue of principle which is fairly easily judged – this is largely a housing estate,' said Ford. 'The possibility of CPOs is effectively pressure to sell. It could go on for ages. The Trump Organization may never make a request. A policy of not telling residents is absolutely unfair.' The provost restated the council's support for CPOs in the 'general public interest'. He ruled out the question going to anyone else.

Trump could always look to Edinburgh for affirmative action. As well as confirming CPOs acquired by local authorities, the Scottish Government could make its own orders. Taking land at Menie might be viewed as consistent with the granting of outline planning permis-sion: it would expedite delivery of a development already judged to be in the public interest. After all, you wouldn't tell someone they could have your car then deny them the key. True, the scheme put before the public inquiry didn't include the four homes in question, but a masterplan including the sites *had* been approved.

Don Jr estimated the Trump Organization had spent $1 million dollars dealing with 'bullshit' – cynical attempts to impede progress at Menie. The company thought the exhaustive planning examina-tion had made any case against the resort un-winnable. They figured

Molly Forbes had been persuaded to take them to the Court of Session over the masterplan because she had few assets: Paradise wasn't much worth should Trump decide to go after his costs. But losing first required a ruling, so for objectors winning the argument wasn't so important. Keeping the argument going was.

That's why TUT was looking to further divide the Mill of Menie plot, excitedly reporting that 5,000 prospective owners had contacted them in the space of two days. They were aiming for 15,000 – three square feet per person. The tactic was to delay and disrupt any attempted land-grab: the validity of an order made by the Ministers could be contested in the Court of Session. Campaign group Road Sense had halted the building of Aberdeen's bypass by challenging the remit of a public inquiry, which had considered the merits of the preferred route rather than the need for the road itself.

As for the length of a judicial review, that would depend on how the CPOs were drafted, the financial bravery of the Bunker's owners, and the disposition of the judge. 'Comprehensive CPOs covering many land ownerships are not uncommon, but each landowner might want his day in court,' said Bob Reid. 'But judges could take a dim view of the law being manipulated in such a fashion and might require a "group action", at least as the first case.' The Trump Organization didn't fear a war of attrition. It was often how Trump got what he wanted. 'We're usually the bigger party,' said George Sorial.

'The recommendation is to refuse,' says John Loveday, turning to item 6B on the Formartine Area Committee agenda.

Item 6B is a council report on the Trump Organization's efforts to comply with dozens of planning conditions laid down by the Scottish Government. The work includes providing a blueprint for the layout of buildings and roads, and an environmental management plan.

Chairman Loveday corrects himself. The recommendation is very much to approve. 'I'll stop before I go any more red-faced,' he says.

A report by head of development services Sonya Galloway couldn't be more effusive. She has judged the masterplan 'a visionary document which establishes key strategic directions, design parameters and provides a framework for managing the overall phased development'. Even SNH is impressed, commenting that the layout is 'more sympathetic and intuitive'.

Councillor Allan Hendry wants to establish if any complaints about vandalism have been made against Trump. He is looking at Paul Johnston as he speaks. Officers say no. 'I would move that we approve the application without any further ado,' says Hendry forcibly.

'People haven't had a chance to ask questions,' says Loveday.

Queries follow about buggies and public access, but little else.

Debra Storr asks the committee to reject the masterplan, claiming it is 'not deliverable'. 'We actually don't know what changes will be needed in the event of non-availability of the land,' she says. Ninety-three of 161 objections – more than half of which have come from outside the North-east – were made 'purely on the grounds that the masterplan did not show the existing homes on the site'. In her report, Ms Galloway has stressed this is a framework to *guide* development.

Storr recounts the burying of the Scottish coastal village of Culbin by a sandstorm in 1694. She directs the Trump Organization to 'history' and wishes them 'good luck' with the masterplan.

It sounds like an imprecation. You expect her to cackle and disappear in a puff of smoke. 'Thanks for your concern,' says George Sorial from the public benches, a few feet away. On this occasion, Loveday lets Sorial's comment go. There is now a palpable sense of weariness over the masterplan. Even Storr seems to have Trump fatigue. 'I know you're all going to disagree with me,' she says of her motion to reject.

And that's just what councillors do, all but Paul Johnston backing Rob Merson's amendment to approve. 'We see a very responsible approach has been taken in meeting the conditions,' says Merson.

Council leader Anne Robertson agrees. 'I do think we need to move this on.'

After travelling maybe 250,000 miles to attend meetings like this, George Sorial would doubtless agree.

'The Formartine Area Committee took a huge step forward today to bring significant investment to the North-east,' says Sorial. 'They should be proud and commended for that. We're certainly very grateful. This is a council that is very business-minded, that understands what we're doing here. That really wants to open the door for not just this investment but other significant investments in the North-east of Scotland.'

Trump is naturally 'very honoured' by the 9-2 vote. 'I pledge to do a truly wonderful job,' he says. 'We just want to get this thing going.' Something is niggling him, though. A Scottish newspaper has reported that his golf courses don't rank among the world's best. Trump's courses do have their accolades.

'Should I send you a list?' he asks.

A lot had changed in the four years since Trump first visited Menie. He had become a father for the fifth time and a grandfather for the first. The United States had a new president and Britain a new prime minister, both elections carrying a semblance of historic change. People still believed in money but their faith had been shaken: the financial markets continued to quiver, Greece requiring a European Union bailout to avoid going bankrupt. The harshest winter in a generation and a flatulent Icelandic volcano had served to remind people in the UK of nature's anarchic streak. Even Tiger Woods was looking vulnerable as he flailed at his ball on his return to golf and quit a tournament for the first time as a professional, complaining of a cricked neck.

The United Nations was now focusing on saving habitats and species as well as the atmosphere, entities people could see and coo over. A report by Pavan Sukhdev, a former senior banker with Deutsche Bank, speculated that the cost-benefit ratio of preserving the Earth's bio-diversity would be even higher than that of cutting carbon emissions. Sukhdev wanted countries and conglomerates to rethink their relationship with natural resources – with fines for anyone who ignored the injunction.

Maldivian President Mohamed Nasheed was calling for protest marches in the United States to persuade the establishment to take climate change seriously. Nasheed, interviewed by video link for a UK book festival, intimated that any species smart enough to trash a planet could salvage it: 'By simply believing in life you can get out of situations. I believe in human ingenuity.'

US biologist Craig Venter may well have agreed. He had just announced the production of the world's first synthetic cell, having persuaded a chemical concoction to set up home in a bacterium shell and start replicating. The pay-off for the Earth? Venter wanted to create algae able to capture CO_2 from the air. Biological sequestration was also being championed by the National Oceanography Centre at the University of Southampton, which proposed spraying the seas with iron sulphate to promote the growth of CO_2-absorbing phytoplankton. The dead blooms, it was hoped, would lie inert on the cold, sunless ocean floor, with the carbon fixed in their bodies.

Political line-ups were changing too. Paul Johnston was expelled from the local Liberal Democrat group, the fourth departure since Trump arrived on the scene. Sam Coull said Johnston had been left with a 'stiletto in his back' after 'the longest execution ever'. Martin Ford, another member of the Democratic Independent Party led by Johnston, called the expulsion 'unjust and unjustifiable'.

Ford had been equally disconsolate after Sue Edwards took just 752 votes out of the 48,825 cast in Gordon at the Westminster election. The SNP came a distant second behind the Lib Dems. The Conservatives snuck into power but secured only one seat in Scotland, causing Alex Salmond to question their mandate to govern north of the border. Not that he had reason to rest up in his homeland: a poll carried out three weeks after the election by TNS-BMRB showed the SNP's support in Scotland down from thirty-five per cent to twenty-nine per cent at the start of the year and Labour's up from thirty-seven per cent to forty-five per cent. Plans for a St Andrew's Day referendum on independence were postponed.

There was some cheer. Salmond was pushing for fiscal autonomy and hailed the biggest North Sea oil find in nine years as proof Scotland could be financially independent. In the twenty-sixth round of exploration licensing, bids for 356 blocks were made, the highest since drilling started in 1964.

At Menie, Neil Hobday's consultancy role (for a rumoured £20,000 a month) was at an end. The Trump Organization issued a statement acknowledging the 'important role' Hobday had played early on, adding: 'Neil is currently pursuing other business interests and his departure was voluntary.' The appointment of Sarah Malone long before any grass had been planted may have compromised Hobday's job as Project Director. Nobody was saying. Trump valued discretion in employees, and the world of international golf development was comparatively small. Trump said Hobday remained a 'friend' of the project and promised to write him a 'very strong reference'.

The investigation into the £50,000 wrecking spree at Menie was dropped but police were kept busy. They were called to the estate after a woman was found riding her horse back and forth across the fifteenth green. It happened the evening before Trump returned to New York. Trump didn't want the rider – held by security guards – charged, just spoken to. Michael Forbes wasn't extended the same clemency when he reportedly removed twenty flags used to mark the estate boundary. Forbes thought the flags were on his land, and handed them over to officers when they turned up at his house, but was still charged with theft after allegedly stealing the flags. He was given a 'formal adult warning letter', used where an officer 'believes a relatively minor crime has been committed and the person involved has no notable history of involvement with the police'.

At Aberdeen Sheriff Court, a jury took four hours to convict nine members of Plane Stupid of breach of the peace. The protestors had been on trial accused of forcing the closure of Aberdeen Airport, preventing an aircraft from landing and taking off, and putting people in a state of fear and alarm. Emerging from court, James Kerr said: 'The law may have found us guilty of breach of the peace but in the court of public opinion we have received overwhelming support. We have been found guilty of breach of the peace but we do not think of ourselves as criminals. We have taken action to prevent climate change.'

Matilda Gifford said: 'Now that the court has heard expert witnesses testify to the imperative need to cut emissions, they are mandated to prosecute the real criminals – the corporations who are profiting from polluting.'

On 29 June, the first of the detailed plans were brought before the Formartine Area Committee for determination. The application for the championship course was recommended for approval by planning officer Sonya Galloway:

> It is noted that the development proposals already consented at Menie which include as an integral part the championship golf course are acknowledged within the forward looking Aberdeen City and Shire Structure Plan 2009 as an asset within the Aberdeen to Peterhead strategic growth area.

The pertinacious Debra Storr moved to reject partly on the grounds that detailed plans were not being brought forward as a whole, her reading of the conditions imposed by the Scottish Government. Rob Merson called the grumble that housing *wasn't* on the table a 'volte-face'. Allan Hendry was surprised there were any plans left to discuss. 'Mr Trump must be sick to the back teeth,' he said.

Storr's motion was seconded by Jim Gifford (Paul Johnston was absent), but only, he said, in 'the interests of democracy'. He didn't support it, and building permission was granted by 8-1 votes.

Afterwards, Sue Edwards complained Sonya Galloway had been 'rolling her eyes at George Sorial' as Storr spoke. I phoned Trump at home within a few hours of the decision. He was getting ready to shoot *The Apprentice* but wanted to talk. He thanked the council, the 'dynamic' people, the 'tremendous' business community. He sounded different – less stagey, more ebullient, unashamedly so. 'Now I just hope we can work together to get the Open to come to Aberdeen,' he said.

A few weeks later, the Great Dunes were being patted into shape.

Chapter 14

TICKING ALL THE BOXES

The preparations are underway. A stand is taking shape next to the first tee. The rigging of scaffolding chimes out across the fairway like a church bell: a proclamatory sound, rich with import. Out on the links, ground staff are spreading sand to suppress coarser grasses so that finer strains can poke through; grass that will be trodden and baked and trodden again until the burnished earth has a golden sheen. Back at the first, tourists photograph the nascent stand, steel poles and rows of empty plastic seats.

The Open is coming and the St Andrews Old Course is awaiting its congregation.

There are three months to go before the championship arrives in the Fife town. Presentation work on the course has been going on for rather longer.

Six hundred years ago people started to clear a path through the gorse as they travelled to and from the medieval harbour in the Eden estuary. Shepherds, left alone with their flock, are credited with inventing the game of golf after using their crooks to knock stones into holes. St Andrews produced the template for the modern game in 1764 when players settled on eighteen holes. Ten years earlier the Royal and Ancient Golf Club was founded under its original name of the Society of St Andrews Golfers. The R&A's squat, sandstone office is next to the first tee.

'You take people to that first tee and they all experience the same buzz, even if they have played plenty of times,' says Mike Woodcock of St Andrews Links Trust, the body that manages the Old Course and the six other public courses. 'They have seen the black-and-white images of Bobby Jones, they know the game as we know it today came from this piece of land. It feels as if you are stepping on a stage. You can play the Old Course in January and there will still be people watching you. You get round to the seventeenth and you might get people applauding you from the hotel and from the road and enjoying it with you . . . and you get to the eighteenth and there are more people with cameras and videos, having their picture taken with you in the background.'

Augusta, Pebble Beach and the Old Course – the three courses people most want to play, says Mike.

'I have taken part in golf shows and events around the world, as far afield as Russia and Mexico, and people either can't wait to tell you they have been here, or that they are coming, or that they want to go. A Japanese TV producer who came to St Andrews said it was the sporting equivalent of seeing the Golden Gate Bridge or the Sydney Opera House. When Jack Nicklaus played the Open for his last professional round at the Old Course in 2005 there were 55,000 people here. When he went on the Swilcan Bridge, Tom Watson, whom he had been paired with, was in tears. It has that effect even on top sportsmen.'

Jack Nicklaus said no other golf course gets 'remotely close' for generating a sense of occasion. Tiger Woods, another double winner at the venue, called St Andrews his 'favourite course in the world'. Mike tries to explain why players of their stature feel that way about the Old Course.

'The defining characteristic is that by and large the Old Course has evolved naturally over time. There are hollows that were originally shaped by sheep sheltering from the wind. Some of the biggest bunkers on the course were made that way. You can be safely on the fairway and not really have a line for a shot at the green, or you can find yourself on the green with a sixty or seventy-yard putt. There are a lot of hanging lies and a lot of mounds and shapes guarding the greens and very subtle borrows on the greens themselves. It is as much a game of chess as it is a game of golf.

'Players have to plot their way around the course and those who win at St Andrews tend to be those who are best able to adapt as Tiger did in 2000 when he managed to avoid finding any of the 112 bunkers on the course in four days of golf.'

We are sitting in the Trust's Pilmour House, near the fifteenth fairway of the Old Course. The course itself is on public land owned by the local authority, having been gifted to the people by King David I in 1123.

Dr Alister MacKenzie spent time surveying the layout of the Old Course before designing Augusta National in Georgia with American Bobby Jones, a winner at St Andrews in 1927. Jones said he wanted the second shot to be 'simpler in proportion to the excellence of the first' by offering more green to aim at or a chance to attack the pin. The mathematical elegance – the just ratios and innate topographical balance – owed much to his Fife forays. Jones wrote of Augusta: 'It will never become hopeless for the duffer, nor fail to concern and interest the expert. And it will be found, like old St Andrews, to become more delightful the more it is studied and played.'

The Old Course isn't much to look at. It takes a rolling ball to emphasise its delicate curves. Mike readily concedes there are tougher courses, more 'visually appealing' courses, not just around the world but here in St Andrews. There is, however, a purity to the way the Old Course plays, a certain fidelity. It is the very embodiment of a sporting chance.

'There are not really any gimmicks out there,' says Mike. 'You can go quite far without finding trouble but if you do find trouble you will be severely punished. It is all about variation; it is about a subtlety of challenge. It is a course that challenges the top professionals but also gives an enjoyable experience to an average player like myself. It never plays the same twice. Every time you play the Old Course, you learn something else new about it.'

Maybe this was how to see the Old Course. As a benevolent playing partner, imparting its wisdom to the patient disciple.

The course is not a work of art, not when it was styled by sheep and people looking for a shortcut to the harbour. Rather, it is a foil to the artist in all golfers, the would-be Bobby Jones. When you step onto the first tee you behold an elemental landscape, lightly inscribed by history: the soil and grass await your narrative. The course is there to inspire rather than intimidate; to engage the golfer in mind and body; to encourage people to do better; perhaps, even, to ennoble. When someone steps from the eighteenth green their head is usually held a little higher, regardless of how they have played.

Trump's visit in May had ended with him playing the first nine holes of Royal Aberdeen, part of the sand sheet that bunches towards Menie. Trump applauded the club for its support – and turned praise for the course into greater approbation for his own. 'The big dunes are in the middle,' he said. 'Royal Aberdeen is at the end, at the smallest part of the dunes. The world considers the front nine of Royal Aberdeen to be the best nine holes of golf anywhere in the dunes, so that's it.'

Listings of great golf courses do exist, compiled by panels of players, designers and scribes. The game's oldest ranking system was established in 1966 by *Golf Digest* magazine. In putting together a shortlist of some 1,000 courses, it contacts golf associations, federations and unions around the world. More than 800 panellists, including the magazine's twenty-eight foreign editors, then evaluate everything from the condition of the grass to the ambience of the fairways. Scoring for 'shot values' carries double the weighting of any other criterion.

In 2009/10 Augusta National edged Pine Valley among US courses. Royal County Down in Northern Ireland was ranked best in the rest of the world, ahead of the Old Course, which was number one in 2005/6. *Golf Digest*'s list tends to change because courses change. Even the great ones are regularly tweaked. Old Tom Morris, who designed Royal County Down, finessed the Old Course.

Golfweek claims to have 'the most respected ranking structure in the industry'. Nearly 500 assessors measure more than 2,200 courses against ten standards, including the 'variety and memorability' of the holes. A 'walk in the park' rating quantifies the 'degree to which the course ultimately is worth spending a half-day on as a compelling outdoor experience'. Of the US's classic courses, Pine Valley and Cypress Point came top in 2010. Royal County Down and the Old Course occupied the same positions for the whole of Great Britain and Ireland but with lower scores than either American course.

Golf Magazine – featuring 'the most thorough and respected rankings in golf' – does produce an absolute list, a biennial Top 100 Courses in the World. In 2009, the top spots went to Pine Valley, Cypress Point, Augusta, the Old Course (the designer described as 'Nature') and Royal County Down. Brian Morgan, one of 100 judges, believes Menie is the 'best piece of land in Scotland' but stops short of comparing it with Pine Valley or Cypress Point (another Alister MacKenzie design) because they are different *types* of courses. Pine Valley is secreted within a New Jersey forest (it barely has room for spectators) while Cypress Point is draped over a serrated Californian headland. That said, Morgan doesn't hesitate to suggest that Menie 'has the potential to be among the world's top ten'.

So far, Bedminster has been Trump's only top-rated course. In 2009 it was fifth in *Golf Digest*'s Best New Private Courses, thirteenth in *Golfweek*'s Best New Courses, and fifty-fourth in *Golf Magazine*'s Top Courses in the US.

Such assessments will always be subject to prejudice and infatuation but the different lists do throw up a recurring feature. The chart-toppers tend to have been around for a long time. Pine Valley opened in 1918, Cypress Point in 1928, Augusta in 1932: the United States has younger cities. Royal County Down welcomed its first golfers in 1889, just four years after Trump's grandfather Friedrich Drumpf arrived in America from Germany. Tested by a number of practitioners over a number of years, they are technically as well as aesthetically complete. Repeated experimentation has corroborated the 'greatest course' theory, converted opinion into an approximation of fact.

Toby Ingleton of *Golf Course Architecture*, a publication dedicated to design, visited the Menie site in June 2010 and was 'very impressed' by the setting. Becoming the best in the world was a different matter:

> Enjoyment of golf is influenced by many different factors and individuals will inevitably have different interpretations. It's a bit like saying I'm going to create the world's best piece of music. Trump could, I suppose, be saying 'this course will be at No. 1 on some magazine's world's best list', but I'd be amazed if that happened with any of those publications that take their rankings seriously. Those courses that regularly appear towards the top of published lists – such as Pine Valley, Augusta National, St Andrews Old and Muirfield – are all steeped in history. The greatest modern courses rarely make a significant impact, with the occasional groundbreaking exception such as Sand Hills in Nebraska.

Trump had, however, espied a shortcut to stateliness, a way of making the newish venerable. If he could secure the Open Championship, he would have just about the biggest endorsement going in golf, the finest accolade of all, perhaps. Casper Grauballe, part of Martin Hawtree's Menie team, thinks no course could ever truly be considered number one without having first hosted a major and withstood the most exacting test of all. He recognises the inchoate brilliance of the land he is working with, but also the advantages of letting the world's best loose on it:

> If you take some of the renowned links courses around the world, you can have a stretch of holes that are great. I think this site has the opportunity to give us the full package. On any other site just to have one of these holes would make the golf course. We've got eighteen of them. There shouldn't be anything stopping it becoming the best in the world but they could say that if it hasn't hosted a major it hasn't been put to the ultimate test.

Brian Morgan suggests the Scottish Open might satisfy the Grauballe Test. If Trump bought the rights and the venue was switched from Loch Lomond (far from the sea) to Menie, it could draw the bulk of the Open field by offering players a chance to warm-up on a links in the week before the main event. Tiger Woods might choose Scotland instead of Ireland to practise. But Grauballe's statement is axiomatic: it takes the ultimate prize to produce the ultimate play.

The trouble with shortcuts is that the route can be uncertain and the ground uneven. Trials can lie along the way.

American golf writer Michael Bamberger was given a tour of Trump's courses and the Menie site. When asked afterwards by Trump to pick his favourite course, Bamberger found himself opting for the one that hadn't been built. He thought Menie and its possibilities 'astonishing', reporting that it felt like 'golf's home'. But Bamberger said Trump raised 'questions of style, right down to how he names his courses' and doubted he would land the US Open or its British equivalent:

> Whatever he builds in Scotland, I don't imagine it's ever getting a British Open. The men at the Royal and Ancient Golf Club, curators of the Open Championship, aren't interested in new and don't care about the best this and the biggest that . . . The very idea of Trump won't fly with them, at least not for the world's oldest golf championship. Taking a page from their book might be a good thing for him, and maybe he will.

When it comes to the R&A, Trump has been attentive and unusually compliant, admitting to being 'very much guided' by the governing body and giving them 'carte blanche' to say what they think of his plans. 'We would hope that we would build something whereby we would be able to get a British Open over a period of time,' he said. 'Not too long.' The R&A is too discreet to talk about Trump. Neil Hobday had defended the R&A's conservatism: 'Whilst they obviously cannot commit, they say they are totally open-minded about it.'

In the spring of 2010, Trump spent £330,000 to have bespoke turf (a mix of coastal grasses like fescue and brown top bent) grown under cover in Lincolnshire, England, for the tees and greens, turf that would be laid like carpet.

'It will slot right in,' said Links Superintendent Paul O'Connor. 'The terrain is mind-blowingly good but we have to complement that with the condition of the greens. Courses are always judged on their greens . . . You want to build a course that would appear to have been there for generations but with proper attention to detail it will be right ahead of the modern game. The course will tick all the boxes. It would undoubtedly be good enough to hold the Open. This is tailor-made for the championship.'

'The Open is out of my hands,' admitted Trump. 'We will present them with a canvas that's the best anywhere in the world. The rest is going to be up to Peter Dawson and the Royal & Ancient.'

Nine venues currently take turns at hosting the Open: St Andrews, Carnoustie, Muirfield, Royal Birkdale, Royal Liverpool, Royal Lytham, Royal St George's, Royal Troon, and Turnberry. Five have fallen off the rota: Prestwick, Musselburgh, Prince's, Royal Cinque Ports, and Royal Portrush in Northern Ireland, which made its only appearance in 1951. Some venues have been found wanting because they cannot accommodate the infrastructure needed to handle tens of thousands of spectators and the demands of the media, as well as the technology that allows players to thump a ball 300-plus yards off the tee. The Old Course has added around 200 yards across six holes since 2000.

Trump's course will have five tee positions on every hole and plenty of space to hit balls before going out. Two access roads and a 450-bedroom hotel should take care of transportation and accommodation demands. The Trump Organization has been quietly pushing for Aberdeen's bypass and the doubling of the trunk road past the Menie Estate to be completed in time for the course opening.

It is also keen to see a runway extension progressed at Aberdeen Airport, one that would allow for direct flights between the city and North America.

Menie, then, has it all.

Except, that is, tradition.

The Open has been at St Andrews a record twenty-eight times. No new course has made the rota since Turnberry in 1977. The Ayrshire links had been maturing for twenty-six years prior to its inclusion, and, perhaps more tellingly, had been a favourite place to knock balls about since the turn of the twentieth century. To find another new entrant you have to go back to 1954 and Royal Birkdale in north-west England. That club was founded in 1889 and the transformation that produced a course worthy of the Open took place in 1932, carried out by J.H. Taylor and a certain Frederick Hawtree, grandfather of Martin.

'The Menie course will have qualities which Royal Birkdale doesn't, namely a very fine view of the sea from many of the holes,' said Hawtree, who worked on Birkdale with his father. 'It is a wonderful site. It has space. It has length. It will certainly be as testing as the existing Open Championship golf courses. The more I go onto the site the more I enjoy the site and believe it will one day make a tremendous golf course.'

Good enough for the Open?

'It may happen one day.'

Good enough to be the world's best?

'It's difficult to say but it's got to be. Here is a man, 3,500 miles away, investing a lot of money in a project which simply can't be a respectable second or third best.'

Martin Hawtree describes Trump's desire to host an Open within his own lifetime as an ambition of 'Damoclean' proportions.

Damocles was the guy in Greek legend who had a bit of bother with a sword. The anecdote goes that Damocles kept flattering his boss Dionysius by telling him what a terrific house he had, how much he liked his clothes and trinkets. Dionysius, perhaps sensing a covetous tone or simply tired of the sycophancy, invited Damocles to be a tyrant for the night. So there's Damocles, luxuriating on a golden couch, tended by nubile waiters and anointers, when he notices hanging above his head a sword, suspended by a single horse hair. Well, that rather puts a damper on the evening, and Damocles leaves. Life as Dionysius isn't the party he had imagined.

In trying to turn a pile of sand into the world's best golf course, in striving to know paradise on Earth, Donald Trump has been sitting under any number of swords, sharpened by protesters and sympathetic politicians. Some of those swords have twirled and glinted and threatened to drop. Unlike Damocles, Trump has so far stayed put. He has risked his money, his time, his reputation. The project might yet be judged a failure – the course great but not the greatest.

It is hard to conceive that Menie – a Scottish links – could be regarded as the world's best without having first hosted an Open, without the ground having been consecrated. The blessing of the R&A would not in itself make it number one; patently, the nine courses on the Open rota cannot all be the mightiest. But should Trump ever find the governing body knocking on his door, asking if one July they might borrow his links – this skelp of land devoid of golfing history or heritage, a venue promoted with vaudevillian gusto to the most reactionary of sports – then it will surely be because there is no finer place on Earth to whack a wee ball with a stick.

APPENDIX A

The Players

Sue Edwards. Aberdeenshire resident and spokeswoman for TUT, which is opposed to building on the dunes and the use of compulsory purchase orders.

Mickey Foote. A member of protest groups Sustainable Aberdeenshire and Tripping Up Trump (TUT). Lives next to the Menie Estate.

Michael Forbes. A quarry worker. Owner of a twenty-three-acre plot of land included in the Menie resort masterplan. Sold one acre to protest group TUT.

Molly Forbes. Michael's mother. Lives near her son in a mobile home called Paradise.

Martin Ford, Debra Storr, Paul Johnston. Aberdeenshire councillors who are among Trump's arch critics. They voted to reject the Menie Estate plans and were objectors at the public inquiry.

Dr Christine Gore. Head of Aberdeenshire Council's planning service. Her officers advise councillors on whether to approve or reject applications.

Tom Griffin. US lawyer who sold the Menie Estate to Trump. Formerly a legal adviser to the oil and gas industry in Aberdeen.

Martin Hawtree. Head of the oldest continuous golf design company in the world. Produced the layout for the Menie championship course. An advisor to the Open Championship.

Neil Hobday. Golf course development consultant. Project Director on the Menie Estate from 2006 to 2010.

John Loveday. Aberdeenshire councillor and chairman of the Formartine Area Committee.

Sarah Malone. Executive Vice President of Trump International – Scotland. Formerly Executive Director of the Gordon Highlanders Museum in Aberdeen.

David Milne. Health and safety consultant. His home – an old Coastguard Station – is included in the Menie Estate masterplan. Has vowed never to sell to Trump.

Brian Morgan. Scottish photographer and golf course development consultant who promoted the potential of the Menie site.

Anne Robertson. Aberdeenshire Council leader who appeared in support of Trump at the public inquiry. Member of the Formartine Area Committee, the local planning board covering Menie.

Alex Salmond. Scotland's First Minister and leader of the Scottish National Party. Member of the Scottish Parliament for Gordon, the constituency that includes the Menie Estate.

George Sorial. Trump Organization's International Development Director. Real-estate lawyer who replaced Ashley Cooper on the Menie Estate project.

Donald Trump. Billionaire Chief Executive of the Trump Organization. New York real-estate developer whose interests include golf courses. Star of The Apprentice and best-selling writer.

Donald Trump Jr. Trump's eldest son. The family representative on the Menie Estate project. Heads up the development team with Sarah Malone and George Sorial.

APPENDIX B

Timeline of Key Events

2006

12 January. Rumours emerge that Trump is in talks with Aberdeenshire Council officers about a golf course development in the North-east of Scotland.

28 April. On a visit to Aberdeen, Donald Trump reveals his plan to build 'the greatest golf course anywhere in the world' at the Menie Estate in Aberdeenshire.

27 November. A plan for two championship golf courses, a 450-room hotel and almost 1,000 holiday homes on the Menie Estate is put forward.

2007

11 September. Aberdeenshire Council's planners recommend supporting the scheme, saying it's an opportunity that 'must be grasped', despite the adverse impacts on the environment.

20 November. The council's local planning board – the Formartine Area Committee (FAC) – backs the plan. Nine days later, the more powerful Infrastructure Services Committee rejects it on the casting vote of Chairman Martin Ford.

4 December. The Scottish Government calls in the application because of its 'national significance'. The move comes a day after First Minister Alex Salmond has met Trump's representatives in Aberdeen.

2008

13 March. Alex Salmond is cleared of any wrong-doing after a parliamentary inquiry into the calling-in of the Trump application.

10 June. Trump is the first witness at a four-week public inquiry into the golf resort plan.

3 November. John Swinney, Cabinet Secretary for Finance and Sustainable Growth, agrees with the public inquiry findings and grants Trump outline permission, subject to forty-six conditions.

2009

7 May. Trump announces a bid to buy four homes – Mill of Menie, Menie Fishing Station, Hermit Point, Leyton Cottage – so the land can be included in the resort plan.

1 September. FAC grants Mr Trump planning permission to include the four homes in his masterplan.

27 October. FAC gives the go-ahead to stabilise the dunes with maram grass.

23 November. Molly Forbes launches a legal challenge against Aberdeenshire Council, claiming that proper planning procedures have not been followed.

2010

6 January. The Court of Session rules that Mrs Forbes has not been able to show good reason to call a halt to work on the resort and her request for an interim interdict is refused.

8 June. FAC approves the masterplan.

29 June. FAC approves the first detailed plans to come forward – the championship course.

1 July. Construction of the championship course starts.

APPENDIX C

Directorate for Planning and Environmental Appeals
Public Local Inquiry report to the Scottish Ministers –
conclusions

This is a large and complex proposal but only the principle of the development is before Scottish Ministers and the environmental information that has been submitted is sufficient to enable the outline planning application to be determined. Further submissions made to the planning authority will have to be subject to additional environmental assessment as part of a multi-stage planning process.

The issues to be determined are whether the proposal is consistent with the relevant provisions of the development plan, in this case North-east Scotland Together – the Aberdeen and Aberdeenshire Structure Plan 2001–2016 and the Aberdeenshire Local Plan 2001; and, if not, an exception to these provisions is justified by other material considerations, which includes the conservation of the environment, of protected land and of biodiversity; the economic and social effect of the development; the need for the residential development; and national policy, in particular the Government's Economic Strategy, the national Planning Framework and NPPG 14 – Natural Heritage; and, if so, whether the proposed development would preserve the setting of the Category B Listed Menie House.

Full compliance with the development plan was never likely with a complex and unforeseen proposal on this scale. Some development plan policies support it, notably those concerned with the delivery of economic development, whilst others do not. The proposal amounts to a significant departure in respect of environmental impact, landscape impact and as the consequence of the proposed residential development. That assessment has been the consistent view of the council throughout. The issue of whether or not outline planning permission is to be granted thus falls to be made by an assessment of material considerations where the test set by NPPG 14 is of overarching importance, being the national policy applying to the country's natural heritage.

The development would have a significant adverse impact on the southern third of the Foveran Links SSSI. Here the dynamism that underpins the designation of the SSSI would, for the majority of the holes in the back nine of the championship course, be halted. Much, though not all, of the geomorphological interest in that affected part of the SSSI would be compromised alongside a major adverse effect on the coherence of the ecological structure and function of the impacted areas compromising the objectives of both designation and overall integrity.

The issue of whether outline planning permission is to be granted therefore falls to be considered against the second element of the national policy contained in NPPG 14. Based on the assessment made independently for the council we are in no doubt that the economic impact of the development would be nationally significant. It could thus make a significant contribution to achieving the Government's overarching purpose set by the Economic Strategy. Additionally the development would also contribute to delivery against the strategy contained in the National Planning Framework and other national, regional and local policies directed at diversification of the economy to achieve wider social benefits as well as the encouragement of tourism, including golf tourism. The development has the potential to deliver major benefits against economic and social objectives at national, regional and local level.

In economic, or business, terms, the residential development is required to cross-fund the development. It is not consistent with current development plan policy, but emerging strategic planning policy proposes development within this corridor. It is a material consideration that a housing development is needed on this scale to realise the economic and social benefits of the overall project; that also appears to have been the assessment of the council.

A significant visual impact within a wide zone of influence is likely and is understandably the cause of considerable concern to some, but not all, who live in the vicinity. However, the design of the golf resort will be decided by Aberdeenshire Council whose objective is to achieve better integration between a design philosophy that is genuinely iconic and the landscape, so as to achieve a reduction in landscape and visual impacts and a better relationship with existing land uses. The proposals have no direct effect on the listed Menie House and the potential effect on its setting is not such as to justify the refusal of outline planning permission.

Because of the relationship with the Ythan Estuary, Sands of Forvie and Meikle Loch SPA Scottish Ministers will have to make an appropriate assessment of the implications in view of that site's conservation objectives. Information concerning the likely impact has enabled SNH to conclude that the proposed development would not have a significant impact on the SPA, providing certain conditions are attached to an outline planning permission.

Our findings contain our conclusions on a number of other important considerations that are material. None affects our overall conclusion that the economic and social advantages of this prospective development at national, regional and local level are such as to justify, uniquely, the adverse environmental consequences caused by a development on this scale and in this location. In reaching that assessment we recognise, given the effect on environmental attributes protected for their national importance, that the national interest is invoked. That properly is a matter for Ministers; our conclusions and recommendation in favour of the outline planning application are offered to assist with that assessment.

APPENDIX D

Official Hole-by-Hole Analysis of the Course
The Championship Course – Hawtree Ltd, 26 May 2010

1. From a raised teeing position the south playing par-4 501 yard first hole wonderfully confines itself in a low valley that sets the tone for the course to come. The fairway skirts high dunes along its left and areas of heathland along its right before arriving at an elevated green location, nestled into a massive dune behind its location.

2. The North Sea is visible for the first time during the walk to the elevated second tees. From the tees on the 446-yard par-4, there is a grand and panoramic view over the golf course and surrounding countryside. The downhill tee shot is to a fairway flanked on the left by low-lying dunes that converge into it and to the right by low-lying heather. The Menie burn, which bisects the fairway, plays an important role in the hole's strategy. Placement of the tee shot as close as possible to the burn means a shorter shot and better angle to the uphill green that is naturally set in a series of low rising mounds. With the prevailing winds into the player's direction of play and an uphill approach this hole will be a stern test.

3. The first hole that plays towards the sea – this par-3 of 175 yards is a dramatic hole that plays through a high-sided valley. From

the elevated tee the topography falls sharply into a dune slack before rising slightly to a green set hard against a dune system along its right and the Blairton burn behind. A lovely viewing window of the sea, created by the high dunes system either side, dominates the hole's backdrop.

4. A formidable par-5 of nearly 525 yards; this challenging hole demands nerves and skill to negotiate it. A slightly raised tee, and with the sea in full view, the fairway is dominated by the coastal dunes along its left and the meandering Blairton burn skirting its right. Despite a wide fairway, both the features will make the hole feel narrow and intimidating but also, visually stunning. The green and its approach is located on a wonderful dune formation, elevated high above the fairway from where there is a panoramic view of much of the championship golf course to the north.

5. A 180-degree change of direction back to the Clubhouse starts with this fine mid-length par-4. A large bunker near the middle of the fairway will demand a whole range of possible choices from the tee; carry it, leave the tee shot short, or maybe skirt it left or right? The resultant decision dictating the length and difficulty of the approach to a green nicely nestled into the sloping hillside. The initial drive carry from the elevated tee is across an area of wetland to a fairway bordered on both sides by swathes of well-developed heather with marram interspersed – perhaps the most prolific example of heather of all the holes on the course. The canting right to left terrain acts as part of the strategy of the ground game and there is a nice contrast between the dune-like landscape of the hole next to the smoother more expansive landscape along the left.

6. As dramatic a par-3 hole to be found anywhere in the world, this short hole is certain to garner attention from its sheer beauty

and difficulty. The elevated tees are located on a dune that reduces in size as it moves to the left, and then massively reforms back to the right into an expansive dune crest that partially hides a generous greensite found well above the Blairton burn on the fourth hole. The vista from the tee is unmatched to the greensite that will be one of the most interesting and daunting, set in a fine series of dunes that will surround nearly three-fourths of the green; with only the front of the green exposed to the slopes and burn below.

7. One of the shorter par-4 holes on the course, the elevated series of tees encounter an undulating, much narrower dune landscape to play through than on the previous holes. The hole presents an option to drive the green from the tee, but a multitude of bunkers must be negotiated and the narrow fairway is bordered by thick areas of marram grass and heather. The greensite is a natural bowl within the dunes with steep drops off its left edge.

8. From the isolated feeling of the seventh hole, the eighth opens up again to fine vistas across the course and countryside. Elevated tees provide another unencumbered view across a hole whose essence and feel is decidedly individual to the others on the course. A medium dune system found nearly the entire left of the fairway helps turn this long par-4 hole right. Along the way there are various oddities, including isolated dune structures, extensive low-lying heather right of the fairway and a high dune structure behind the green. The elements – dunes, low lying and medium lying heather, openness, compelling topography, extreme length of hole, bold dunes back-dropping the green – all add up to make this a remarkable hole.

9. An inspiring finishing hole for the front nine, the ninth is the second par-5 hole, reaching nearly 562 yards in length. After a

generously wide landing area, the fairway narrows, winding its way through steep-sided dunes as it proceeds to the greensite. Much like the seventh, the marram grass-covered dunes create a sense of isolation and are very much part of the hole's essence.

10. The start of the back nine sets the tone for a decidedly different feeling course. From a set of tees that are found among swathes of heather, the course's general elevation starts to rise from this point allowing more views to the sea. The fairway is split in two on this par-5 hole, a natural wetland between the two fairways creating what is a rare feature on links courses, but strongly strategic. The more difficult target being the island fairway on the right, but from here the approach is shorter and with a clearer view of the green. From the left fairway, an easier target from the tees, the approach is long and blind. Low dunes border much of the hole's left edge before suddenly rising up to high conical peaks that dominate the approach and green location. The magnitude and shape of the dunes is so impressive that it forms an iconic feature to the green's surrounds.

11. A lengthy par-4 of nearly 456 yards, the dog-leg right eleventh finds itself on the edge of the dome system and the open pastureland to the left. The tee shot carries over areas of sand and marram to a fairway that will have an authentic recreation of a large dunes structure to the left helping to ensure a continuity of the links course feeling that thrives throughout the rest of the hole. The green is set into a complicated area of small dunes and will be a narrow but a deep target.

12. The drive from the main tee complex nestled against some high steep sided dunes is to the highest fairway on the course. The fairway rises upwards to a crest on the horizon that has the most unequalled view across the entire golf course site, sea and

countryside. A large created dune in the left rough helps turn the hole to the right and the fairway follows the slope of the terrain to a greensite located against a small butt dune. The valley far below the green will be extended across the approach and areas of bare sand mixed with marram will offer a new and exciting change of landscape.

13. A fine short hole that plays due east towards the sea, the 230-yard par-3 thirteenth is another memorable hole. From a series of tees from where there are panoramic glimpses of the North Sea, the tee shot is across a wide valley with the greensite located at the far side of it. Behind the greensite is a curious array of small mushroom-shaped sand dunes; an unusual but beautiful backdrop. The green is angled such that the golfer is encouraged to shape their shot left to right, particularly if the pin is positioned back right. Three bunkers guard the entire right and front of the green. The horizon line towards the sea, along with the dunes behind the green, is a fine setting for this stunning short hole.

14. The most undulating hole on the course with widespread views of the sea and coastline to the North; the fourteenth provides drama and beauty. From elevated tees the views are unparalleled in golf. The hole plunges downward into a natural dune valley to the heaving, tumbling action of the fairway below – movement that continues all the way to a green located on a natural platform above. Marram grass abounds on this hole and is the major obstacle to avoid in front or either side of a fairway that is without doubt, the most undulating of all on the course. At 437 yards the hole is formidable in length, possesses memorable topography and unforgettable views.

15. A superb par-4 of 412 yards, this hole naturally dog-legs left through a fine valley bordered to the right by a large and fluid dune system that begins as a smooth and sweeping feature before

finishing in tall dune peaks of irregular character. The left side of the hole is gentler in nature but still high enough to give a sure indication of the fairway. The hole gradually arcs at an angle from right to left with rough and sandy areas dominating the carry and left edge. Golfers will have to make a choice of how much they dare to carry; the longer the carry, the shorter and consequently easier the approach. The surface of the fairway will be simple; a sharp contrast to the fourteenth and a good example of the ever-changing topography and landscape the site offers.

16. At this point in the round the turn is made south, back in the direction of the clubhouse for the last three holes. This is a short par-3 with the tee complex set in a large dune; the different tee positions offer varying angles of play into a green that is set against a hillside right, with a series of echeloned cross bunkers moving from right to left. At 200 yards and with a wind generally in the face of the players, the hole will play longer than it appears.

17. A long and very demanding par-4, the tee shot is relatively level but to a fairway similar in stature to the fourteenth – strongly undulating. While it is bordered by high dunes along its left edge, the right of the hole will have gentler contours with landscaping in the form of bare areas of sand and marram blending together. The approach will be one of the toughest on the golf course – uphill and into the wind, a sharp drop off along much of its left edge and a tiered green set into the slope. The green will be open and receptive to long iron approaches but any shots slightly off target are sure to find the approach and greenside bunkers.

18. At 631 yards, with wind against the golfer, the final hole will provide a memorable and strong finish to the round. The elevated

tees ensure a beautiful view of the entire hole with wetland ponds bordering much of the fairway's left side and areas of heathland and marram adjacent to its right edge. Forty yards short of the green a burn angled from left to right, will be formed. It will offer a range of different choices for the approach shot. Those attempting to reach the green must carry its far edge while those leaving their approach short of the burn will then have a tricky pitch to a well protected green surrounded with swathes of heather. A fine and dramatic finishing hole to a challenging and memorable championship golf course.

FURTHER INFORMATION

Please consult the following sources for additional reading.

Aberdeenshire Council Report on Trump Plan:

http://www.aberdeenshire.gov.uk/committees/detail.asp?ref_no=8
02572870061668E80257391005F27C1

Evening Express Poll of Residents (Researcher):

http://www.ideasinpartnership.co.uk

Local Government and Communities Committee Report:

http://www.scottish.parliament.uk/nmCentre/news/
news-comm-08/clgc08-s3-002-MenieSummary.pdf

Trump Public Local Inquiry Documentation:

http://www.aberdeenshire.gov.uk/planning/inquiry/index.asp

Directorate for Planning and Environmental Appeals Report to the Scottish Ministers:

http://www.aberdeenshire.gov.uk/planning/inquiry/CINABS001.
pdf

Trump Masterplan:

http://www.aberdeenshire.gov.uk/planning/apps/detail.asp?ref_no=APP/2010/0423#proposal

Architecture and Design Scotland Report on Masterplan:

http://www.ads.org.uk/what_we_do/design_review/reports/684_trump-international-golf-course-and-resort

Lady Smith Judgement:

http://www.scotcourts.gov.uk/opinions/2010CSOH1.html

Scottish Green Party Poll on Compulsory Purchase:

http://www.scottishgreens.org.uk/news/show/6396/harvie-visits-menie-as-public-swing-against-trump-project

WWF, *Living Planet Report*:

http://assets.panda.org/downloads/living_planet_report_2008.pdf

United Nations Population Fund Report:

http://www.unfpa.org/swp/2009/en/pdf/EN_SOWP09.pdf

Institute of Mechanical Engineers Report:

http://www.imeche.org/NR/rdonlyres/77CDE5E4-CE41-4F2C-A706-A630569EE486/0/IMechE_MAG_Report.PDF

Planning (Scotland) Act, 2006:

http://www.opsi.gov.uk/legislation/scotland/acts2006/pdf/
asp_20060017_en.pdf

Financial Crisis:

BBC. 'Timeline: Credit crunch to downturn'. http://news.bbc.
co.uk/1/hi/business/7521250.stm

Niall Ferguson. *The Ascent of Money: A Financial History of the World*. Penguin, 2008.

Climate Change:

Editorial. 'Copenhagen climate change conference: "Fourteen days to seal history's judgment on this generation"'. http://www.guardian.co.uk/commentisfree/2009/dec/06/copenhagen-editorial

John Coleman. 'Global Warming Has Failed The Scientific Test'. http://ihatealgore.com/?p=849

Steven D Levitt and Stephen J Dubner. *Superfreakonomics: Global Cooling, Patriotic Prostitutes and Why Suicide Bombers Should Buy Life Insurance*. Allen Lane, 2009.

Peter Taylor. *Chill, A Reassessment of Global Warming Theory*. Clairview, 2009.

Miscellaneous:

Michael Bamberger. 'The Trump Tour'. http://www.golf.com/golf/tours_news/article/0,28136,1628264-0,00.html

Alex Frangos. 'Trump on Trump: Testimony Offers Glimpse of How He Values His Empire'. http://online.wsj.com/article/NA_WSJ_PUB:SB124261067783429043.html

Peter Macari. 'Contested Call'. http://www.journalonline.co.uk/Magazine/53-6/1005388.aspx

Jeremy Rowan Robinson and Elaine Farquharson-Black. *Compulsory Purchase and Compensation - The Law in Scotland.* Sweet and Maxwell, 2009.

Alex Shoumatoff. 'The Thistle and the Bee'. http://www.vanityfair.com/culture/features/2008/05/trump200805

Donald Trump with Meredith McIver. *Trump: Think Like a Billionaire.* Random House, 2004.

Donald Trump with Meredith McIver. *Trump: Never Give Up.* Wiley, 2008.

Organisations:

http://www.trippinguptrump.com

http://www.trump.com